AFRICAN
DIVINATION SYSTEMS

African Systems of Thought

General Editors
Charles S. Bird
Ivan Karp

Contributing Editors
Thomas O. Beidelman
James Fernandez
Luc de Heusch
John Middleton
Roy Willis

AFRICAN DIVINATION SYSTEMS

WAYS OF KNOWING

Edited by Philip M. Peek

INDIANA UNIVERSITY PRESS
Bloomington & Indianapolis

The paper used in this publication meets the minimum requirements of American
National Standard for Information Sciences—Permanence of Paper for Printed
Library Materials, ANSI Z39.48-1984.

∞™

Manufactured in the United States of America

Library of Congress Cataloging-in-Publication Data

African divination systems : ways of knowing / edited by Philip M.
Peek.
    p.   cm. — (African systems of thought)
  Includes bibliographical references.
  ISBN 0-253-34309-7 (cloth : alk. paper)
  1. Divination—Africa, Sub-Saharan. [1. Africa, Sub-Saharan—
Social life and customs.] I. Peek, Philip M.   II. Series.
BF1773.2.A4A37   1991
133.3'0967—dc20   76/20   90-39421
                                                                    CIP

1   2   3   4   5   95   94   93   92   91

To William Bascom

Contents

Acknowledgments

Over the extended gestation period of this volume, a number of debts have been acquired. I thank Ivan Karp for his continual encouragement and the many others, most especially my collaborators, who have persevered to complete this project. Our thanks to the editors at Indiana University Press and to various readers, most especially Paula Girshick Ben-Amos, for many helpful suggestions. I am grateful for several Drew University Faculty Research grants which supported the manuscript preparation and for Deborah Cahalen's aid in preparing the final draft. Inevitably, one must acknowledge the patience of one's spouse and family— "Hey! How does this sound?" can only be asked so many times. Thank you, Pat, Megan, and Nathan. Finally, my sincere appreciation to my colleagues without whose work and forbearance there would be no book for which to offer acknowledgments. With our dedication to William Bascom, we salute his thoughtful and thorough pioneering research on Yoruba divination systems. My thanks to one and all.

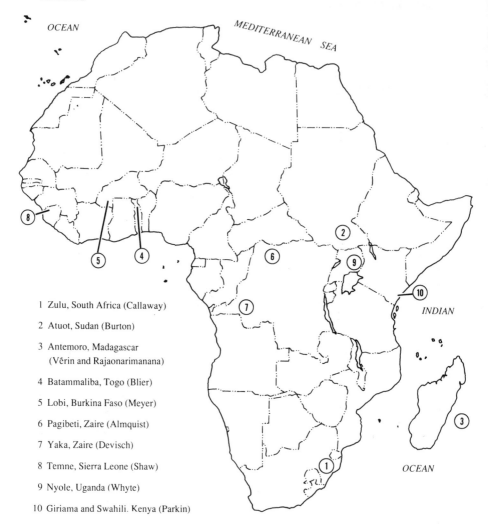

ATLANTIC

OCEAN

MEDITERRANEAN SEA

INDIAN

OCEAN

1 Zulu, South Africa (Callaway)

2 Atuot, Sudan (Burton)

3 Antemoro, Madagascar
   (Vérin and Rajaonarimanana)

4 Batammaliba, Togo (Blier)

5 Lobi, Burkina Faso (Meyer)

6 Pagibeti, Zaire (Almquist)

7 Yaka, Zaire (Devisch)

8 Temne, Sierra Leone (Shaw)

9 Nyole, Uganda (Whyte)

10 Giriama and Swahili. Kenya (Parkin)

Political map of Africa showing location of peoples whose divination systems are highlighted, with authors in parentheses.

Philip M. Peek

Introduction

The Study of Divination, Present and Past

Every human community recognizes a need for the special knowledge gained through divination. While this need is hardly of the same order as the need for food and shelter, it is nonetheless universal. Murdock, for instance, includes divination among the features found "in every culture known to history or ethnography" (1945:124).

Prometheus's gift of fire to humankind is well known, but his gift of the arts of divination has almost been forgotten, even though his name, meaning "forethought," reflects the importance of this contribution to Greek culture (Oswalt 1969:249–51). Other great civilizations have granted similar prominence to divination. Anthologies by Caquot and Leibovici (1968) and Loewe and Blacker (1981) include contributions on divination's critical role not only in the classical world but also in the Americas, India, Tibet, Japan and China, Africa, ancient Egypt and the Middle East, Judaism and Islam, and the Germanic world.

Although divination practices continue worldwide, remarkably little research has been done on these systems of knowledge, including those in Africa, the focus of this collection. Mbiti's observation remains valid: "With few exceptions, African systems of divination have not been carefully studied, though diviners are found in almost every community" (1970:232).

Ways of Knowing

Foremost among the concerns which shaped this volume is that, given the pivotal role of divination in African cultures, the study of divination systems must assume a central position in our attempts to better understand African peoples today.[1] As will be demonstrated, the sheer volume of information gained from recent thorough investigations of these systems reveals how much knowledge we lost as a result of earlier prejudices against divination. Throughout Africa—whether in

the city or in the country, no matter the religion, sex, or status of the individual
—questions, problems, and choices arise for which everyday knowledge is insufficient and yet action must be taken. The information necessary to respond effectively is available, but often only through a diviner. That is why divination continues
to provide a trusted means of decision making, a basic source of vital knowledge.

A divination system is a standardized process deriving from a learned discipline
based on an extensive body of knowledge. This knowledge may or may not be
literally expressed during the interpretation of the oracular message. The diviner
may utilize a fixed corpus, such as the Yoruba Ifa Odu verses, or a more diffuse
body of esoteric knowledge. Divining processes are diverse, but all follow set
routines by which otherwise inaccessible information is obtained. Some type of
device usually is employed, from a simple sliding object to the myriad symbolic
items shaken in diviners' baskets. Sometimes the diviner's body becomes the vehi-
cle of communication through spirit possession. Some diviners operate self-ex-
planatory mechanisms that reveal answers; other systems require the diviner to
interpret cryptic metaphoric messages. The final diagnosis and plan for action
are rendered collectively by the diviner and the client(s).

Divination sessions are not instances of arbitrary, idiosyncratic behavior by diviners. A divination system is often the primary institutional means of articulating
the epistemology of a people. Much as the classroom and the courtroom are primary sites for the presentation of cultural truths in the United States, so the diviner
in other cultures is central to the expression and enactment of his or her cultural
truths as they are reviewed in the context of contemporary realities. The situating
of a divination session in time and space, the cultural artifacts utilized (objects,
words, behaviors), the process of social interaction, and the uses made of oracular
knowledge all demonstrate the foundations of a people's world view and social
harmony. Divination systems do not simply reflect other aspects of a culture; they
are the means (as well as the premise) of knowing which underpin and validate
all else. Contemporary Africans in both urban and rural environments continue
to rely on divination, and diviners play a crucial role as mediators, especially
for cultures in rapid transistion.

A second concern of the shapers of this volume was that African divination
research had become lost in an almost exclusively functionalist mode, which assumed the practice to be at best simply supportive of other social systems and
at worst irrational and detrimental to its adherents. Every study presented here
emphatically demonstrates the centrality of divination. Divination systems are not
simply closed ideologies founded on religious beliefs but are dynamic systems
of knowledge upon which the proper ordering of social action is based. Looking
at these systems from this standpoint, we begin to understand why divination
is so often chosen over other means of decision making.

We intend this volume to contribute to current discussions in comparative epistemology and the anthropology of knowledge, cross-cultural psychology and cognition studies, and semiotics and ethnoscience as well as to religious studies and
more traditional anthropological topics. Although divination systems are not solely
manifestations of religious beliefs, a sacred world view is nonetheless a key ele-

ment. It is virtually impossible to discuss social interaction, self-identity, and cognitive process in an African context without consideration of divination, especially diviner-client interaction and the modes of analysis employed. Political and sociological studies of African societies need to recognize the role of divination systems in the enactment and validation of African legal systems and political structures. Investigation of a divination complex reveals a wealth of historical data in divinatory texts, esoteric terminology, and diviner's paraphernalia. Because many diviners are also herbalists, their diagnostic and treatment methods can aid the study of traditional healing systems. No aspect of life is *not* touched by divination, and so the process becomes critical to any study of African cultures and peoples.

With our emphasis on divination as a system of knowledge in action, we are reminded that our scientific tradition is but one way of knowing and that we can gain much from other systems proven effective over the centuries. African divination systems involve a combination of (as we commonly label cognitive processes) "logical-analytical" and "intuitive-synthetical" modes of thinking, while in the European tradition the separation of these modes is rigidly maintained.

In addition, the European tradition tends to characterize the diviner as a charismatic charlatan coercing others through clever manipulation of esoteric knowledge granted inappropriate worth by a credulous and anxiety-ridden people. Instead, we have found diviners to be men and women of exceptional wisdom and high personal character. The critical input of the divinatory congregation, especially that of the consulter/adviser and the particularizing discussions between diviner and client(s), serves to demythologize the domineering diviner image. By approaching divination as a dynamic, determining process, we are no longer limited to simple product analysis of the divinatory diagnosis.

Another guiding principle of the contributors to this book was to provide an overview of sub-Saharan African cultures and contemporary divination scholarship. The contributions are based on extensive fieldwork among peoples from Burkina Faso, Kenya, Madagascar, Sierra Leone, South Africa, Sudan, Togo, Uganda, and Zaire. Not only do these studies provide new theoretical approaches to a variety of divination systems; they also present much new ethnographic material, including several divination forms never described previously. While we hope that this anthology will aid in focusing future research on divination, we did not attempt to confine it to a single analytical approach. Most contributions, nonetheless, are in concert with what Devisch (1985) terms internal, semiotic and semantic, and praxeological approaches. Therefore, despite the diversity of peoples, divination systems, scholars, and academic orientations represented, a number of significant common points emerge to unify the collection.

Although each essay discusses numerous aspects of a divination system, the essays are grouped to enhance their major contributions, and section introductions provide brief analytic and comparative commentaries to highlight the groupings. The first section, as a kind of prelude to the whole volume, is devoted to one of the earliest recorded accounts of the process of becoming a diviner. Taken from Henry Callaway's classic ethnographical study, *The Religious System of the Amazulu*, it describes a future diviner's experiences and the cultural institutions

which validate and channel them. Further data on the selection and training of
African diviners are found throughout the volume.

The two essays constituting the second section provide comparative regional
studies of divination as a search for knowledge. First is John W. Burton's analysis
of divination among the Nilotic peoples of the Sudan, especially the Atuot, for
whom divination provides the primary interpretation of their experience and the
source of their philosophy. Pierre Vérin and Narivelo Rajaonarimanana, using archival and field material, then discuss the development and diffusion of the Antemoro divination system in Madagascar and the influence of Arabic divination on
African systems.

The third section focuses on divination as the major—often the sole—expression
of a social system and the means of maintaining its governing norms; in other
words, the social system exists *through* divination. Rudolph Blier describes the
central role of the diviner-consultant in the health care system of the Batammaliba
of northern Togo, from selection and training to diagnostic practice. Piet Meyer
presents the divination system of the Lobi from Burkina Faso, who are totally
dependent on the suprahuman powers revealed only through divination. The next
two essays, although both deal with Zairean peoples, reveal very different divination systems. Alden Almquist, in the context of the Pagibeti culture and hunting
ethos, analyzes the criteria employed to choose among divinatory mechanisms.
René Devisch demonstrates how the divination system of the Yaka, while determining the causes of their misfortunes, also maintains their social structure, especially
aspects of matrilineal inheritance and ascent.

The fourth group of essays is primarily concerned with how knowledge and
truth are generated by the special sensibilities of divination and then subjected
to the cooperative, transformational interaction of diviner and client(s) through
the full divinatory process. Rosalind Shaw critiques the imposition of European
rationality on other cultures' systems of knowledge and analyzes the construction
of truth through the "authorizing process" of divination among the Temne of Sierra
Leone. Susan Reynolds Whyte discusses the ways in which divination, through
control of oracular knowledge by the consulter/adviser, defines social relationships
between Nyole men and women of Uganda. David Parkin's study of the oracular
speech of the Giriama and Swahili diviners of Kenya demonstrates how these
bricoleurs transform the confusion of simultaneous events into a comprehensible
sequencing of significant factors.

My own contribution in the fifth section proposes a way to understand the
diverse symbolic elements and the unique cognitive process of these systems of
knowledge. This analysis suggests that the divinatory enterprise establishes a non-
normal mode of cognition through the manipulation of cultural symbols of anoma-
lousness, liminality, and inversion in order to receive non-normal communication,
which is then mediated by diviner and client(s) to permit effective practical response.

James W. Fernandez provides a final overview in which he analyzes the evocative
and efficacious ways in which "figuring out" takes place in divination through
the critical roles of metaphoric speech and primary process knowing, which the

diviner then synthesizes with secondary process knowing to determine the client's plan of action. Fernandez's personal reflection on the nature and value of divination among African peoples provides an apt conclusion to the volume.

Background to the Study of Divination

Because European and American scholarship has granted divination only marginal status in human affairs and presumed it to be magical in nature, one must glean those factors which have affected divination research from broader discussions of religion. In the later nineteenth century, several prominent themes, including evolutionism and secularism, shaped anthropology's approach to non-European belief systems; but most influential was positivism, which accepted only verifiable observations as "truths" and automatically denied any ideas of religious or esthetic causality.[2] These ideologies, coupled with the "moral crisis" of the times (Evans-Pritchard 1965:100–101; Langness 1987:11–12) and the urgency to be more "scientific" in all endeavors, hardly promoted the sensitive study of non-European religions.

In *Primitive Cultures*, Tylor simply enumerates myriad divinatory methods which "survive" only as games of chance (1958, vol. 1:78–83, 119–33). Clearly "Mr. Tylor's Science" had little tolerance for the arts of divination anywhere; he completely ignores contemporary European use of divination. Other early anthropologists, including Frazer, Malinowski, and Radcliffe-Brown, offer nothing on divination. Although Fortune records much on Dobu divination (1963), he defines divination as "a method of arriving at a judgment of the unknown through a consideration of incomplete evidence" (1931:174). I will discuss the persistence of this attitude in England in my review of Evans-Pritchard and the British social anthropologists.

Outside strictly academic circles at the turn of the century, other scholars reflected ambivalence about divination. Henri Junod, a missionary whose research on the Thonga appeared in 1898, allows that "the Bantu mind" has invented an extremely comprehensive and responsive divination system: ". . . the art of bone-throwing is by no means child's play, nor mere quackery by which astute soothsayers deceive their credulous followers" (1927:568). Nevertheless, he concludes: "I am convinced that, however high the degree of astuteness engendered by the divinatory bones may be, they have been extremely detrimental to the intellectual and moral welfare of the Natives" (572). A fellow missionary in southern Africa, Henry Callaway, while agreeing about divination's effectiveness, did not accept Junod's final evaluation (see section I).

The status of divination study in France was not as dire as in England, but one might have expected more attention to be paid to the topic.[3] The philosopher Lévy-Bruhl concluded that divination works for its practitioners but on the basis of a type of logic different from that of educated Europeans (1966); he thereby erroneously excluded "the mystical in our own culture as rigorously as he excluded the empirical in savage cultures," according to Evans-Pritchard (1965:91). Durkheim's approach to religion as a system of ideas and values that could be studied objectively presents a far more sympathetic perspective than had developed in England. In fact, Durkheim and Mauss singled out divination as a core area for research as early as 1903:

> There is nothing more natural, moreover, than the relation thus expressed between divination and the classification of things. Every divinatory rite, however simple it may be, rests on a pre-existing sympathy between certain beings, and on a traditionally admitted kinship between a certain sign and a certain future event. Further, a divinatory rite is generally not isolated; it is part of an organized whole. The science of the diviners, therefore, does not form isolated groups of things, but binds these groups to each other. At the basis of a system of divination there is thus, at least implicitly, a system of classification. (1967:77)

The tragic loss of Durkheim and most of his students during and shortly after World War I greatly disrupted the development of French ethnology. Still, it is curious that Griaule and his colleagues did not emphasize Dogon divination more than they did, especially given Griaule's concern with "typical" modes of knowledge (Clifford 1983). Although both Griaule (1937) and Paulme (1937) wrote on divination and one of the group's major publications, *The Pale Fox,* is named after the divining agent itself, Dogon divination never performed the organizing function for their research that it could have. As Douglas notes, "The technique [of divination] was well demonstrated, but only by the use of hypothetical examples. They neither knew how the Dogon used it to solve *their* dominant preoccupations, *nor* how to use it to solve their *own* problems as investigators" (1979:137).[4] Nevertheless, major studies of divination systems were published by Trautmann (1940), Maupoil (1943), and Delachaux (1946). More recently, important research has been pursued by Retel-Laurentin (1969) and Adler and Zempléni (1972) (see Devisch 1985).

Surprisingly, the broad theoretical orientation of American cultural anthropologists did not encourage consideration of divination; their studies of traditional religions barely touch the topic. Evans-Pritchard suggests that Americans ignored religious systems because they were primarily concerned with the emotions of religious activity (1965:38–39).[5] An intellectual atmosphere similar to that which stifled divination study in England evidently predominated in the United States, as illustrated by Lessa and Vogt's characterization of divination as mere coin flipping—a description they have left unchanged since the first edition of their anthology over thirty years ago (1979:333). Little work was done by American anthropologists on the topic until Bascom began to publish his lifelong research on the Ifa divination system of the Yoruba (1941). Although Bascom avoided theoretical pronouncements, the extent of his work surely indicated the value of studying divination systems. Gebauer (1964), Moore (1979), Park (1967), Fernandez (1967), and Bohannan (1975) published significant analytical studies, but a cohesive body of research never developed. Fernandez's afterword to this volume offers an honest self-appraisal of the attitudes toward divination held at that time.[6] Even with the development of ethno-science, such epistemologies as manifest in divination systems were not approached; nor have the fields of symbolic and cognitive anthropology turned to this topic, although the Colbys' recent work on Maya divination (1981) and Daniel's on Tamil divination (1984:chap. 5) may signal a change.

The Influence of Evans-Pritchard

Returning to England to review the work of Evans-Pritchard and the British social anthropologists, we will gain a better insight into the absence of extensive study of African divination systems. Evans-Pritchard's influential *Witchcraft, Oracles and Magic among the Azande*, published in 1937, was the first serious treatment of divination; it, along with his other writings, confronts several theoretical issues in the study of non-European religions. Here we can only comment on a few key issues raised in his phenomenological study of Zande divination and discussions of the dichotomization of religion and rationality by anthropologists.[7]

Evans-Pritchard's critique of the biases affecting the study of religion is found throughout his writings; the argument was formed rather early (Douglas 1981). In the introduction to *Nuer Religion*, he addresses the most basic problem:

> So strong has been rationalist influence on anthropology that religious practices are often discussed under the general heading of ritual together with a medley of rites of quite a different kind, all having in common only that the writer regards them as irrational; while religious thought tends to be inserted into a general discussion of values. Here the view is taken that religion is a subject of study *sui generis*, just as are language or law. (1967:viii)

Religion has to be studied as a system, and Evans-Pritchard stresses that the ethnographer's religious orientation is critical, "for even in a descriptive study judgement can in no way be avoided" because those who "give assent" to religious beliefs write differently than those who do not (1967:vii).[8] He cites anthropologists' aggressive agnosticism as the cause of the fundamental skepticism encountered in the study of African religions (and thus of divination). Most anthropologists were raised in strongly religious homes,[9] but as adults they became atheists or agnostics for whom religion was an illusion (Evans-Pritchard 1965:15). Why then did they persist in the study of religion?

> They sought, and found, in primitive religions a weapon which could, they thought, be used with deadly effect against Christianity. If primitive religion could be explained away as an intellectual aberration, as a mirage induced by emotional stress, or by its social function, it was implied that the higher religions could be discredited and disposed of in the same way. (Evans-Pritchard 1967:15)[10]

The cultural event which generated so much of Evans-Pritchard's soul searching and later debate among others[11] was the poison oracle of the Azande of southern Sudan, which involves the administration of poison to a chicken whose subsequent behavior provides a response to the matter under investigation (Evans-Pritchard

1968:281–312). A series of propositions are presented after the chicken has been poisoned; for example, "If such is the case, poison oracle kill [or spare] the fowl." The chicken's movements and fate—whether or not it dies—are interpreted in relation to the continuous questioning. "The main duty of the questioner," Evans-Pritchard points out, "is to see that the oracle fully understands the question put to it and is acquainted with all facts relevant to the problem it is asked to solve. They address it with all the care for detail that one observes in court cases before a prince" (297). The oracle thus serves to establish accountability, to determine the cause (usually witchcraft) of misfortune.

After describing several sessions, Evans-Pritchard develops a lengthy interrogation of the Azande poison oracle from every imaginable angle (313–51). Although the unidentified skeptic with whom he debates might be his English audience or possibly Lévy-Bruhl, one cannot avoid the impression that the debate is ultimately internal.[12] Evans-Pritchard assures us that while there are Zande skeptics and manipulators, Zande religion is not only internally consistent and rational but "Zande Man" constantly makes self-interested utilitarian use of his oracles in order to respond to witchcraft. To reach such conclusions, Evans-Pritchard has to distinguish between the "mystical" and the "objective" in Zande thought and argue that the Zande kept the two realms separate. He believes that Malinowski and Durkheim erred in portraying the operation of the magical world in the world of the practical (or the sacred in the profane) because each world follows its own rules.[13] This position parallels Evans-Pritchard's criticism of agnostics for turning "theological" facts into "sociological" facts in the study of religion. But his inability to appreciate that other peoples may not share the rigid European dichotomization of science and religion and may utilize different modes of thought, often in alternating fashion, is exactly what has generated much criticism today.[14] Later we shall argue that Evans-Pritchard's analysis fails specifically because divination makes definite use of both modes of thinking.

Finally, Evans-Pritchard seems to have wearied in his defense of the Azande; by the end of his discourse on the poison oracle he observes that further formulation of Zande beliefs would simply "expose their hollowness" (347). Reflecting his own positivist stance (reminiscent of Junod's conclusions), he writes:

> Their blindness is not due to stupidity, for they display great ingenuity in explaining away the failures and inequalities of the poison oracle and experimental keenness in testing it. It is due rather to the fact that their intellectual ingenuity and experimental keenness are conditioned by patterns of ritual behavior and mystical belief. Within the limits set by these patterns they show great intelligence, but it cannot operate beyond these limits. (338)

What a difference if he had only allowed at this point that this description could apply to most individuals in any culture!

Evans-Pritchard maintains that the anthropologist should only describe not explain religion—"his problems are scientific, not metaphysical or ontological" (1965:

17). Nevertheless, at the end of *Theories of Primitive Religion* he quotes Bergson extensively on the instinctual nature of religious behavior and, although he is critical, the prominence of place suggests agreement and continues an argument he presented earlier.[15] This stance is consistent with his understanding of societies as moral systems. Perhaps finally Evans-Pritchard's colleagues and students only heard his questioning of the poison oracle's logic. They certainly did not join in his agonizing introspection and in the end Evans-Pritchard considered himself alone in perceiving these dilemmas in the study of religion (1966:170).

British anthropologists continued to study African religions despite Evans-Pritchard's warnings, but it was always clear *how* religion was being approached, as Middleton's first line in his preface to *Lugbara Religion* indicates: "This book does not seek to present Lugbara religion as a system of theology, but to make a sociological analysis of the place of ritual and belief in Lugbara social life" (1964:v).[16] British anthropologists were primarily concerned with the relationship of witchcraft to social systems, following as they did Evans-Pritchard's conclusion that witchcraft accusations were means of adjusting social relationships and allocating responsibility.[17] Their publications constitute a formidable body of scholarship on witchcraft, but it developed at the expense of research on other aspects of religion (divination is only marginally treated[18]) and the consideration of religions as systems (see Kuper 1985:138–39). It is extraordinary that so much attention could be devoted to witchcraft and so little to divination, especially when it is still the only means of detecting witchcraft for many African peoples. Ironically, British (and other) anthropologists have produced study after study which simply offer "then the matter was decided by a diviner" and nothing more. In fact, the basic research guide *Notes and Queries on Anthropology* makes only two brief references to divination in nearly four hundred pages of advice to fieldworkers. Studies of divination appeared occasionally, of course; but even Turner, whom we can praise for his insights into Ndembu basket divination, never attended a divination session (Werbner 1972:231).

Although British social anthropologists working in Africa produced significant studies of religion, religion (and thereby divination because it was considered only in its spiritual dimensions)—was portrayed as derivative of the social system, primarily understood through kinship and government. And if religious belief and practice "worked" (by supporting kinship structure, allowing emotional release, and so on), then it did not matter whether religion was "logical."

But even more striking is the number of British anthropologists who treated divination with great derision. "When he divined for me, I deliberately misled him," Lienhardt writes (1970:69). Beattie informs us that the diviner was well aware that "he was simply putting on an act" (1967a:64). Fortes characterizes divination as "the game" (1966:421), while Middleton refers to a spirit-possessed diviner's speech as "gibberish" (1971:271). And Parrinder cannot believe that anything is revealed by divination's "haphazard methods" (1976:122). Unless we also accept similarly contentious characterizations of polygynous marriages or initiation ceremonies as a legitimate part of the ethnographic literature on African cultures, we must question why these mocking comments about divination exist at all. One is forced to recall Evans-Pritchard's critical observations.

Another theme emerged in Britain which contributed to the limitations of divination studies. Whether as a defensive response to the French ethnologists' revelations of complex African cosmologies or as an independently developed position, British anthropologists did not accept the existence of coherent, autonomous systems of knowledge in Africa. As Forde states in the introduction to *African Worlds*, "there need be no complete integration of belief and doctrine, still less the domination of conduct in all spheres by a single system of beliefs or basic ideas" (1963: vii). A "nationalistic" interpretation of the differences between French rationalism and British empiricism may seem overly simplified, but that is exactly what several scholars maintain, as became apparent in the discussions at the 1960 conference that fostered *African Systems of Thought* and in Richards's review of the book (1967).[19]

Whatever the causes, British study of African cultures demonstrates the continued domination of positivist functionalists' assumptions. Concerning anthropologists' ambivalence toward religion, Gell observed that "there has always been something scandalous about magic, fascinating and repellant at the same time" (1974:16; see also Lewis 1974). Some anthropologists' response has been to deny religion a central role in African cultures. Obviously anthropologists should not debunk others' beliefs (as illustrated above), but the alternative is not necessarily "a conversion experience" (Turner 1975:32) or the use of a "mystical idiom" when discussing divination (Evans-Pritchard 1968:320).

What we do need is increased reflexivity by anthropologists and more attention paid the anthropology of knowledge (Jackson 1978; Crick 1982). For example, a comparison of Christian and Jewish scholars of African religions might be very informative (Evans-Pritchard 1960:16). Westerlund (1985) demonstrates the value of comparing theological studies by Anglophone (usually Protestant) East and West African scholars and those by Francophone (usually Catholic) Central African scholars. Surely Richards's attempt (1967) to answer why the French find symbol systems and cosmologies in Africa while the British only encounter social systems and subsistence patterns must be pursued further.[20] Perhaps Douglas is correct in depicting British anthropologists as diviners delving behind formal appearances to find the reality of unrecognized contradictions of ideal social interaction (1979: 138–39). She develops this comparison in praise of British anthropologists, but Jules-Rosette uses the analogy of social scientists and diviners as they each seek meaningful patterns in apparently random and contradictory elements to critique Western scholarly prejudice when it validates its "oracular reasoning" with a "veil of objectivity" (1978:563–68). Similar observations about the "authorizing process" in truth making by these "specialists" are raised in this volume by Shaw and Fernandez. Others have also compared anthropologists and diviners; Turner humbly observes that his work on the Ndembu "may perhaps be said to reveal an anthropological diviner in action, at the beginning of a long seance that has by no means been concluded" (1975:30).[21]

Typologies of Scholarship and Divination Forms

A review of contemporary scholarship and typologies of divination forms reveals further conceptual problems in the anthropological study of African divination systems. In his excellent critical survey, Devisch (1985) categorizes the major approaches to the study of divination in Africa under the headings "(structural)-functionalist," "external, cognitive," and "internal, semiotic and semantic" and distinguishes each anthropologist's varying use of different models. In the first grouping Devisch (54–62) separates psychological analyses which emphasize therapeutic functions of divination (e.g., reduction of anxiety) and sociological analyses which stress sociopolitical functions (e.g., reestablishing social order). He also notes those studies which seek divination's function in correspondences of a culture's divination forms and features of social structure or cultural change.[22]

Although external cognitive approaches (Devisch's second category, 62–68),[23] consider "the expressive and explanatory function of divination, seen as a conceptual system, a system of thought, a way of knowing" (62). they remain variations of the functionalist orientation in their literal interpretations and assumptions of Western science's universality. They assume order as an individual and group goal and thus "offer the epistemological complement of the structural-functionalist interpretation of divination" (62) by focusing on sociopolitical order, moralizing trends, or a "pre-scientific way of knowing." Because other systems of knowledge are expected to adhere to Western positivist scientific principles, they are, of course, found lacking; therefore, these approaches ultimately portray divination as "illogical" and "non-rational." In this category are those anthropologists whom Gell terms "apologists" (1974:17; see also p'Bitek 1970:40).[24]

Devisch sees more promise in his third grouping of internal, semiotic, and semantic approaches (68–76),[25] which allow divination's methods and symbolic models to stand on their own and not simply be representations of social structures. The appropriate analysis should focus on the esthetic elements, semiotic patterning, dramaturgical features, and transformational processes of the diviner and the divinatory congregation. Devisch's "praxeological approach" (demonstrated, I believe, by most of this volume's essays) also takes into account the specific divination event, differing types of divination, clients' problems, and the subsequent dynamics of the sessions which lead to practical action in the larger cultural context (77). Finally, this helpful review questions divination's transcultural use—how a system rooted in culture-specific symbolism serves clients from different cultures, as is so often the case. I analyze the common use of "foreign" diviners in the final essay in this volume.

Rigid dichotomizations separating states of consciousness and human and spiritual or suprahuman realms have contributed to the inadequacies of typologies of divination systems, although the tremendous variety of divinational forms defies any easy categorization. Divination systems employ virtually anything that can register change with subsequent pattern alternations being interpreted. DeWaal Malejift (1968:216–24) distinguishes interpretation of signs, divination via human experiment, and divination in altered states of consciousness. Lessa and Vogt (1979: 333) separate inspirational (possession) and noninspirational divination (interpretation of both fortuitous and deliberate events), and Zuesse (1987:376) cites intuitive, possession, and wisdom divinational forms.[26]

African-based typologies reflect a similar pattern of ideas. Crawford (1967: 179–81) proposes a tripartite division of forms, allowing that the same diviner may employ all threes: psychic (involving possession), psychological (diviner interviewing client), and causal (chance cast of objects). Reflecting the dichotomizations suggested by Lessa and Vogt (1979) and Zuesse (1979:212ff), Zahan (1979: 86) categorizes diviners as "interpreters" (an intellectual process) and "messengers" (a mediumistic process). Devisch (1985:51–54) distinguishes "interpretative," "mediumistic," and "oracular-interpretative" divination. In the first form the diviner manipulates divinatory vehicles and decodes their communication according to an established scheme. For mediumistic divination, with its "transformation in the diviner's consciousness," Devisch accepts Bourguinon's distinction (1968) of trance, possession trance, and shamanistic trance. Between the interpretive and mediumistic forms are a variety of oracular-interpretative forms in which "mediumistic phenomena or oracular mediums" intervene (but not through the diviner), as in ordeals and the movement or configuration of significant objects.[27]

Other principles are present which might guide our categorizations. Blier (1983) notes that many divinatory processes involve locomotion, by tracing movement (fox's tracks among the Dogon), interpreting resistance (Zande rubbing boards), or even using associated implements (East African sandal divination). Or we could consider the opposition of open-ended analogical systems (such as Ndembu basket divination) and fixed response digital systems (based on a yes/no binary such as the Zande poison oracle).

Such a diversity of organizational schemes would seem to reinforce the stereotype of divination's capriciousness: divination is whatever practitioners call divination. Actually, careful choices are made in each culture among many possible methods, mediums, and materials for divination, and these choices must be studied closely. But with each culture employing several divination forms and diviners often utilizing different types in the same session, previous typologies are unsatisfactory because the cognitive modes they attempt to distinguish usually overlap. In fact, a key to our understanding of divination is found in the continual reference to an intermediate category between the poles of mathematical calculation and spirit mediumship. All analyses try to distinguish those forms involving ecstatic states from those performed in normal states of consciousness, yet the only real difference between them is that in ecstatic states the occult powers "speak" through the diviner rather than the divinatory apparatus. All divination forms involve a non-normal state of inquiry which then requires a "rational' interpretation of the revealed information by the client if not by the diviner. Thus, as Devisch and Shaw assert, in response to Turner, both "analytical" and "revelatory" dimensions are present (see their essays in this volume).

It is far more fruitful to focus on the total process generated rather than try to distinguish the individual mechanical causes of the oracular diagnosis because they are similar means to the same end. Obviously more attention must be paid to emic typologies. Some resolution of our difficulties may be possible when we have learned more about which form of divination correlates with which kind of problem. For example, is Shaw correct to suggest in her essay that analytic divination forms are used for more formal legalistic problems while revelatory forms are used for more occult-oriented issues?

Although many aspects of divination are treated in this volume, we have by no means exhausted all dimensions of this multifaceted topic. We must immediately acknowledge the scarcity of research by Africans on divination systems. This situation must be rectified, but it is certainly understandable given the negative portrayals of divination by European and American anthropologists and theologians (see p'Bitek 1970 and Westerlund 1985). Abimbola'a publications on Yoruba Ifa divination are among the few such studies available. Important new work is being published on African philosophy by Africans, such as Hountondji (1983), and by teams of Africans and non-Africans, such as Ruch and Anyanwu (1984) and Hallen and Sodipo (1986) (which suggests the value of cross-cultural cooperation for such topics); but unfortunately these works do not treat divination.

As any area of study refines its efforts, more questions than answers result. Of the many dynamic elements in divination, the dramaturgical and linguistic are least understood. More biographies of those exceptional individuals who become diviners are needed. More regional studies of divination complexes would clarify the relationships among divination systems. Divination must be studied in the larger context of decision making in daily life. Although Gluckman suggests that divination articulates a people's theory of morality and distinguishes between occult and legal responsibility (1972), its study can no longer be limited to religious contexts. The association of divination with judicial systems is critical, as Huizinga discussed years ago (1950). What are the decision-making mechanisms available to each society and how do they differ in terms of sources and types of knowledge? The correlations of social structure with divination (Park 1967) and spirit mediumship (Greenbaum 1973) can now be better pursued. Are there distinct types and users of divination among cultures with differing subsistence strategies and political systems? Are Edgerton (1974) and Goldschmidt (1986) correct that divination is more prevalent among pastoralists than farmers?

Even more important, we must learn more about different African cultures' systems of knowledge. Are different types of knowledge available from unique sources with distinct methods of acquisition and criteria of validation? How do these concepts correspond to each culture's theories of personality and behavior, religion, and the natural world? Certainly efforts by cross-cultural psychologists must incorporate indigenous epistemologies in order to avoid the dead ends of imposed frames and mechanisms in their study of cognitive processes.[28] A more complete study of divination systems, as provided by the essays included here, demonstrates that we can undertake the documentation of the intellectual histories of African societies. Data are available to trace the development of different ideologies and epistemologies, and we have an obligation to fulfill this challenge.

Many African peoples maintain that "real" knowledge is hidden, secret, available only to certain people capable of using it properly. Frequently that knowledge is only revealed through divination. Thus we return to the basic issue which this volume addresses: how can we possibly gain an understanding of contemporary African peoples and their ongoing search for sufficient knowledge to complete their life patterns unless we try to understand their sources of knowledge, their ways of knowing?

All who have contributed to this volume intend to convince others to reconsider their relegation of divination to a peripheral and exclusively religious role in culture. We especially hope that African scholars will reject the biases which have so misrepresented African epistemologies and will return to their own elders to ensure that African systems of knowledge are part of the total record of the human enterprise. We reaffirm p'Bitek's challenge that "the African scholar must endeavor to present the institutions of African peoples as they really are" (1970:7), and we hope this collection of essays contributes toward that end.

Notes

1. This volume developed from a panel on divination systems at the 1981 African Studies Association meeting, where Alden Almquist, Rudolph Blier, John W. Burton, and Piet Meyer first presented their papers. My sincere thanks to Mark Whitaker for his helpful comments on this introduction.

2. See Evans-Pritchard (1966:155–61) and Ray (1976:2–7). As Evans-Pritchard concludes, "It was in such a climate of Comtism, utilitarianism, Biblical criticism, and the beginnings of comparative religion that social anthropology, as we now know it, came into being" (161).

3. There was, for example, Bouché-Leclercq's monumental *Histoire de la divination dans l'antiquité*, 4 vols. (1879–82).

4. Douglas (1979) also suggests correspondences between the surrealist poets and the Dogon of Griaule and his collaborators, and Clifford explicitly develops the idea in his discussion of "Ethnographic Surrealism" (1988). Griaule, one recalls, first published on the Dogon in surrealist journals such as *Minotaure* (1933).

5. Elsewhere Evans-Pritchard observes that American anthropologists all regarded religious belief as illusion because "religion is superstition to be explained by anthropologists, not something an anthropologist, or indeed any rational person, could himself believe in" (1966:162).

6. Even today, accounts such as Grindal's (1983) and Stoller and Olkes's (1987) are exceptional, as most anthropologists do not publish their paranormal experiences (see Lewis 1974 and Long 1977: 371–96). They also avoid work on divination by parapsychologists, such as Stanford (1972).

7. For more thorough comments on the personal and professional dimensions of this complex individual, see Beidelman (1974), Lienhardt (1974), Douglas (1981), and Burton (1983).

8. Interestingly, van Binsbergen and Schoffeleers raise the issue of their contributors' religious faith but conclude that the papers reflect no clear influence (1985:36). A survey

of this volume's contributors, who represent a wide range of religious attitudes, suggests a similar conclusion.

9. For example, Tylor's family was Quaker and Frazer's Presbyterian, while Durkheim's was rabbinical.

10. Evans-Pritchard never addressed his own personal belief, which was a constant throughout his life: his father was an Anglican reverend; he was strongly impressed by the missionaries he met in Africa; and he converted, not unexpectedly, to the Roman Catholic Church in 1944 (Lienhardt 1974; Douglas 1981:43; Burton 1983:175, 184 n.5).

11. See Cooper (1975), Salmon (1978), and Ahern (1982). Hallpike (1979) also has generated much discussion.

12. Yet Evans-Pritchard used the oracle regularly and "found this as satisfactory a way of running my home and affairs as any other I know of" (1968:270).

13. Fortes (1966), Gluckman (1972), and Gell (1974) argue this position even more strongly.

14. Lévi-Strauss (1966:3) and Zuesse (1987:375) argue against the opposition of magic and science; Marwick (1973) and Singleton (1979) effectively dispute the use of this rigid dichotomization when discussing other epistemologies.

15. Evans-Pritchard cites Benjamin Kidd's *Social Evolution* (1894) to the effect that "social evolution or progress" came about due to religious systems and that "through the operation of the law of natural selection the race must grow ever more and more religious" (1966:166–67).

16. But Middleton does oppose Evans-Pritchard's portrayal of coherent systems of belief among the Zande and Nuer (Karp 1980); probably Lienhardt (1970) shares the most affinity with Evans-Pritchard's approach.

17. For example, Middleton and Winter's *Witchcraft and Sorcery in East Africa* (1963) (with Evans-Pritchard's foreword), Beattie and Middleton's *Spirit Mediumship and Society in Africa* (1969), Douglas's *Witchcraft Confessions and Accusations* (1970; both the book and the conference on which it was based were dedicated to Evans-Pritchard), and Gluckman's aptly titled *The Allocation of Responsibility* (1972).

18. Even Forde's *African Worlds* (1963; subtitled *Studies in the Cosmological Ideas and Social Values of African Peoples*) and Fortes and Dieterlen's *African Systems of Thought* (1972) contain only passing references to divination.

19. As Richards summarizes the matter, "It is then because of his basic functional assumptions, the way in which he has traditionally worked and the data with which his note-books are filled, that the empirical hackles of the British ethnographer tend to rise when the autonomy, consistency and logic of primitive systems of belief are stressed" (1967: 294–95).

20. "Thus Griaule and Dieterlen describe the lay-out of Dogon fields in relation to a pattern of ideas and not as providing a more or less efficient use of land for food. . . . The system sought after was a system of ideas" (Richards 1967:295). Richards's discussion has been insightfully extended by Southall (1972), Douglas (1979:124), and Clifford (1988).

21. Turner dedicated *Revelation and Divination in Ndembu Ritual* (1975) "to Muchona, friend and educator," the diviner who was his primary informant.

22. Among others, Devisch cites Beattie (1967b) and Turner (1975) as emphasizing psychological interpretations; Middleton (1964), Evans-Pritchard (1968), Harwood (1970), and Gluckman (1972) for sociological interpretations; and Bourguignon (1976) and Rigby (1975) for comparisons to social systems.

23. Here Devisch cites Evans-Pritchard (1968), Turner (1975), Horton (1967), and Mendonsa (1978).

24. Others who have questioned the functionalist bias include Hallpike (1979:493), Ahern (1981:115, n.12), MacGaffey (1981:238–40), Crick (1982), Winkelman (1982:37), Shaw (1985), and several contributors to this volume. Even Evans-Pritchard queried how

religion could be "functional" if all its religious dimensions were denied, as they had been by agnostic anthropologists (1966:167).
   25. Devisch cites Turner (1975), Young (1977), and Werbner (1973).
   26. Ahern (1981) suggests distinguishing interpersonal divination (reading mechanisms for their encoded messages from suprahuman powers) and the calculation of causal connections from impersonal extant factors (as in geomancy).
   27. See also an excellent discussion by "G.K.P.," which recommends similar categories (*Encyclopedia Britannica* 1974:916–20).
   28. Most "comparative" research in the social sciences remains focused on how "they" respond to our modes of thinking and behaving, although cross-cultural psychology is beginning to question this tradition, as illustrated by Lloyd and Gay's *Universals of Human Thought: Some African Evidence* (1981).

References

Abimbola, 'Wande. 1967. "Ifa Divination Poems as Sources for Historical Evidence." *Lagos Notes and Records* 1 (1).
———. 1976. *Ifa: An Exposition of Ifa Literary Corpus*. Ibadan: Oxford University Press.
———. 1977. *Ifa Divination Poetry*. New York: Nok.
Adler, A., and A. Zempléni. 1972. *Le bâton de l'aveugle: Divination, maladie et pouvoir chez les Moundang du Tchad*. Paris: Hermann.
Ahern, Emily Martin. 1981. *Chinese Ritual and Politics*. Cambridge: Cambridge University Press.
———. 1982. "Rules in Oracles and Games." *Man* n.s. 17 (2):302–12.
Bascom, William R. 1941. "The Sanctions of Ifa Divination," *Journal of the Royal Anthropological Institute* 71 (1–2):43–54.
———. 1969. *Ifa Divination: Communication between Gods and Men in West Africa*. Bloomington: Indiana University Press.
———. 1980. *Sixteen Cowries: Yoruba Divination from Africa to the New World*. Bloomington: Indiana University Press.
Bastide, Roger. 1968. "La divination chez les Afro-Américains." In *La Divination*, vol. 2, ed. A. Caquot and M. Leibovici, 393–427. Paris: Presses Universitaires de France.
Bauer, Dan F., and John Hinnant. 1980. "Normal and Revolutionary Divination: A Kuhnian Approach to African Traditional Thought." In *Explorations in African Systems of Thought*, ed. Ivan Karp and Charles S. Bird, 213–36. Bloomington: Indiana University Press.
Beattie, John. 1967a. "Consulting a Nyoro Diviner: The Ethnologist as Client." *Ethnology* 6(1): 57–65.
———. 1967b. "Divination in Bunyoro, Uganda." In *Magic, Witchcraft and Curing*, ed. John Middleton, 211–31. Garden City, N.Y.: Natural History Press.
Beattie, John, and John Middleton, eds. 1969. *Spirit Mediumship and Society in Africa*. London: Routledge and Kegan Paul.
Beidelman, Thomas O. 1974. "Sir Edward Evan Evans-Pritchard (1902–1973): An Appreciation." *Anthropos* 69:554–67.
———. 1986. *Moral Imagination in Kaguru Modes of Thought*. Bloomington: Indiana University Press.
Benham, Marian S. 1896. *Henry Callaway M.D., D.D. First Bishop for Kaffraria. His Life-History and Work: A Memoir*, ed. Rev. Canon Benham. London: Macmillan.

Binsbergen, Wim van, and Matthew Schoffeleers. 1985. "Introduction: Theoretical Explorations in African Religion." In *Theoretical Explorations in African Religion*, ed. W. van Binbergen and M. Schoffeleers, 1–49. London: KPI/Routledge and Kegan Paul.

p'Bitek, Okot. 1970. *African Religions in Western Scholarship*. Nairobi: East African Literature Bureau.

Blier, Suzanne Preston. 1983. "African Geomancy: Art and the Idiom of Knowledge Revelation." Paper presented at the African Studies Association meeting, Boston.

Bloch, Maurice. 1968. "Astrology and Writing in Madagascar." In *Literacy in Traditional Society*, ed. J. Goody, 278–97. Cambridge: Cambridge University Press.

———. 1986. *From Blessing to Violence: History and Ideology in the Circumcision Ritual of the Merina of Madagascar*. Cambridge: Cambridge University Press.

Bohannan, Paul. 1975. "Tiv Divination." In *Studies in Social Anthropology*, ed. J. H. M. Beattie and R. G. Lienhardt, 149–66. Oxford: Clarendon Press.

Boshier, Adrian K. 1974. "African Apprenticeship." In *Parapsychology and Anthropology*, eds. A. Angoff and D. Barth, 273–93. New York: Parapsychology Foundation.

Boston, J. S. 1974. "Ifa Divination in Igala." *Africa* 44(4): 350–60.

Bouché-Leclerq, A. 1879–82. *Histoire de la divination dans l'antiquité*. 4 vols. Paris: Leroux.

Bourguignon, Erika. 1968. "Divination, transe et possession en Afrique transsaharienne." In *La Divination*, vol. 2, ed. André Caquot and Marcel Leibovici, 331–358. Paris: Presses Universitaires de France.

———. 1976. "Spirit Possession Belief and Social Structure." In *The Realm of the Extra-Human: Ideas and Actions*, ed. Agehanada Bharati, 17–26. The Hague: Mouton.

Burton, John W. 1983. "Answers and Questions: Evans-Pritchard on Nuer Religion." *Journal of Religion in Africa* 14(3): 167–86.

Calame-Griaule, G. 1965. *Ethnologie et langage: La parole chez les Dogon*. Paris: Gallimard.

Callaway, Henry. 1871–72. "On Divination and Analogous Phenomena among the Natives of Natal." *Journal of the Royal Anthropological Institute* 1:163–85.

———. 1970. *The Religious System of the Amazulu* (1870), facsimile reprint. Cape Town: C. Struik.

Caquot, André, and Marcel Leibovici. 1968. *La Divination*. 2 vols. Paris: Presses Universitaires de France.

Clifford, James. 1983. "Power and Dialogue in Ethnography: Marcel Griaule's Initiation." In *Observers Observed*, ed. G.W. Stocking, Jr., 121–56. Madison: University of Wisconsin Press.

———. 1988. *The Predicament of Culture*. Cambridge, Mass.: Harvard University Press.

Colby, Benjamin N., and Lore M. Colby. 1981. *The Daykeeper: The Life and Discourse of an Ixil Diviner*. Cambridge, Mass.: Harvard University Press.

Cooper, David E. 1975. "Alternative Logic in 'Primitive Thought.'" *Man* n.s. 10:238–56.

Crawford, J. R. 1967. *Witchcraft and Sorcery in Rhodesia*. London: Oxford University Press.

Crick, Malcolm R. 1982. "The Anthropology of Knowledge." In *Annual Review of Anthropology*, vol. 11, 287–313.

Daniel, E. Valentine. 1984. *Fluid Signs: Being a Person the Tamil Way*. Berkeley: University of California Press.

Davis, S. 1955. "Divining Bowls, Their Uses and Origin: Some African Examples and Parallels from the Ancient World." *Man* 55(143):132–35.

Delachaux, Théodore. 1946. "Méthodes et instruments de divination en Angola." *Acta tropica* 3(2).

Devisch, René. 1985. "Perspectives on Divination in Contemporary Sub-Saharan Africa." In *Theoretical Explorations in African Religions*, ed. W. van Binsbergen and M. Schoffeleers, 50–83. London: KPI/Routledge and Kegan Paul.

Douglas, Mary. 1979. "If the Dogon . . ." *Implicit Meanings: Essays in Anthropology*, 124–41. London: Routledge and Kegan Paul.

———. 1981. *Edward Evans-Pritchard*. New York: Penguin Books.

Douglas, Mary, ed. 1970. *Witchcraft Confessions and Accusations*. Association of Social Anthropologists Monographs, 9. London: Tavistock Publications.

Drewal, Margaret Thompson, and Henry John Drewal. 1985. "An Ifa Diviner's Shrine in Ijebuland." *African Arts* 16(2):60–67, 99–100.

Durkheim, Emile, and Marcel Mauss. 1967. *Primitive Classification* (1903). Chicago: University of Chicago Press.

Edgerton, Robert B. 1974. "Pastoral-Farming Comparisons." In *Culture and Personality*, ed. Robert A. Levine, 345–68. Chicago: Aldine Press.

Encyclopedia Britannica. 1974. "Divination" (by G.K.P.), 916–20. Chicago: Encyclopedia Britannica.

Evans-Pritchard, E. E. 1960. Introduction. In Robert Hertz, *Death and the Right Hand* (trans. R. and C. Needham), 9–24. Aberdeen: Cohen and West.

———. 1965. *Theories of Primitive Religion*. London: Oxford University Press.

———. 1966. "Religion and the Anthropologists." *Social Anthropology and Other Essays*, 155–71. New York: Free Press.

———. 1967. *Nuer Religion* (1956). Oxford: Clarendon Press.

———. 1968. *Witchcraft, Oracles, and Magic among the Azande* (1937). Oxford: Clarendon Press.

Fernandez, James W. 1967. *Divinations, Confessions, Testimonies—Confrontations with the Social Superstructure among Durban Africans*. Occasional Papers of the Institute for Social Research (Winter-Spring), University of Natal.

Forde, Daryll, ed. 1963. *African Worlds: Studies in the Cosmological Ideas and Social Values of African Peoples*. London: International African Institute and Oxford University Press.

Fortes, Meyer. 1966. "Religious Premises and Logical Technique in Divinatory Ritual." *Philosophical Transactions of the Royal Society of London* series B 251: 409–22.

Fortes, Meyer, and G. Dieterlen, eds. 1972. *African Systems of Thought*. London; Oxford University Press.

Fortune, Reo. 1931. "Divination." In *Encyclopedia of the Social Sciences*, vol. 5, 174–75. New York: Macmillan.

———. 1963. *Sorcerers of Dobu* (1932). New York: Dutton.

Gebauer, Paul. 1964. *Spider Divination in the Cameroons*. Milwaukee, Wis.: Milwaukee Public Museum Publication in Anthropology, no. 10.

Gell, Alfred. 1974. "Understanding the Occult." *Radical Philosophy* 9:17–26.

Glaze, Anita J. 1981. *Art and Death in a Senufo Village*. Bloomington: Indiana University Press.

Gluckman, Max. 1972. "Moral Crises: Magical and Secular Solutions." In *The Allocation of Responsibility*, ed. Max Gluckman, 1–50. Manchester: Manchester University Press.

Goldschmidt, Walter. 1986. *The Sebei: A Study in Adaptation*. New York: Holt, Rinehart and Winston.

Greenbaum, Lenora. 1973. "Societal Correlates of Possession Trance in Sub-Saharan Africa" and "Possession Trance in Sub-Saharan Africa: A Descriptive Analysis of Fourteen Societies." In *Religion, Altered States of Consciousness, and Social Change*, ed. E. Bourguignon, 39–57, 58–87. Columbus: Ohio State University Press.

Griaule, M. 1933. "Introduction Méthodologique." *Minotaure* 2:7–12.

———. 1937. "Notes sur la divination par le chacal." *Bulletin du Comité d'Etudes Historiques et Scientifiques de l'Afrique Occidentale Française* 20 (1–2):113–41.

Griaule, Marcel, and Germaine Dieterlen. 1963. "The Dogon of the French Sudan." In

African Worlds, ed. D. Forde, 83–110. London: International African Institute and Oxford University Press.

Grindal, Bruce T. 1983. "Into the Heart of Sisala Experience: Witnessing Death Divination." *Journal of Anthropological Research* 39(1):60–80.

Gussler, Judith D. 1973. "Social Change, Ecology, and Spirit Possession among the South African Nguni." In *Religion, Altered States of Conciousness, and Social Change*, ed. E. Bourguignon, 88–126. Columbus: Ohio State University Press.

Hallen, Barry, and J. O. Sodipo. 1986. *Knowledge, Belief and Witchcraft: Analytic Experiments in African Philosophy*. London: Ethnographica.

Hallpike, C. R. 1979. *The Foundations of Primitive Thought*. Oxford: Clarendon Press.

Harwood, Alan. 1970. *Witchcraft, Sorcery and Social Categories among the Safwa*. London: Oxford University Press.

Herskovits, M. J. 1938. *Dahomey: An Ancient African Kingdom*. 2 vols. New York: J. J. Augustin.

Horton, Robin. 1964. "Kalabari Diviners and Oracles." *ODU* 1(1):3–16.

———. 1967. "African Traditional Thought and Western Science." *Africa* 37(1):50–71 and 37(2):155–87.

Hountondji, Paulin J. 1983. *African Philosophy: Myth and Reality*. Trans. Henri Evans and Jonathan Rice. Bloomington: Indiana University Press.

Huber, H. 1965. "A Diviner's Apprenticeship and Work among the Bayaka." *Man* 66: 46–48.

Huffman, Thomas N. 1985. "The Soapstone Birds from Great Zimbabwe." *African Arts* 18(3):68–73, 99–100.

Huizinga, J. 1950. *Homo Ludens: A Study of the Play-Element in Culture* (1938). New York: Roy Publishers.

Jackson, Michael. 1978. "An Approach to Kuranko Divination." *Human Relations* 31(2):117–38.

Jules-Rosette, Benneta. 1978. "The Veil of Objectivity: Prophecy, Divination, and Social Inquiry." *American Anthropologist* 80(3):549–70.

Jung, C. G. 1973. "Synchronicity: An Acausal Connecting Principle" (1952). In Collected Works of C. G. Jung, vol. 8. Princeton, N.J.: Princeton University Press.

———. 1974. Foreword to *The I Ching or Book of Changes*, 3d ed. Trans. R. Wilhelm and C. F. Baynes. Princeton, N.J.: Princeton Univerity Press.

Junod, Henri. 1927. *The Life of a South African Tribe. Vol. 2: Mental Life*. 2d ed. London: Macmillan.

Karp, Ivan. 1980. Introduction to *Explorations in African Systems of Thought*, ed. Ivan Karp and Charles S. Bird, 1–10. Bloomington: Indiana University Press.

Kuper, Adam. 1985. *Anthropology and Anthropologists: The Modern British School*, rev. ed.. London: Routledge and Kegan Paul.

Langness, L. L. 1987. *The Study of Culture*, rev. ed. San Francisco: Chandler and Sharp.

Lee, S. G. 1969. "Spirit Possession among the Zulu." In *Spirit Mediumship and Society in Africa*, ed. J. Beattie and J. Middleton, 128–56. London: Routledge and Kegan Paul.

Lessa, William A., and Evon Z. Vogt. 1979. Introduction to chap. 7. In *Reader in Comparative Religion*, 4th ed., ed. Lessa and Vogt, 332–34. New York: Harper and Row.

Lévi-Strauss, Claude. 1966. *The Savage Mind*. Chicago: University of Chicago Press.

———. 1967. *Structural Anthropology*. New York: Doubleday Anchor.

Lévy-Bruhl, Lucien. 1966. *Primitive Mentality* (1923). Boston: Beacon Press.

Lewis, I. M. 1970. "A Structural Approach to Witchcraft and Spirit-Possession." In *Witchcraft Confessions and Accusations*. ed. M. Douglass, 293–309. London: Tavistock.

———. 1974. "The Anthropologist's Encounter with the Supernatural." In *Parapsychology and Anthropology*, ed. A. Angoff and D. Barth, 22–35. New York: Parapsychology Foundation.

Lienhardt, Godfrey. 1970. *Divinity and Experience: The Religion of the Dinka*. Oxford: Clarendon Press.

———. 1974. "E-P: A Personal View." *Man* n.s. 9:299–304.

Lloyd, Barbara, and John Gay. 1981. *Universals of Human Thought: Some African Evidence*. Cambridge: Cambridge University Press.

Loewe, Michael, and Carmen Blacker, eds. 1981. *Oracles and Divination*. Boulder, Colo.: Shambhala

Long, Joseph K., ed. 1977. *Extrasensory Ecology: Parapsychology and Anthropology*. Metuchen, N.J.: Scarecrow Press.

McClelland, E. M. 1982. *The Cult of Ifa among the Yoruba*. Vol. 1: *Folk Practice and Art*. London: Ethnographica.

MacGaffey, Wyatt. 1981. "African Ideology and Belief: A Survey." *African Studies Review* 24(2–3):227–74.

Mack, John. 1986. *Madagascar: Island of the Ancestors*. London: British Museum.

McLean, David A., and Ted J. Solomon. 1971. "Divination among the Bena Lulua." *Journal of Religion in Africa* 4(1):25–44.

Marwick, M. G. 1973. "How Real Is the Charmed Circle in African and Western Thought?" *Africa* 43(1):59–70.

Maupoil, Bernard. 1943. *La géomancie à l'ancienne Côte des Esclaves*. Paris: Institute d'Ethnologie.

Mbiti, John. 1970. *African Religions and Philosophy*. New York: Doubleday Anchor.

Mendonsa, Eugene L. 1978. "Etiology and Divination among the Sisala of Northern Ghana." *Journal of Religion in Africa* 9(1):33–50.

———. 1982. *The Politics of Divination*. Berkeley: University of California Press.

Middleton, John. 1964. *Lugbara Religion: Ritual and Authority among an East African People*. London: Oxford University Press.

———. 1971. "Oracles and Divination among the Lugbara." In *Man in Africa*, ed. Mary Douglas and Phyllis M. Kaberry, 262–78. New York: Doubleday Anchor.

———. 1973. "Some Categories of Dual Classification among the Lugbara of Uganda" (1968). In *Right and Left: Essays on Dual Symbolic Classification*, ed. R. Needham, 369–90. Chicago: University of Chicago Press.

Middleton, John, and E. H. Winter, eds. 1963. *Witchcraft and Sorcery in East Africa*. London: Routledge and Kegan Paul.

Moore, Omar Khayyam. 1979. "Divination—A New Perspective." In *Reader in Comparative Religion*, 4th ed., ed. William A. Lessa and Evon Z. Vogt, 376–79. New York: Harper and Row.

Morris, Martha B. 1976. "A Rjonga Curing Ritual: A Causal and Motivational Analysis." In *The Realm of the Extra-Human: Ideas and Actions*, ed. Agehananda Bharati, 237–60. The Hague: Mouton.

Murdock, George P. 1945. "The Common Denominator of Cultures." In *The Science of Man in the World Crisis*, ed. Ralph Linton, 123–42. New York: Columbia University Press.

Nadel, S. F. 1970. *Nupe Religion* (1954). New York: Schocken Books.

Ngubane, Harriet. 1977. *Body and Mind in Zulu Medicine*. London: Academic Press.

Oswalt, Sabine G. 1969. *Concise Encyclopedia of Greek and Roman Mythology*. Glasgow: Collins.

Park, George K. 1967. "Divination and Its Social Contexts." In *Magic, Witchcraft and Curing*, ed. J. Middleton, 233–54. Garden City, N.Y.: Natural History Press.

Parrinder, Geoffrey. 1976. *African Traditional Religion*. New York: Harper and Row.

Paulme, D. 1937. "La divination par les chacals chez les Dogon de Sanga." *Journal de la Société des Africanistes* 7:1–15.

Peek, Philip M. 1982. "The Divining Chain in Southern Nigeria." In *African Religious Groups and Beliefs*, ed. S. Ottenberg, 187–205. Meerut, India: Folklore Institute.

Ray, Benjamin. 1976. *African Religions: Symbols, Ritual, and Community*. Englewood Cliffs, N.J.: Prentice-Hall.

Redmayne, Alison. 1970. "Chikanga: An African Diviner with an International Reputation." In *Witchcraft: Confessions and Accusations*, ed. M. Douglas, 103–28. London: Tavistock.

Retel-Laurentin, A. 1969. *Oracles et ordalies chez les Nzakara*. Paris: Mouton.

Reynolds, Barrie. 1963. *Magic, Divination and Witchcraft among the Barotse of Northern Rhodesia*. Berkeley and Los Angeles: University of California Press.

Richards, A. I. 1967. "African Systems of Thought: An Anglo-French Dialogue" (review article). *Man* n.s. 2(2):286–98.

Rigby, Peter. 1975. "Prophets, Diviners, and Prophetism: The Recent History of Kiganda Religion." *Journal of Anthropological Research* 31(2):116–48.

Roumeguère-Eberhardt, Jacqueline. 1968. "La divination en Afrique australe." In *La Divination*, vol. 2, ed. A. Caquot and M. Liebovici, 359–72. Paris: Presses Universitaires de France.

Royal Anthropological Institute of Great Britain and Ireland. 1967. *Notes and Queries on Anthropology* (1951). 6th ed. London: Routledge and Kegan Paul.

Ruch, E. A., and K. C. Anyanwu. 1984. *African Philosophy*. Rome: Catholic Book Agency.

Salmon, Merrilee H. 1978. "Do Azande and Nuer Use a Non-standard Logic?" *Man* n.s. 13(3):444–54.

Shaw, Rosalind. 1985. "Gender and the Structuring of Reality in Temne Divination: An Interactive Study." *Africa* 55(1):286–303.

Singleton, M. 1979. "*Dawa*—Beyond Science and Superstition (Tanzania)." *Anthropos* 74(5–6):817–63.

Southall, Aidan. 1972. "Twinship and Symbolic Structure." In *The Interpretation of Ritual*, ed. J. S. La Fontaine, 73–114. London: Tavistock.

Stanford, R. G. 1972. "Suggestibility and Success at Augury: Divination from 'Chance' Outcomes." *Journal of the American Society for Psychical Research* 66(1):42–62.

Steiner, Franz Baermann. 1954. "Chagga Truth: A Note on Gutmann's Account of the Chagga Concept of Truth." *Africa* 24:364–69.

Stoller, Paul, and C. Olkes. 1987. *In Sorcery's Shadow: A Memoir of Apprenticeship among the Songhay of Niger*. Chicago: University of Chicago Press.

Sussman, Robert W., and Linda K. Sussman. 1977. "Divination among the Sakalava of Madagascar." In *Extrasensory Ecology: Parapsychology and Anthropology*, ed. Joseph K. Long, 271–91. Metuchen, N.J.: Scarecrow Press.

Suthers, Ellen Moore. 1987. "Perception, Knowledge, and Divination in Djimini Society, Ivory Coast." Ph.D. dissertation, University of Virginia.

Trautmann, René. 1940. *La divination à la Côte des Esclaves et à Madagascar: Le Vôdoû Fa–Le Sikidy*. Dakar: Institut Français d'Afrique Noir.

Turner, Victor W. 1967. "Muchona the Hornet, Interpreter of Religion" (1959). In *Forest of Symbols: Aspects of Ndembu Ritual*, 131–50. Ithaca, N.Y.: Cornell University Press.

———. 1975. *Revelation and Divination in Ndembu Ritual*. Ithaca N.Y.: Cornell University Press.

Tylor, Edward Burnett. 1958. *The Origin of Culture* (1871). 2 vols. New York: Harper Torchbooks.

Vansina, Jan. 1971. "The Bushong Poison Ordeal." In *Man in Africa*, ed. M. Douglas and P. M. Kaberry, 245–61. New York: Doubleday Anchor.

———. 1978. *The Children of Woot: A History of the Kuba Peoples*. Madison: University of Wisconsin Press.

deWaal Malejifit, Annemarie. 1968. *Religion and Culture*. New York: Macmillan.

Werbner, Richard P. 1972. "Sin, Blame and Ritual Mediation." In *The Allocation of Responsibility*, ed. Max Gluckman, 227–55. Manchester: Manchester University Press.
———. 1973. "The Superabundance of Understanding: Kalanga Rhetoric and Domestic Divination." *American Anthropologist* 75(5):1414–40.
Westerlund, David. 1985. *African Religion in African Scholarship*. Monograph no. 7, Studies Published by the Institute of Comparative Religion at the University of Stockholm. Stockholm: Almquist and Wiksell International.
Winkelman, Michael. 1982. "Magic: A Theoretical Reassessment." *Current Anthropology* 23(1):37–66.
Young, Alan. 1977. "Order, Analogy, and Efficacy in Ethiopian Medical Divination." *Culture, Medicine and Psychiatry* 1(2):183–99.
Zahan, Dominique. 1983. *The Religion, Spirituality, and Thought of Traditional Africa*. Chicago: University of Chicago Press.
Zuesse, Evan M. 1979. *Ritual Cosmos: The Sanctification of Life in African Religions*. Athens: Ohio University Press.
———. 1987. "Divination." In *The Encyclopedia of Religion*, ed. M. Eliade, 375–82. New York: Macmillan.

PART ONE

Becoming a Diviner

> When people come to a fork, they must choose
> exactly where they want to go. It is a place of
> choice. Usually they have foreknowledge of the
> way to go. Everyone has such knowledge. But
> the diviner goes between the paths to a secret
> place. He knows more than other people. He has
> secret knowledge.
>
> Victor W. Turner, "Muchona the Hornet,
> Interpreter of Religion"

Who are those extraordinary individuals who become diviners, who take that other path? How are they chosen? How are they prepared? The following excerpt from Henry Callaway's texts about becoming a diviner illustrates the critical initial stage in a diviner's life and allows us to review a classic example of early European ethnography.

Callaway arrived in Natal as a missionary in 1854 and immediately began recording Zulu customs and language with his primary translator and informant, Umpengula (Benham 1896:77). He published "A Kaffir's Autobiography" in 1861, but his first major contribution was a Zulu folktale collection. Callaway realized that these tales were a means of "discovering what was the character of the mind of the people" (228), a theme he directly pursued in his most important work, *The Religious System of the Amazulu*, published in 1870. In the preface, he declares: "My object is to show that they have a well-defined religious system." This work was to include four sections covering traditions of creation, ancestor worship, divination, and "medical magic" and witchcraft. Callaway presents his informants' accounts verbatim in Zulu with parallel English translations and only occasional footnotes. The disparaging comments characteristic of his contemporary, the missionary Henri Junod, are absent.

A year later, Callaway offered an analysis of divination in which, as a nineteenth-century religious "man of science," he sought to understand human spirituality in its broadest sense. Callaway asserted that "there is a power of clairvoyance, naturally belonging to the human mind, or, in the words of a native [Zulu] speaking on this subject, 'There is something which is divination within man'" (1871–72:165, 168–69). This perspective was not well received at the Royal Anthropological Institute and, despite Edward Tylor's support, Callaway never received funds to complete publication of the fourth section of his *Religious System*. He returned to southern Africa but conducted no further research before ill health forced his retirement to England in 1887.

Callaway records four types of Zulu diviners (1970:259–374 and 1871–72:177–79; see also Fernandez 1967 and Fernandez's afterword to the present anthology). The first type, the *iziniyanga zesitupa*, or "thumb-doctor," gives diagnoses that are answered by people striking the ground with rods. A second type is the *iziniyanga ezadhla impepo*, "those who ate *impepo*" (see Callaway's excerpt, note 5). A third type includes the *omabukula iziniti*, who use sticks, and the *amatambo*, who use bones. Stick diviners employ three sticks, which leap toward the client and fix themselves on "that part of the body which corresponds with that which is diseased in the patient" (1871–72:178) In bone divination, animals' bones (each assigned a meaning) are cast and the diviner interprets their arrangement. Found throughout southern Africa, bone divination is described in detail by Junod (1927:539–72) and others. Lastly, there are the *abemilozi* or *inyanga yemilozi*. These diviners use *imilozi* ("familiar spirits")— "*amatongo* or spirits of the dead, who wait on a particular diviner, and speak in a low whistling tone . . . they are . . . spirits who live with a man" (Callaway 1970:348 n.l).

Whatever the divination method, clients are ready to criticize poor diviners who speak recklessly (1871–72:178). If a diviner fails in his diagnosis, the Zulu call him "the diviner who is a man" (i.e., *only* a man), or they may say, "He has wandered. He is lost" (1970:330 n.79, 289). A diviner's work is often compared to following a trail: "Now he will proceed carefully, following that footprint of truth. . . . Like a man who has lost his cattle, having found a footprint he will return again and again to it, till he succeeds in connecting it with others, and thus form a continuous track, which leads him to the lost property" (1970:324). Such imagery is encountered throughout Africa, both in terms of tracking down the truth and of discovering the proper pattern of factors relevant to the client's problem.

A diviner must go beyond his clients' responses and reveal the unknown. A good diviner "sees a difficult thing at once" and has a "clearness of perception" (*kcakcambisa*; literally, "to make white") (1970:321 n.74). According to Ngubane, a Zulu diviner's initiation is "a series of sacrifices and treatment with white medicines [which] all aim at promoting her illuminations" (1977:87). Ngubane's research among the Nyuswa Zulu generally confirms Callaway's texts except that Callaway's informants spoke only of male diviners while Ngubane asserts that "divination is a woman's thing [paternal ancestor spirits only return through daughters], and if a man gets possessed he becomes a transvestite, as he is playing the role of a daughter rather than that of a son" (1977:57 and 142). Callaway never mentions whether informants dressed as women, but Lee reports that young males dressed as women during their initiation (1969:140 and pl. 9). This critical matter of diviners' cross-gender identification is discussed in Peek's essay in this volume.

We would benefit from more life histories of diviners like those provided by Redmayne (1970), Turner (1967), and some of this volume's contributors. Callaway's record of Zulu diviners' initial experiences remains one of the most complete personal accounts available and corresponds to data reported for mediumistic diviners elsewhere in Africa. Because of the dangers associated with being a diviner, the "call," which comes from the ancestors or suprahuman powers, may at first be ignored (see the essays by Burton and Meyer below). An individual's selection may be signaled by patterned non-normal behavior (see Blier's essay) or, as among the Bena Lulua, by a period of illness or misfortune (McLean and Solomon 1971:38). Suspicions about such signs are confirmed through divination, as reported by Muchona, the Ndembu diviner (Turner 1967 and 1975:247–49). Insanity or even death for the chosen individual may result if the correct response is not made (Morris 1976:243). High intelligence, good memory, and especially personal control must be manifest as well, even for mediumistic diviners (see Zuesse 1979:210–11 and Bauer and Hinnant 1980:224).

Future diviners usually undergo a lengthy period of formal training. Yoruba diviners are trained for at least ten years in the branches of knowledge on which Ifa divination is based (Abimbola 1976; see also Bascom 1969:81–90 and McClelland 1982:85–95). Yaka diviners complete a rigorous year-long training in medicinal preparations and the special divination language (Huber 1965). With or without formal training, diviners are ceremonially presented to the community, often following an initiation ceremony. Complementing Callaway's record of male Zulu diviners' preparation are Ngubane's study of the initiation of Zulu women diviners (1977) and Boshier's account (1974). Symbols of death and rebirth dominate the elaborate initiation ceremonies of the Bena Lulua of Zaire (McLean and Solomon 1971:39–42). Middleton (1964, 1971) and Zahan (1983:83–86) provide further information on mediumistic diviners' initiations. When a diviner concludes training or initiation, she or he is tested publicly. Yoruba *babalawo* are examined extensively on the branches of Ifa knowledge, while Zulu diviners must demonstrate the clarity of their special vision by readily finding lost objects (as is done by Ndembu diviners: Turner 1975:261–62).

From Madagascar to Togo most diviners continue learning and refining their skills throughout their lives, sharing their expertise and studying with more renowned diviners. This common practice reminds us that these are shared epistemologies, not simply idiosyncratic behaviors and personal intuitions. In fact, the Yoruba and Malagasy have divination schools, and the Bena Lulua have formal diviners' associations headed by "queens" (McLean and Solomon 1971:26).

References

See reference list at end of main introduction.

Henry Callaway

The Initiation of a Zulu Diviner

The condition of a man who is about to be an *inyanga*[1] is this: At first he is apparently robust; but in process of time he begins to be delicate, not having any real disease, but being very delicate. He begins to be particular about food, and abstains from some kinds, and requests his friends not to give him that food, because it makes him ill. He habitually avoids certain kinds of food, choosing what he likes, and he does not eat much of that; and he is continually complaining of pains in different parts of his body. And he tells them that he has dreamt that he was being carried away by a river. He dreams of many things, and his body is muddled[2] and he becomes a house of dreams.[3] And he dreams constantly of many things, and on awaking says to his friends, "My body is muddled to-day; I dreamt many men were killing me; I escaped I know not how. And on waking one part of my body felt different from other parts; it was no longer alike all over." At last the man is very ill, and they go to the diviners to enquire.

The diviners do not at once see that he is about to have a soft head.[4] It is difficult for them to see the truth; they continually talk nonsense, and make false statements, until all the man's cattle are devoured at their command, they saying that the spirit of his people demands cattle, that it may eat food.

So the people readily assent to the diviners' word, thinking that they know. At length all the man's property is expended, he being still ill; and they no longer know what to do, for he has no more cattle, and his friends help him in such things as he needs.

At length an *inyanga'* comes and says that all the others are wrong. He says, "I know that you come here to me because you have been unable to do any thing for the man, and have no longer the heart to believe that any *inyanga* can help you. But, my friends, I see that my friends, the other *izinyanga*, have gone astray. They have not eaten *impepo*.[5] They were not initiated in a proper way. Why have they been mistaken, when the disease is evident? For my part, I tell you the *izinyanga* have troubled you. The disease does not require to be treated with blood.[6]

As for the man, I see nothing else but that he is possessed by the Itongo.[7] There is nothing else. He is possessed by an Itongo. Your people[8] move in him. They are divided into two parties; some say, 'No, we do not wish that our child should be injured. We do not wish it.' It is for that reason and no other that he does not get well. If you bar the way against the Itongo, you will be killing him. For he will not be an *inyanga*; neither will he ever be a man again; he will be what he is now. If he is not ill, he will be delicate, and become a fool, and be unable to understand any thing. I tell you you will kill him by using medicines. Just leave him alone, and look to the end to which the disease points. Do you not see that on the day he has not taken medicine, he just takes a mouthful of food?[9] Do not give him any more medicines. He will not die of the sickness, for he will have what is good[10] given him."

So the man may be ill two years without getting better; perhaps even longer than that. He may leave the house for a few days, and the people begin to think he will get well. But no, he is confined to the house again. This continues until his hair falls off. And his body is dry and scurfy; and he does not like to anoint himself. People wonder at the progress of the disease. But his head begins to give signs of what is about to happen. He shows that he is about to be a diviner by yawning[11] again and again. And men say, "No! Truly it seems as though this man was about to be possessed by a spirit." This is also apparent from his being very fond of snuff; not allowing any long time to pass without taking some. And people begin to see that he has had what is good given to him.

After that he is ill; he has slight convulsions, and has water poured on him, and they cease for a time. He habitually sheds tears, at first slight, and at last he weeps aloud, and in the middle of the night, when the people are asleep, he is heard making a noise, and wakes the people by singing; he has composed a song, and men and women awake and go to sing in concert with him.

In this state of things they daily expect his death;[12] he is now but skin and bones, and they think that tomorrow's sun will not leave him alive. The people wonder when they hear him singing, and they strike their hands in concert. They then begin to take courage, saying, "Yes, now we see that it is the head."[13]

Therefore whilst he is undergoing this initiation the people of the village are troubled by want of sleep; for a man who is beginning to be an *inyanga* causes great trouble, for he does not sleep, but works constantly with his brain; his sleep is merely by snatches, and he wakes up singing many songs; and people who are near quit their villages by night when they hear him singing aloud, and go to sing in concert. Perhaps he sings till the morning, no one having slept. The people of the village smite their hands in concert till they are sore. And then he leaps about the house like a frog; and the house becomes too small for him, and he goes out, leaping and singing, and shaking like a reed in the water, and dripping with perspiration.

At that time many cattle are eaten. The people encourage his becoming an *inyanga*; they employ means for making the Itongo white, that it may make his divination very clear. At length another ancient *inyanga* of celebrity is pointed out to him.[14] At night whilst asleep he is commanded by the Itongo, who says to him, "Go to So-and-so; go to him, and he will churn for you emetic-*ubulawo*,[15] that you may be an *inyanga* altogether." Then he is quiet for a few days, having gone to the *inyanga* to have *ubulawo* churned for him; and he comes back quite another man, being now cleansed and an *inyanga* indeed.

And if he is to have familiar spirits, there is continually a voice saying to him, "You will not speak with the people; they will be told by us every thing they come to enquire about." And he continually tells the people his dreams, saying "There are people[16] who tell me at night that they will speak for themselves to those who come to enquire." At last all this turns out to be true; when he has begun to divine, at length his power entirely ceases, and he hears the spirits who speak by whistlings[17] speaking to him, and he answers them as he would answer a man; and he causes them to speak by asking them questions; if he does not understand what they say, they make him understand every thing they see. The familiar spirits do not begin by explaining omens which occur among the people; they begin by speaking with him whose familiars they are, and making him acquainted with what is about to happen, and then he divines for the people.

This then is what I know of familiar spirits and diviners.

If the relatives of the man who has been made ill by the Itongo do not wish him to become a diviner, they call a great doctor to treat him, to lay the spirit, that he may not divine. But although the man no longer divines, he is not well; he continues to be always out of health. This is what I know. But although he no longer divines, as regards wisdom he is like a diviner. For instance, there was Undayeni. His friends did not wish him to become a diviner; they said, "No; we do not wish so fine and powerful a man to beocme a mere thing which stays at home, and does not work, but only divines." So they laid the spirit. But there still remained in him signs which caused the people to say, "If that man had been a diviner, he would have been a very great man, a first-class diviner."

As to the familiar spirits, it is not one only that speaks; they are very many; and their voices are not alike; one has his voice, and another his; and the voice of the man into whom they enter is different from theirs. He too enquires of them as other people do; and he too seeks divination of them. If they do not speak, he does not know what they will say; he cannot tell those who come for divination what they will be told. No. It is his place to take what those who come to enquire bring, and nothing more. And the man and the familiar spirits ask questions of each other and converse.

When those who come to seek divination salute him, he replies, "O, you have come when I am alone. The spirits departed yesterday. I do not know where they are gone." So the people wait. When they come they are heard saluting them, saying, "Good day." They reply, "Good day to you, masters." And the man who lives with them also asks them saying, "Are you coming?" They say, they are. It is therefore difficult to understand that it is a deception, when we hear many voices speaking with the man who has familiar spirits, and him too speaking with them.

The Way in Which a Person Begins to Be a Diviner

Uthlabo[18] is known by causing a sensation of perforation[19] of the side; and the man says, "I have pain under the armpit, beneath the shoulder-blade, in my side, in the flesh. It causes the feeling as if there was a hole there; the pain passes through my body to each side."

The men ask, "What is this disease? for it resembles nothing but *uthlabo*."

He replies, "Yes, yes; I too say it is *uthlabo*; it is that which comes out[20] from the side of my body and will not let me breathe, neither will it let me lie down."

At length the doctor who knows the medicines for *uthlabo* cures it. But black people call it also *ukxulo*,[21] and say it is a caused by the Itongo.[22] And when a man is constantly affected[23] by *uthlabo*, black men say the Itongo is walking in him; Amatongo are walking in his body. If the disease lasts a long time, they at length go to enquire of diviners. They come and say, "He is affected by the Itongo. He is affected by his people who are dead.[24] There was one of them who was an *inyanga*; and this man has the Itongo in this body; his people wish him to have a soft head,[25] and become a diviner, when he has been initiated."

The diviners say, "Do not give him any more medicines. Do you not see when you get *uthlabo*-medicines for him, the disease does not cease? When you give him medicine, do you not thereby increase the disease? Leave him alone. His people are in him. They wish him to dream."

And if one of his people who is dead was an *inyanga*, the diviners who come to divine call him by name, and say, "So-and-so is in him; it is he who says he is to be an *inyanga*. It is a great *inyanga* that possesses him." That is what the diviners say. They say, "The man who was an *inyanga*, who is walking in his body, was also an *inyanga* who could dig up poisons.[26] He used to dig them up. And since he who used to dig up the poison of the sorcerers by which they destroyed others has taken possession of this man, he too as soon as he has been initiated will have a white Itongo,[27] and will dig up poisons as So-and-so, one of his people, used to do. Leave him alone as regards medicines. Throw away medicines, and give him no more; you will kill him if you do. You think they will cure him. They will not cure him. He is purposely thus affected. The Amatongo wish him to become a white[28] *inyanga*. Be quiet, and see if the Amatongo do not give him commands at night in his sleep. You will see him come home in the morning, not having seen him go out, having had medicines revealed to him which he will go to the mountains to dig up; you will see he has dug up cleansing-*ubulawo*, and he will churn it and make it froth and drink it, and cleanse himself by it, and so begin to be an *inyanga*. And at other times he will be commanded to fetch *impepo*, which he will go to the marsh to pluck."

The Amatongo tell him to kill cattle, for the dead are very fond of demanding flesh of one whom they wish to make an *inyanga*. He slaughters them for his people who are dead. And others enter his kraal.[29] He slaughters constantly, and others again come in in their place, the cattle being derived from his treatment of disease, and from divining, and digging up poisons. When men are perishing, being destroyed by sorcerers, he goes and digs up the poisons, and purifies those whom the sorcerers are poisoning.

When the Amatongo make a man ill, he cries, "Hai, hai, hai."[30] They cause him to compose songs, and the people of his home assemble and beat tune to the song the Amatongo have caused him to compose—the song of initiation, a song of professional skill.

Some dispute and say, "No. The fellow is merely mad. There is no Itongo in him." Others say, "O, there is an Itongo in him; he is already an *inyanga*."

The others say, "No; he is mad. Have you ever hidden things for him to discover by his inner sight, since you say he is an *inyanga*?"

They say, "No; we have not done that."

They ask, "How then do you know he is an *inyanga*?"

They say, "We know it because he is told about medicines, which he goes to dig up."

They reply, "O! he is a mere madman. We might allow that he is an *inyanga* if you had concealed things for him to find, and he had discovered what you had concealed. But you tell us what is of no import, as you have not done this."

As they are talking thus and disputing about concealing things for him to find, at night when he is asleep he dreams that the man of his people who is dead, and who is causing him to begin to be an *inyanga*, tells him saying, "They were disputing with each other, saying you are not an *inyanga*."

He who is beginning to be an *inyanga* asks, "Why do they say I am not an *inyanga*?"

He replies, "They say you are not an *inyanga*, but a mere mad man; and ask if they have hidden things for you to discover, since the others say you are an *inyanga*." He says, "Tell me who they are who say so."

He replies, "So-and-so and So-and-so were disputing."

The man asks, "Do you say they lie when they say so?"

He replies, "Be quiet. Because they say so, I say you shall be a greater *inyanga* than all others, and all men in the world shall be satisfied that you are a great *inyanga*, and they shall know you."

The man who is beginning to be an *inyanga* says, "For my part I say they speak the truth when they say I am mad. Truly they have never hidden anything for me to find."

Then the man who was an *inyanga*, he who is initiating him, says, "Just be quiet. I will take you to them in the morning. And do you appear on a hill; do not come upon them suddenly; but appear on a hill which is concealed, and cry 'Hai, hai, hai;' cry thus on the hill which is concealed, that they may hear. When you cry 'hai, hai, hai,' if they do not hear, then go on to a hill which is open; do not expose yourself much; as soon as you expose yourself, cry 'Hai, hai, hai,' so that they may just hear. When they hear that it is you, go down again from the hill, and return to the one which is concealed. So I say they will see and understand that they have spoken of a man who is beginning to be a doctor; they shall know by that, that when they said you were a mad man and not an *inyanga* they were mistaken."

So he does so. He cries, "Hai, hai, hai," on a hill which is hidden; they do not hear him distinctly; they hear only a continual sound of *"Nkene, nkene, nkene, nkene."*[31] One of them says, "It sounds as though there was some one singing." Others say, "We do not hear. We hear only an echo."

The Itongo comes to him and tells him that they cannot hear, and bids him go out a little on the open hill, and then return again to the hill which is hidden.

So he departs at the word of the Itongo, and goes out to the open hill, and cries "Hai, hai, hai;" and they all hear that it is he. They are again disputing about him, and as soon as they hear that it is he, they say, "Can it be, sirs, that he comes about the matter we were disputing about, saying, he is mad?"

Others[32] say, "O, why do you ask? He comes on that account, if indeed you said he was not an *inyanga*, but a madman."

The great man of the village to which the *inyanga* is approaching, says, "I too say he is mad. Just take things and go and hide them, that we may see if he can find them."

They take things; one takes beads, and goes and hides them; others take picks, and go and hide them; other hide *assagais*; others bracelets; others hide their sticks, others their kilts, others their ornaments, others their pots; others hide baskets, and say, "Just let us see if he will find all these things or not." Others hide cobs of maize; others the ears of *amabele*, or sweet cane, or of *ujiba*, or the heads of *upoko*.

Some say, "O, if he finds all these things, will he not be tired? Why have you hidden so many?"

They say, "We hide so many that we may see that he is really an *inyanga*."

They reply, "Stop now; you have hidden very many things."

They return home, and wait. Then the Itongo tells him on the concealed hill; for it had already said to him, "Keep quiet; they are now hiding things; do not begin to appear. They wish to say when you find the things that you saw when they hid them. Be quiet, that they may hide all the things; then they will satisfied that you are an *inyanga*." Now the Itongo tells him, "They have now hidden the things, and gone home. It is proper for you now to go to the home of the people who say you are mad and not an *inyanga*."

So he comes out on the open mountain, and runs towards their home, being pursued by his own people who are seeking him, for he went out during the night, and they did not hear when he went out very early in the morning, when it was still dark, when the horns of the cattle were beginning to be just visible.[33] He reaches their home, and his own people who are looking for him, and have now found him, come with him. On his arrival he dances; and as he dances they strike hands in unison; and the people of the place who have hidden things for him to find, also start up and strike hands; he dances, and they smite their hands earnestly.

He says to them, "Have you then hid things for me to find?"

They deny, saying, "No; we have not hidden things for you to find."

He says, "You have."

They deny, saying, "It is not true; we have not."

He says, "Am I not able to find[34] them?"

They say, "No; you cannot. Have we hidden then things for you to find?"

He says, "You have."

They deny, declaring that they have not done so. But he asserts that they have.

When they persist in their denial, he starts up, shaking his head. He goes and finds the beads; he finds the picks, and the kilts, and the bracelets; he finds the cobs of maize, and the ears of the *amabele* and *ujiba* and of *upoko*; he finds all the things they have hidden. They see he is a great *inyanga* when he has found all the things they concealed.

He goes home again as soon as he has found all the things, and not one thing remains outside where they had hidden it. On his return to their home from the river whither he had gone to find what was hidden, he is tired, and the Amatongo say to him, "Although you are tired, you will not sleep here; we will go home with you." This is what the Amatongo say to the *inyanga* when he is tired with finding the things.

The *inyanga*'s people who accompany him say, "Just tell us if he is not an *inyanga*?"

And he says, "I have found all the things which you hid; there is nothing left outside; all things are here in the house. I was commanded to come to you, for you said I was not an *inyanga*, but a madman, and asked if my people had hidden things for me to find. Just say who told me the things about which you were speaking. You said I was mad. You thought you were just speaking. Do you think the Amatongo do not hear: As you were speaking, they were listening. And when I was asleep they told me that I was a worthless *inyanga*, a mere thing."

Then the people make him presents. One comes with beads and gives him; another brings a goat; another an *assagai*; another a bracelet; another brings an ornament made of beads, and gives him. The chief of the village gives him a bullock; and all the chief men give him goats, because he had come to their village at the bidding of the Amatongo.

Notes

This excerpt from *The Religious System of the Amazulu* (Cape Town: C. Struik, 1970, pp. 259–80) may be a combination of several informants' accounts. Callaway's original notes have been kept while occasionally changing his punctuation, deleting his comparative references, and italicizing the Zulu terms. Also added are clarifications from elsewhere in Callaway's original texts and some editorial comments in square brackets. Parallel Zulu texts are not reproduced.

1. *Inyanga*, a diviner.

2. *Dungeka*: *Ukudunga* is to stir up mud in water, so as to make the water turbid,

or muddy; and is hence applied by metaphor to confusion or muddling of mind by trouble, disturbance of a family or a village by contention and quarrelling, and, as above, to general derangement of the body from disease.

3. "A house of dreams," meaning that he dreams constantly, that dreams take up their abode with him. Many dreams are supposed to be caused or sent by the Amatongo [ancestors], but not all.

4. "A soft head," that is, impressible. Diviners are said to have "soft" heads.

5. *Impepo* is of two kinds—white and black. The black is first used as an emetic to remove all the badness and causes of dimness from the system. The white is burnt as incense when sacrificing to the Amatongo; *izinyanga* use it as an emetic to prevent the return of dimness of the inner sight after the use of the black *impepo*; they also eat it; and place it under their heads at night, that they may have clear, truthful dreams. They believe that by the use of this medicine they are enabled to divine with accuracy. Hence to have "eaten *impepo*" means to be a trustworthy diviner.

6. "Treated with blood," that is, of sacrifices.

7. *Umhlaba*, "the earth," is a name given to the Amatongo, that is, the Abapansi, or Subterraneans; i.e., "ancestral spirits" [see Callaway 1970:147–48 n.14].

8. "Your people move in him," that is, the Amatongo. Or, he is possessed by your people.

9. When he takes medicines, he eats nothing and is worse than usual. When he leaves off medicines, he is better and takes a little food.

10. "What is good," viz., the power to divine.

11. Yawning is considered a sign of approaching inspiration by the Itongo. [Callaway's reference to the effects of a troll's yawns found in Icelandic legends are deleted.]

12. Lit., "It is now seen by the morning," viz., that he is still alive. They retire to rest doubtful whether they shall find him still living at daybreak.

13. Lit., "We see the head," viz., that it is affected in that way which is followed by the power to divine.

14. That is, by the Itongo in a dream.

15. *Ubulawo*, "a class of medicines, used for cleansing and brightening. Medicines used with the view of removing from the system something that causes dislike [black *ubulawo*], and introducing into it something that will cause love [white *ubulawo*]. [See Callaway 1970:142–43 n. 10.]

16. "People," viz., the dead, the Amatongo.

17. The supposed voice of the familiar spirits is always in a shrill, whistling tone; hence they are called *imilozi*.

18. *Uhlabo*, the name of a disease, from *ukuhlaba*, to stab, because it is attended with a stabbing pain or stitch in the side. It is applied either to pleurodynia or pleurisy.

19. *Isibobo*, "a hole;" that is, the patient feels as though a hole has been made in his side with a sharp instrument. The same sensation that we call a "stitch in the side."

20. He speaks of the disease as though it was a knife, or something of that kind; he personifies it.

21. *Ukxulo*: the same as *uhlabo*, from *ukukxula*, "to stab."

22. We may compare the following faith in evil Nats, which seem to hold very much the same position in the East as the Amatongo among the Amazulu. . . . [The long quotation about the role of Nats in Burma is deleted.]

23. *Tandwa*, lit., "loved." [It is significant that Callaway chooses not to enter this meaning in the text (although he has at least informed us of it) because this is certainly the more appropriate term for the relationship of the diviner and these powers.]

24. That is, the Amatongo.

25. To have a soft or impressible head, that is, to be an *inyanga*.

26. *Ukumbulula*.—Sorcerers are supposed to destroy their victims by taking some portion of their bodies, as hair or nails; or something that has been worn next [to] their person,

as a piece of an old garment, and adding to it certain medicines, which is then buried in some secret place. They are at once the subjects of disease, and suffer and die. The power alluded to above is that of discovering and digging up this poison. Very similar to the practice of sorcerers amongst ourselves, who used to make an image of wax or clay of the person they wished to kill, and treat it with poisons, etc., and every thing done to the image was felt by their victim. [Callaway's example of such practices from Danish tradition is deleted.]

27. That is, an Itongo who shall influence for good, and enable him to see *clearly* and help others. They also speak of an Itongo *elimnyama*, a dark or black Itongo, that is one that is jealous, and when he visits any one causes disease and suffering without giving any reason for his doing so. It is said, *"Li lwe li tulile,"* that is, "It fights in silence," —contends with people without telling them what to do to pacify it. They suppose that sorcerers are aided by the Amatongo of their house to practice sorcery with skill and effect; but such Amatongo are not said to be black or dark, but white, because they reveal with clearness their will to their devotee.

28. As we speak of "white witches;" [he should become] an *inyanga* who shall see clearly, and use his power for good purposes. [While this may well be true, Callaway has elsewhere cited white solely in terms of clarity of divinatory vision.]

29. By sacrificing to the Amatongo he obtains their blessing; they enable him to treat disease and to divine successfully; and thus he obtains many cattle, which enter his kraal instead of those he has sacrificed.

30. *Haiya*, to cry as the diviner; a continued repetition of "Hai, hai, hai."

31. *Nkene*, from *ukunkeneza*, "to echo."

32. That is, who were not present at the former discussion.

33. *Ku'mpondo zankomo*, "It is the horns of a bullock;" a saying to express the earliest dawn, when the horns of the cattle are just becoming visible.

34. Lit., "take out," viz., from the place of concealment.

PART TWO

The Search for Knowledge

The right conduct of affairs will need, first of
all, the use of divination. . . .
       Marcel Griaule and Germaine Dieterlen,
         "The Dogon of the French Sudan"

An understanding pervades African societies that the true reasons for all events can be known, but sufficient knowledge is seldom available through mundane means of inquiry; therefore, divination is employed to ensure that all relevant information is brought forward before action is undertaken. Because of its primacy, divination is counted among the most ancient traditions of African cultures, as it is of other cultures.

Virtually every civilization has linked divination's advent to the introduction of other necessary technologies and arts (see Caquot and Leibovici 1968 and Loewe and Blacker 1981). In Madagascar, Andriamamelo, the mythical founder of the Merina royal dynasty, discovered metal working and "is also represented as a master of astrology, an advanced technique of civilization, which he is said to have discovered" (Bloch 1986:106). The ancient Greeks recorded that Prometheus gave them much technical knowledge, including the arts of divination. Other Greek traditions about divination concern the blinding of Tiresias as punishment by the gods, who then granted him extraordinary vision through divination. These accounts contain remarkable similarities to the associations with divination encountered in African cultures, such as liminality and androgyny, which are discussed later in this volume by Peek.

Despite divination's centrality, accounts of its origins are not easily found. The detailed Yoruba historical traditions about Ifa are an exception (see Bascom 1969; Abimbola 1976; McClelland 1982). Usually there are only marginal comments, such as Lienhardt's reference (1970) to the time before the Dinka had diviners as intermediaries between worlds. For the Atuot of the Sudan (see Burton's essay below) and the Lobi of Burkina Faso (see Meyer's essay), an original world of harmony was disrupted by improper human behavior, for which God punished the people by giving them ignorance, illness, and death. While God "blinded" humans to the "real" reasons for events, simultaneously divination was made available so they might "see" and still find meaning and order in their lives.

Nadel offers an interesting comment on divination's primordial role in the scheme of things for the Nupe:

> Although Nupe divination is marked off as being "of God," it is not numbered among the other, similar "things of the world," that is, of creation. Nor are there any legends explaining its origin or appearance on earth. This ambiguity seems in keeping with the peculiar role of divination in Nupe religious practice. Divination is clearly one of the tools bestowed by God upon man so that he may be better fitted to cope with the practical problems of life on earth; but these include also the problem of handling successfully all the other transcendental tools. And just because divination is such a twofold "prerequisite" and is basically indispensable, its presence is simply taken for granted. (1970:65)

Oral traditions and early European accounts confirm that many divination systems are centuries old, and while some have changed significantly, most demonstrate great stability and antiquity. Using Shona divining tablet markings, Huffman interprets similar markings on soapstone birds from the Great Zimbabwe ruins, thus suggesting a seven-hundred-year time depth for that divination system (1985).

The history of a people can be gained from divination texts and traditions, as Abimbola demonstrates with Ifa divination verses (1967). Vansina utilizes divination customs to illuminate Bushong and Kuba histories (1971, 1978). Drewal and Drewal reconstruct an Ifa diviner's family history from his shrine (1985).

Too seldom are distinctions drawn between indigenous and foreign forms, as noted by Horton (1964) for the Kalabari Ijo and by Mendonsa (1982) for the Sisala. The pioneering studies by Junod (1927) and Evans-Pritchard (1968) do, however, comment on origins of Thonga and Zande divination types among their neighbors. For southern Africa, Zuesse discusses the origins and distribution of *hakata* dice and basket divination forms (1979) and surveys were done by Reynolds (1963:102–21), Roumeguère-Eberhardt (1968), and Greenbaum (1973). In reconstructing Dahomean history, Herskovits concludes that the Abomey kings introduced Fa (a cognate of the Yoruba Ifa system) to replace older divination forms and to validate their political control (1938). Comparative studies of African divination systems often offer only contextless enumerations, such as Lévy-Bruhl's cataloging of divination forms (1966) and Davis's study of divining bowls (1955). There are a few studies of specific divination types, such as Bourguignon's on mediumistic forms (1968) and Peek's on the divining chain complex in southern Nigeria (1982). Bascom (1969:1–12 and 1980) and Bastide (1968) provide comparative studies of African-American divination forms.

In the course of demonstrating divination's critical role in the search for knowledge, the two essays in this section prove the value of regional studies of divination systems. Burton analyzes the relationship of Atuot divination to practices among other Nilotic peoples of the Sudan (thus permitting comparison with Evans-Pritchard's work on the Nuer and Lienhardt's on the Dinka). For the Atuot, inter-ethnic antagonisms are reflected in the origins and behaviors of the *jao*, the spiritual beings who are the most common agents of misfortune. Although the *jao* cause misfortune, they enable the Atuot to "see" the true consequences of human actions through their possession of diviners.

In Madagascar it is the ancestors who guide human action through divination, as Vérin and Rajaonarimanana show in their discussion of the development and diffusion of divination by Antemoro diviners. Diviners mediate between the living and the ancestors as they reveal each individual's *vintana*, or "destiny." The multifaceted integration by the Antemoro of Arabic astrology and the indigenous system based on lunar months is evident in the diviner's ancient guides in Arabico-Malagasy script, which incorporate astrological information, *sikidy* figures, and traditional medicinal preparations (see Sussman and Sussman 1977; Bloch 1968; Mack 1986). This process is similar to that of the Ethiopian *awdunigist* diviner, who also uses synoptic texts to guide his numerological diagnoses (Young 1977).

Vérin and Rajaonarimanana's use of archival materials as well as ethnographic data gives a diachronic perspective on the existing epistemology's adaptation of the Arabic system. For years Islamic divination practices were assumed to be the source of sub-Saharan African traditions. Certainly there has been Arabic influence in East Africa, as Whyte and Parkin note (see their essays in this volume), and in Nigeria (see Bascom 1969; Boston 1974; Nadel 1970); but in Madagascar, as elsewhere, Arabic systems probably were either appended to indigenous systems or absorbed in a syncretic process by the diviners to augment their divinatory repertoires.

Future research on African systems of divination will benefit greatly from historical and comparative approaches, especially in regionally based studies. The recording of African peoples' histories will rely more and more on the indigenous texts generated by divination sessions. In the search for knowledge, divination illuminates individual client histories as well as maintaining and adjusting group traditions. Therefore, such texts both contain and comment directly on a culture's historical record.

References

See reference list at end of main introduction.

John W. Burton

Nilotic Cosmology and the Divination of Atuot Philosophy

This essay is concerned with a universal human dilemma as experienced and interpreted by a particular cultural and linguistic community, the Atuot in southern Sudan. The problems the Atuot address through the means to be described below are universal in the sense that personal misfortune is a perpetual rather than an extraordinary element of human existence. In the Nilotic Sudan—the homeland of the peoples known as Shilluk, Anuak, Dinka, Nuer, and Atuot—a common source of misfortune is believed to be possession of a person by one or another *jok*, which these people regard as a suprahuman spirit. The remedy is sought in divination. The closely related Shilluk and Anuak languages use the term *jok* (plural, *jao*) to refer to a refraction of the creator divinity, while in the Nuer, Dinka, and Atuot languages *jok* typically connotes a lesser or earthly spiritual agent that either possesses or is owned by a mortal human being. Permutations of this conception are evident not just in the Nilotic Sudan but throughout Nilotic Africa (see Ogot 1961).

Given the ubiquity of possession by a *jok* and of the use of diviners to resolve the problem, an understanding of this element of life in the Nilotic Sudan entails an understanding of both phenomenological and spiritual realities. When one examines social facts recorded for the Shilluk, Anuak, Dinka, Nuer, and Atuot, one is inevitably engaged in a study of regional variations on a theme. Unfortunately, both the quality and the quantity of firsthand accounts of possession and divination among these peoples are uneven. A careful review of published studies suggests that further research among the Shilluk and Anuak peoples on this topic would surely be welcomed and would amply reward the efforts demanded. Nevertheless, enough research has already been conducted in Dinka, Nuer, and Atuot communities to allow a number of general conclusions.

In Dinka, Nuer, and Atuot cosmology, an ordered and consistent division of the moral and suprahuman world is imagined. The terms *Nhialic*, *Kwoth*, and *Decau* connote a creator divinity that is omnipotent, though generally removed from the mundane affairs of secular life. While petitions and invocations uttered at collective blood sacrifices invariably make final reference to this divinity (or God, as Evans-Pritchard called it), only in dire situations is the divinity petitioned directly (see Burton 1980b). A category of spiritual powers closely associated with the divinity also is imagined by these peoples. Variously called "heavenly" or "free" divinities, these powers affect everyone in a like manner.

This spiritual division is mirrored by a category one may term earthly powers. They manifest in domestic contexts and are more numerous than the spiritual agents. Since they are further removed from divinity, they are imagined to be inferior (see Evans-Pritchard 1956; Lienhardt 1961; Burton 1981). This earthly category of suprahuman phenomena actually defines the world of Nilotic possession and divination and thus is the focus of discussion in this essay.

Nilotic divination is a process in which (1) an individual is believed to be possessed by a spiritual agent; (2) a different individual is called upon to diagnose the spiritual agent that has brought on the particular physical or moral dilemma; and (3) a community of opinion is established in regard to social accountability and ritual recourse as a consequence of possession. The afflicted individual and the community to which he or she belongs commonly are transformed significantly by the experience.

The majority of such possessions manifest in physical maladies. Given the wide variety of illnesses in southern Sudan, Nilotic divination must be characterized as an open spectrum, a continually evolving system to account for unexpected and uncontrollable circumstances. As Lienhardt writes, "Some Dinka assert that the free divinities are comparatively recent introductions, and they are certainly prepared for revelations of new free divinities which may enter Dinkaland at particular times and places" (1961:164; cf. Evans-Pritchard 1956:63–105).

The quintessential illustration of this general and, one must assume, perpetual phenomenon is reported for the Mandari, who live on the southern fringes of Dinka and Atuot territories. Indeed, a central portion of Buxton's study of Mandari cosmology and religion (1973:64–113) is concerned with understanding a "foreign" possession cult associated with *jok*. Buxton states:

> The Mandari claim that during the last few decades new forces affecting health and well-being have made an appearance in their country. The Mandari category designation for these forces which are manifest in multiple form is *jok*. . . .
> Certain punitive expeditions carried out against Aliab and Atuot are seen as directly instrumental in bringing powers to Mandari country. . . . One of these armed forays was against a group of Atuot who were camping in open bush . . . a number of Atuot were killed and wounded. The Mandari constantly return to this incident declaring "The blood of people with *jok* was spilt on our soil, so the angry *jok* belonging to the dead and dying Atuot were loosed in Mandari."
> (1973:66)

Buxton further notes that "the word *jok* is now used to describe any illness thought to have spread or to have been picked up from a neighboring tribe" (67).

Buxton's comments highlight two important facts about possession and divination in the Nilotic Sudan. First, death and the experience of dying are associated with the destruction or collapse of a moral community. In other words, possession threatens both the individual and the larger group. Throughout the region *jao* are associated with immoral and amoral phenomena which affront community standards. Second, the recurrent notion that one or another *jok* originates from beyond the boundary of a specific linguistic community underscores the vital significance of the concept of community in the definition of local social experience. At a further remove, possession and its associated interpretations may be cited as one factor in local perceptions of ethnic difference.

Unfortunately, Evans-Pritchard, writing on the Nuer, had relatively little to say in this regard. Lienhardt and Deng, on the other hand, observed and recognized the central role that possession and divination assume in the Dinka's definition of social and individual experience, so that rather than being epiphenomena of spiritual existence, possession and divination were seen as central to an understanding of Nilotic religions in general. In Lienhardt's words,

> When faced with the failure of sacrifice to produce the required result which is the proximate occasion of sacrifice, [Dinka suggest] that "Divinity has refused" or, more likely, that the power which was really the grounds of the man's sickness was not correctly identified. So, what is required is another sacrifice, and not alternative action. (1961:291)

And when experience contradicts expectation, the limits of human agency are explicitly recognized. As Deng writes:

> Diseases or other evils are not always corrected successfully. In each case, the Dinka find an easy answer in the refusal of divinities to be appeased, or perhaps in the failure of the diviner to have discovered the cause. It would seem that where the organic disease is one that psychological cure cannot effect, or where the patient's condition is too serious, the diviner's psychological cure is likely to be ineffective. In these cases, some diviners are honest enough to tell the relatives that they can do nothing—and that the man must die. (1971:131)

From a different perspective one can argue that the divination experience is ultimately a dialectic between an individual's sense of identity and a social definition of experience, dividing the social personality and in consequence redefining the moral community. Both socially and individually, Nilotic divination draws attention to change and adaptation in social relationships. It does not recreate a community but rather redefines the context of social life.

To the individual who becomes the focus of this attention the diviner is a medium through which a process of psychological projection is made public. Among the Atuot, as among the Nuer, Dinka, Shilluk, and Anuak, the diviner is an individual within whom a power or a number of powers is always latent. The diviner has the ability to dissociate this power at will, thus inviting other powers to possess the self. When the individual affliction is identified as one or another spiritual agent, the grounds and reasons for its existence become manifest in the afflicted. Divination externalizes the self. The "inner" experience of possession must involve a division of existence between the self and the power; the diviner then leads a public gathering through an enactment of that division through a ritual of blood sacrifice. Thus the inner division of experience is externally confirmed. A suprahuman agent is recognized and, in the best of hopes, a unity of self is recreated—or perhaps *reconfigured* is a more appropriate term (see Lienhardt 1961: 152–53).

The preceding remarks, I believe, are generally applicable in comparative studies of the divination experience in the Nilotic Sudan. The comments and observations that follow offer evidence of one variation on this common theme.

In their image of a mythical world, the pastoral Atuot of southern Sudan convey the impression that there were at one time none of the radical dichotomies which now figure as common features of experience. The sky and earth were conjoined; life in its present sense did not exist because there was no death. The general order of existence was an order of unity and completeness.

That primordial world was violently transformed when human beings first acted with self-conscious intention, when, in a sense, the individual emerged from the collectivity. A woman who was pounding grain to prepare a meal self-indulgently sought, in a sudden burst of avarice, to make more than was needed. Common instances of personal misfortune are often defined by the same circumstances. An interpretation of what the Atuot see as an essential human proclivity, to seek gain at another's expense or to suffer misfortune because of some other's antisocial behavior, is fundamental to an understanding of Atuot divination.

One Atuot myth recounts how, at the moment human greed was first manifested, people became blind to its source. In this story, an avaricious man was speared in his side, and as his blood gushed from his mouth he was unable to see the cause of his demise. The mythical image in some instances closely corresponds to daily experience; it offers a reason for performing and participating in rituals of divination.

Atuot certainly do not collectively proclaim a unified philosophy any more than do ordinary folk in any society; each adult is a philosopher of sorts, cognizant of general causes and principles, yet resigned to recognize and act upon the limits of human knowledge. Each adult equally defines his or her philosophy through a process of conjecture and enacts a series of social relationships on the expectation of positive or negative reciprocity. Atuot do, however, share more specific notions relating to misfortune, expiation, and vengeance. These moral and religious precepts, which are defined by their shared knowledge about the source of jealousy and greed, figure in Atuot cosmology as *jao*.

Elsewhere I have described a number of rituals the Atuot perform in association with the spiritual powers (Burton 1980a, 1981). The problem I now wish to address in this context is rather more analytic. I hope to convey an understanding of how what I call Atuot philosophy is a phenomenon reflected in a diverse variety of rituals centered on the problem of divining one or another source of misfortune. There is an Atuot proverb that can be glossed as "everyone has something in his heart." This points to two divergent themes. On one hand the Atuot are agreed, as most peoples seem to be, that there is an order of sociability and reciprocity that everyone ought to observe and respect. On the other hand there is at the same time a shared opinion that "what is mine" may interfere with "what is yours," even though this opinion may be understood and interpreted by different people toward different ends. It is in the context of divination that these differences are publicly acknowledged. And that is the point of this essay: the experience of divination results in a philosophy; the latter is the result of the former. Beattie made the same point: "In a general sense, most people act out their rituals first, and philosophise about them afterwards" (1980:30).

In the myth about the man who died from the thrust of a spear, his people were living in a camp by the riverside, fishing. Nearby lived "the powers," who were engaged in the same activity. This man became jealous of the powers and the catches of fish they had accumulated. When the powers had gone off to fish one morning, he stole some of the fish they had left behind. When they returned, one power protested this injustice and went "up to God," complaining that "people have now become very strong and are stealing our fish." God replied, "I will close their eyes." When the man died suddenly, his people said among themselves, "What is it that is killing us that we cannot see?" (Burton 1981:79). God in his paternal role (as Atuot sometimes view him) also sought to protect the interests of human beings when he saw them mourning the death of one of their fellows. He selected one man among the many who were blind and gave him the ability to "see" powers. And thus originated the first *tiet*, or diviner.

Commonly a person may consider becoming a diviner after he or she has been possessed by a malignant power and later regained health. It is usually men rather than women who choose to do so. (By far the majority of *tiet* I knew personally or learned of were men; women may become *tiet* but always call upon a man to assist in the rite of sacrifice.) The decision is entirely personal, and clearly the majority of formerly possessed individuals do not choose to become practitioners. Those who do first serve in an informal manner as apprentices under the supervision of a person who has already established a reputation for knowing the ways of powers and for dealing with them effectively.

The apprentice's assumption of knowledge about the *jao* is marked by a ritual performed in his hut by his teacher. This ritual entails the sacrifice of a goat, the flesh of which is said to be favored by these powers. The younger man, holding the goat close to his chest as though suckling it, sits on the lap of the teacher, who sings to the accompaniment of his rattle. The animal is then immolated, and its carcass is severed from head to tail. Half goes to each man to be consumed the same evening. The initiate then remains inside his hut for a short period; six days is a figure often cited.

This sacrificial rite is essential, the Atuot explain, for the man to gain the ability to look for, and later see, a *jok* within the walls of a hut or inside the body of an individual. It is then known that the younger man *ca puoce tiet*, "has come to know the ways of powers." The theme of separation, seclusion, and reintegration is evident in this rite of initiation. When the new *tiet* later performs a ritual of divination or exorcism, he acts as a mediator between two worlds, separated from the human realm in order to establish communication with the suprahuman.

The term *tiet* is derived from *tet*, "hand." During the divination ritual the *tiet* holds a rattle in his hand, but it is said to be the *jok*, the suprahuman power within his body, that shakes the rattle, not the *tiet* himself. As the Atuot say, "This is the *jok* moving within him." His own consciousness apparently becomes subordinate to the *jok* that is presumed to control his behavior.

A short text offered by the diviner Mayan Acuot may help in understanding this basic feature of Atuot divination:

> A *tiet* sees *jok* as you see people in the reflection of water. This is how it comes to your eyes. It comes with the thing that was taken [*kue jaal ke a diet ma yen ca lom*]. The *jok* comes to claim its property. The *tiet* will know the reason because he can see it. If a man steals a cow the *jok* comes and says, "This is mine." The *jok* says, "I am coming because of this and that."

Because *jao* are considered to be spiritual manifestations of an individual's inner state of consciousness—manifestations that may enter and act upon another individual—they can be spoken of as active spiritual agents (see Burton 1981).

As Mayan Acuot indicated, divination involves two separate though closely related phenomena. First, the *tiet* must come to know in the course of his work which of the many *jao* in the Atuot pantheon has taken possession of an individual. The *jao* identified by the Atuot generally correspond to diseases as defined by Western medical knowledge. *Thong alal*, for example, is the spiritual power Atuot experience as generalized fever. *Abiel*, the power that speared the man in the myth, is known by the symptoms we associate with amoebic dysentery. *Agok* possession resembles the symptoms of cerebral-spinal disease. (The term *agok* also means "monkey," and a friend once drew, at my request, a picture of a person possessed by *agok*; it shows a man lying on the ground with a monkey on his back.) Second, the *tiet* claims as an important part of his competence the ability to name the individual who was initially responsible for "sending" a power that brought on the symptoms. It should be stressed that the experience of possession by a *jok*—to the degree that this experience can be translated by a foreigner who does not claim to have been similarly possessed—always manifests in a physical malady rather than a psychic transformation of the self.[1]

To describe the situation that gives rise to divination, Atuot use the phrase *ca dom ke jao*, which indicates that a power seizes, commandeers, or takes complete control over a person. When that happens, a *tiet* is called, and he normally arrives that evening at the homestead of the afflicted.

A group of people who share some relationship of kinship with the possessed gather nearby. The composition of this gathering depends on a number of factors. For example, in the case of Akoi, who had experienced spontaneous abortion a number of times, her affines as well as her natal kin were present. Her husband's kin presumed that her apparent inability to carry out a normal term of pregnancy was due to her mother's brother's dissatisfaction with the number and quality of cattle he had received as bridewealth at the time of her marriage. The identity of the power in question may also be a factor. If it is revealed to be a minor power, few may attend the divination. Conversely, possession by a "strong" or "hot" power entails the support of more kin.

Akoi's case reflects traditional ethics ("everyone has something in his heart"), but contemporary dimensions of experience also figure in Atuot divination. I was present at one seance (discussed below) that focused on a young boy who had become paralyzed from the waist down. The *tiet* indicated that the sick boy's elder brother, who had been a guerrilla soldier, had stolen and slaughtered an ox belonging to another man, a rather common practice during the civil war in southern Sudan. It was assumed that the owner of the ox had sent a *jok* to malign the young boy as vengeance.

From a functionalist viewpoint the custom of sending a power to harm another individual would appear to be decidedly antisocial, since an innocent person is made to suffer for another's misdeeds. Yet all those kin of the afflicted who can attend the ensuing divination ritual are expected to do so. Thus one can propose that what is publicly witnessed at a divination or exorcism is a positive assertion of shared moral sentiments. And the quest to ensure well-being takes place in the homestead, a setting that has strong symbolic associations with women and the genesis of life in Atuot cosmology. Significantly, it is commonly the case that women and young children are the victims of a *jok* (see Burton 1980a). In this light it is important to note that women who have some degree of relationship to the afflicted often become possessed during divination to aid the *tiet* in his work. Thus, whereas Atuot will casually inform the foreigner that it is the *tiet* who carries out the task of divination, it is in fact a public event frequently entailing the active participation of women.

One evening my wife and I sat with some Atuot friends outside their homestead while a *tiet* slowly walked around the perimeter of the hut, softly singing a number of songs intended to "wake up" the *jok* within him. It is from his own *jok* or a number of other powers that a *tiet* gains the strength to exorcise a malignant spirit. After a short while the *tiet* came to sit on the ground near a small boy who could no longer walk. As the *tiet* shook his rattle, onlookers began to clap in rhythm to the songs he sang.

After a few hours, the *tiet* called out "*Arum!*" The power in question, Abiel, had been encountered and had entered the diviner's body. He then called for a *gam long*, someone to catch his words (literally, "to hold the voice of the *jok*") and repeat them for the public gathering. The *tiet* now became the mouthpiece of the *jok*, a medium between the human and suprahuman realms.

Figure 1. Mayan, an Atuot diviner, leads songs during a divination session in Abaang village, Sudan, November 1976. *Photo by John W. Burton.*

Figure 2. An afflicted Atuot woman, Akoi, has the power drawn out of her body by Marial, a diviner, in Yirol village, Sudan, February 1977. *Photo by John W. Burton.*

As the power shook the diviner's rattle, the *gam long* delivered the words of the *jok* to the people through the medium of the *tiet*. The boy's mother and father then entered into a dialogue with the power.

Jok: Greetings, people. I am going.

Mother: Abiel, show us something. Do not leave silently like this. Tell us something; bring a word.

Jok: People are not active in these times. Who can I make a dance with? [I.e., too few people are present.]

Mother: Tell me only one thing.

Jok: The ox was shot in the pool with a gun.

Mother: Tell me something about it. No one will show me the way except you, Abiel. You, Abiel of my father, power of my grandfather. . . .

Jok: I have finished the word.

Father: Tell us that the ox was shot at the pool.

Jok: The ox was shot at the pool.

Father: What is it that brought this problem?

Jok: There was also a *jok* that was with you—they came together. I am leaving.

Mother: Do not leave—finish the word.

Jok: I will answer them tomorrow. All the people should come. The words are finished.

Father: What is the *jok* that has come now?

Jok: No more words.

Mother: You will not say the words properly. If you say it tomorrow, it will be good. This household has remained without people. If his death will come, you had better tell us so we can leave it. Do not deceive us.

Jok: People die even if there are others there to help. That is it. The *jok* is missing. Did you hear? I am only the messenger. . . . You will settle this tomorrow when *agok* [a power] and *thong alal* [another power] come. They will come and settle the words. This is my word. I am leaving. Sleep will come within two days and we will sacrifice this goat laughing [i.e., in celebration of a successful exorcism].

Mother: I want sleep [health]. We can only ask for sleep.

Jok: Did the boy not walk at one time?

Mother: Yes, he did walk.

Jok: If he walked one time, there is no problem. I do not want to kill your cow [i.e., goat] in vain. Do you understand? I will kill it so that people will talk of it later [i.e., it will not be done until things are properly organized; people will not have to ask in vain why the animal was killed if nothing good came of it].

Father: This is true. I will keep quiet because you have said you are messenger. Agok is still away. We will get it tomorrow. Everything comes because of the feud. Long ago when there was a fight a person went to get a *jok*. When he [the man who killed the ox] was made responsible, he could not leave what he was told to do. He was given orders—that was Anya nya.

Jok: So it is. We will make it tomorrow.

Then followed another long chorus of songs, and the goat that had been tethered for sacrifice was brought back inside the house.

The following night people gathered again. After the standard chorus of songs, the *tiet* announced *"Arum!"* and all became silent.

> *Father*: We want to know what is giving sickness.
>
> *Jok*: The land is confused.
>
> *Mother*: The sickness has been here for months.
>
> *Jok*: The land is confused, it is confused by all the human beings. There is Nuer over there—they kill people. People who live in the forest, the Anya nya, have also confused things. [Both statements vaguely recall the original world where unity and harmony were the norm, before a violent transformation into opposites.] This is what I will tell you. The ox was killed by your son with a gun. Do you understand? This is why the word came to the *tiet*. This is what brought Abiel. This was done by your brother.
>
> *Father*: He is my brother, I cannot deny this. All the things that happened, all those things, were not done by him alone. How did it come, when so many cattle were killed by the Anya nya? No one knew that it was going to fall on him alone.
>
> *Jok*: It is *jok* belonging to your people of Luac here. It is your own *jok* that is bringing this. The day you sacrifice the goat, that is the day I will give the name of the man. People of this land are hating themselves.

My wife and I left Atuot country before we learned the results of this process of divination, though I doubt whether this fact diminishes the import of the text. A person may or may not recover from possession and the malignancy it often entails. What is more significant, it seems to me, is that Atuot assume diviners possess an insight into underlying causes which common folk do not claim to perceive directly. That powers exist and affect individual experience is a proposition young children come to accept, sitting as they do on the sidelines during the associated rituals.

The real problem was revealed by the father in the dialogue: "Everything comes because of the feud. Long ago when there was a fight. . . . No one knew it was going to fall on him alone." Thus, one interpretation of the myth cited earlier would be that at the moment the individual is conscious of identity and individuality, enmity is inevitable. Some person will inevitably suffer the consequences of some other's action.

As I understand it, Atuot are indirectly positing an underlying order of phenomena through the process of divination. What one person wants another already has. A third person can complicate things all the more. The rare individual who calculates his relations with others so that none suffers is, in a sense, blessed. Far more commonly, individuals seek their own ends and the transgression of the rights or expectations of another occurs. Of course there are those among the Atuot, as in any society, who seek just this end, to disrupt the affairs of others in order to advance their own selfish interests. At the same time, vengeance through a power can be unintentional, as evidenced by the brother of the hungry guerrilla. Retribution for what is perceived to be insult and greed can be more direct and consciously intended, as suggested by the case of Akoi, the wife who sought children denied by a curse of her own brother.

In either of these situations the decision to accept the veracity of the diviner is a reflective exercise. He speaks publicly as a medium. Persons hearing him have the option of considering any number of alternative interpretations. However, once a truth has been agreed upon, or in the Atout's own words, when "a word has been seen," there is no recourse to an alternative interpretation. The facts of the matter have been too plainly evident. The word of the diviner may be cited as an axiom, upon which future divinations for the causes and implications of moral dilemmas are founded.

Were it possible to compile a complete inventory of this type of data over an extended period, it would indeed be possible to speak in definite terms about an Atuot philosophy. I propose that each datum would entail the same transformation of order into its opposite. More specifically, it is possible to observe that the immediate result of divination is a public disclosure of personal animosity, a process that is mirrored in the mythical world. People are still blind to the immediate cause of misfortune, as imagined in a world that was long ago transformed by the behavior of self-motivated people. In the situation of divination Atuot attentively reflect upon how misfortune may be both the cause and the result of intention. Collectively, these suppositions are the beginnings of an unfolding philosophy.[2]

Notes

An earlier version of this essay appeared in 1982 in the *Journal of Religion in Africa* 13(1):1–10. Philip M. Peek, Peter Rigby, and L'Ana H. Burton offered helpful suggestions for this final draft. Anthropological field research among the pastoral Nilotic-speaking Atuot of southern Sudan was made possible with funds awarded by the Wenner-Gren Foundation for Anthropological Research and the Social Science Research Council, whose assistance is gratefully acknowledged. Additional support for preparing the results of research for publication came from a National Endowment for the Humanities stipend and a grant from the Mellon Foundation.

1. The power of psychic transformation is known as *ring*. I have discussed it elsewhere (Burton 1979, 1981).

2. The present comments pertain specifically to possession by a *jok*. There are terms in the Atuot language which can be glossed by the English words *witchcraft* (*apeth*) and *sorcery* (*roadh*), and both offer a means of accounting for misfortune. A somewhat different concept, one that is more relevant to this discussion, is implied by the word *ayuio*. Kulang Takping explained: "*Ayuio* is said to be a *jok* in some people. It is jealousy. A person with *ayuio* may want to own something very much, even though it is not his, nor could

it be. The thing itself will later go bad. If you are cooking a piece of meat and *ayuio* comes wanting it, the meat will burn in the fire or it will fall to a dog. It just happens like that." See Burton (1985).

References

Beattie, J. M. H. 1980. "On Understanding Sacrifice." In *Sacrifice*, ed. M. F. C. Bourdillon and M. Fortes, 29–44. London: Academic Press.

Burton, John W. 1979. "Atuot Totemism." *Journal of Religion in Africa* 10:95–107.

―――. 1980a. "The Village and the Cattle Camp: Aspects of Atuot Religion." In *Explorations in African Systems of Thought*, ed. I. Karp and C. Bird, 268–97. Bloomington: Indiana University Press.

―――. 1980b. "Sacrifice: A Polythetic Class of Atuot Religious Thought." *Journal of Religion in Africa* 11:93–105.

―――. 1981. *God's Ants: A Study of Atuot Religion*. Vienna/St. Augustin: Studia Institut Anthropos.

―――. 1985. "Why Witches? Some Comments on the Explanation of 'Illusions' in Anthropology." *Ethnology* 24(4):281–96.

Buxton, J. 1973. *Religion and Healing in Mandari*. Oxford: Clarendon Press.

Deng. F. M. 1971. *The Dinka of the Sudan*. New York: Holt, Rinehart and Winston.

Evans-Pritchard, E. E. 1956. *Nuer Religion*. Oxford: Clarendon Press.

Lienhardt. R. G. 1961. *Divinity and Experience: The Religion of the Dinka*. Oxford: Clarendon Press.

―――. 1970. "The Situation of Death: An Aspect of Anuak Philosophy." In *Witchcraft Confessions and Accusations*, ed. M. Douglas, 279–92. London: Tavistock.

Ogot, B. A. 1961. "The Concept of *Jok* among the Nilotes." *African Studies* 20:123–30.

Pierre Vérin and Narivelo Rajaonarimanana

Divination in Madagascar

The Antemoro Case and the
Diffusion of Divination

Divination remains a fundamental necessity in the everyday lives of the Malagasy people, whatever their religious affiliation. Since February 28, 1868, when the queen and her prime minister converted to Christianity (Chapus and Mondain 1953:163), divination as well as the "idol cults" have been said to be disappearing from the realm of the "acceptable" beliefs, and it is now assumed, mostly among local Protestant circles, that divination has been completely rooted out in the Uplands. Nevertheless, divination practices are still in use, not only in the "pagan" coastal areas but also in the very heart of Imerina and Betsileo country, even though they may appear inconspicuous to the casual observer.

Divination as practiced in Madagascar has aroused scholarly interest for more than one hundred years. As early as 1877 Lars Dahle published some texts about *sikidy* divination in his *Specimens of Malagasy Folklore*, and several years later he wrote an important contribution on *sikidy* and *vintana* (1886). In subsequent years, many investigators have touched on divination in Madagascar; the Grandidiers' three-volume bibliography of Madagascar (1905–57) lists more than three hundred items concerning Arabico-Malagasy documents and divination materials. Unfortunately, much of the relevant archival material remains untranslated.

Our aim in this essay is not only to provide a synthesis of previous contributions but also to devise a new approach to understanding the divination system. Contrary to what many authors have contended, the intellectual process through which the diviner draws his conclusions is not an uncritical, mechanical use of the column configurations of the *sikidy* system. In fact, the scholar who has obtained a correct list of *sikidy* configurations is only beginning the research. Materials in the native archives which we are deciphering and translating show clearly that the diviner, after arranging the seeds, has at his disposal several options for interpreting his client's destiny. Examples of the choices made, as recorded by Vig (1977) and

Hébert (1965), are discussed below. In addition to describing the complex calculation and diagnostic processes of Malagasy divination, we will comment on the origins and diffusion of the Antemoro system, focusing on how it developed in relation to the Malagasy world view.

After independence, the Western-educated elite who took over from the French in the 1960s established legal procedures to deal with "witchcraft practices" in the country.[3] To enforce the antisorcery laws, the police confiscated bead necklaces, charms, and even books of divination written in the Arabico-Malagasy script.[4] These actions demonstrate a confusion on the part of the officials between divination and sorcery. Most Malagasy make a clear-cut distinction between the *mpamosavy*, the deviant sorcerer, and the *ombiasy*, the benevolent medicine man who practices divination in order to identify the causes of disease and evil and to cure them.

Ombiasy is the general term for a diviner,[5] but according to his ways of investigation he is either an *mpanandro* or an *mpisikidy*. The *mpanandro* relies on astrology to define favorable and unfavorable days; he recommends the proper procedures to be followed so that his clients may achieve the results desired. *Mpanandro* is best translated as "chooser of the day," but the translation of the term used in the southeast, *mpamintanana*, more dramatically reveals the true significance of this individual: "destiny maker."[6] The *mpisikidy* has a quite different function: he seeks the cause of disorders and evils which happen in the lives of his clients by using a form of geomancy. (Sometimes an *ombiasy*, with the aid of sacred texts, performs both roles, as will be discussed below.) The *mpisikidy* employs a divination system, termed *sikidy* (west, *sikily*), which has parallels throughout Africa (Trautmann 1939) and is thought to have come from Arabia (Ferrand and Vérin 1985:947).[7] In Madagascar this system underwent a significant cultural reinterpretation and now continues to serve the people as a crucial channel of communication with the ancestors.

The ancestors' role is all-important. In the traditional religion of the Malagasy, which has no supreme god who can enforce sanctions against a forbidden action, this duty is performed by the ever-present ancestors, who linger around the individual. The Arabico-Malagasy manuscripts of the Antemoro refer to two types of ancestors. The better known ones are linked to living beings by well-documented genealogies, but there are also those whose names are unknown who, it is said, sometimes assume the appearance of genies or spirits.[8] Communication between a person and his ancestors occurs constantly, whether or not a diviner is present. The diviner, when called upon, becomes a witness who interprets the signs, which may be direct expressions of the individual's *vintana* ("destiny") or may appear through the *sikidy* configurations.

In the cases of collective misfortune or individual disease, the *mpisikidy* tries to find out the cause. "Mechanical" causes in the Western sense do not exist for most Malagasy. Misfortunes are attributed to the ancestors' dissatisfaction with the behavior of their descendants who, deliberately or not, have transgressed against customary rules and commited *tsiny* (southwest, *havoa*; southeast, *tahina*), a "sin" that entails a mythical sanction. Channels of communication between the ancestors and the living other than divination are also recognized; warnings may come, for instance, through dreams and possession. But if the ancestors have not shown themselves by these other means, they may always be questioned through *sikidy*. After discovering the origin of the disorder, the *mpisikidy* provides the appropriate solution: offerings (*sadaka*), sacrifices (*sorona* or *joro*), charms to be carried (*ody*; west, *aoly*), or stored remedies (*hazary, fanafody*). Taboos (*fady*; west, *faly*) are also to be observed. The diviner is even charged with helping his patient avoid a recurrence of the trouble.

The *mpanandro*, like the *mpisikidy*, gives advice about events to be dealt with in the future but each employs different investigative techniques. Also, while the *mpisikidy* provides remedies, the *mpanandro* does not. The role of the *mpanandro* is particularly decisive in the case of a birth. This diviner explains to the family the *vintana* of the child and tells them the astrological name and the taboos attached to the new person.

The astrological procedures of the *mpanandro* are quite similar throughout the island, and we strongly suspect that they all came from the same place. According to Flacourt, Matatane country in southeastern Madagascar (around the Matitanana River) where the Antemoro (or Antaimoro) live was a center of astrological study as early as the fourteenth century (1661:172, 195).[9] This area was also the site of early Arab settlements, although strict Islamic observances were lost centuries ago.[10] Historical evidence shows that Antemoro diviners, bearers of the astrological system, infiltrated nearly all the ancient kingdoms of Madagascar beginning in the sixteenth century. The *ombiasy* Andriamisara, who helped found the Sakalava empire around 1650, was said to be a member of the royal family (Fagereng 1948). Some ambitious kings sent delegates to Matitanana in the heart of Antemoro country to obtain the services of highly reputed *ombiasy* who could help increase their power. For instance, in 1790 Andrianampoinimerina, the king of Imerina, sent for Andriamahazonoro, a gifted *ombiasy*, who was incorporated into the noble family (Ferrand 1905).[11] Today, although many persons claim to be *ombiasy*, only the Antemoro diviners are considered true professionals. The area is still a famous place of learning where specialists go for training and then return to their home communities with a common body of knowledge. Now we can better understand the degree of similarity of divination forms found throughout Madagascar. For centuries Matitanana has remained a training center for diviners who have migrated widely, usually attaining important positions in their home communities and with various royal families.

Vintana, "destiny," is the center of interest for traditional Malagasy astrology, which attempts to determine the influence of the stars on terrestrial events and to predict the future from it.[12] The Antemoro system is different from the Western practice of casting individual horoscopes, though its goal is similar: to situate the individual in relation to cosmic forces. A knowledge of individual-cosmic relationships is considered essential to determine what decision should be made. According to the Malagasy world view, things as well as human beings have destinies which are controlled by the ancestors and may need to be explored. The destiny of a house, a cattle pen, or a collective tomb as well as the destiny of a newborn child fits into an astrological framework under the supervision of the ancestors. Once the time of birth or origin and the time of an action are established, the appropriate *vintana*, which will explain past, present, and future occurrences, can be learned.

For each individual there are auspicious and inauspicious lunar months, days, and hours. Arabic astrology has them written in the zodiacal calendar and on home decorations. As noted by Jacques Dez (1984:74; see also 1983), the adjustment of the Arabic system to the Malagasy system establishes a correspondence between the traditional agricultural months (*volana*) and the astrological months (*vintana*). But the adaptations do not stop there. The Malagasy have spatialized the temporal scheme represented by the *vintana*, assigning the major aspects of destiny (*reny vintana*) to the four corners of the house and its minor aspects (*zana-bintana*) to the walls (Dahle 1877a; Délivré 1974:148; Vig 1977:1). One can follow the aspects of destiny as they revolve around the earth or around a house (fig. 1). The rectangular Malagasy house is always oriented with the long sides running north-south. This orientation has both cosmic and social significance, and this double significance extends to tombs, cattle pens, and even villages, whose design also is generally rectangular.

How did such a transfer take place? Many links are missing in the chain of representations of the *vintana* over the centuries. It is easy to understand how there could have been a synthesis of the monthly calendars, but why was the *vintana* system imposed on Malagasy buildings? Among the Arabs, the zodiac is inscribed within a circle (Al-Biruni 1964). But in India the zodiac is represented in a rectangular form. As Indian influence is well documented in Malagasy cultural history, we may imagine that this Indian rectangle was directly associated with the rectangular shape of Malagasy houses and tombs, which shelter the individual from birth to death and afterward. Therefore, it appears that just as the Islamic astrological model meshed with the Malagasy lunar calendar, so the Indian representation of the zodiac found correspondence with Malagasy building forms.

The year starts with Alamahady (Arabic terms for the months are still used in Madagascar). This first month is always represented by the northeast corner. The other eleven months follow Alamahady clockwise in fixed order. Of the cardinal points, the northeast is considered the most favorable, and that corner is dedicated to ancestors, sacred offerings, and prayers. Important people are honored there also.[13] The other eleven *vintana* have their own powers, and each consists of two or three *zana-bintana*, which also have their representations around the house (fig. 2).

Each month contains two or three *kitsary*, or astrological "houses," of good or bad omen. These *kitsary* elements also refer to days. While the localization of the months is stable, the days rotate clockwise as necessary. In figure 2, for example, the meaningful event occurred on a day in the first part of Adaoro. To find out the astrological value of that day, one counts off twenty-eight days (or *kitsary*), moving clockwise from the day of the event (number one) and reaching the last part of Alahamady, which has a given value. If the value of this *kitsary*

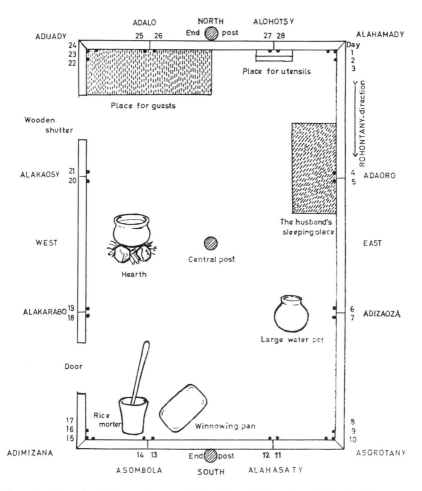

Figure 1. Plan of a Malagasy house with locations of the *vintana* ("destiny") and days of the month indicated, beginning in the northeast corner. *From Ruud 1960; used by permission.*

28 is negative—if it constitutes a bad omen—the diviner picks up the necessary objects connoting the sacrifice to be performed (Vig 1977:13).

The correspondences, positive and negative, for these movable days are myriad, but all are described in the *ombiasy*'s sacred texts, written in Arabico-Malagasy. Although the *ombiasy* is bound by the recipes given in the texts, interpretations are adjusted to specific situations. To offer some idea of the complexity of the calculations and correlations performed by the Antemoro diviner, we reproduce an illustration obtained by Vig (fig.3).

This sketch of a house interior, with north at top, depicts the intricate relationships of the months and days, the associated *vintana*, and the appropriate offerings

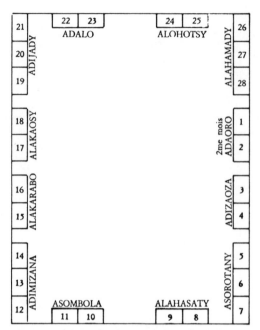

Figure 2. Schematic representation of minor
aspects *(zana-bintana)* of *vintana* within a
house for an event starting in Adaoro. *From
Vig 1977; used by permission.*

and animal sacrifices. Each day of the week also corresponds to a specific *sikidy* configuration. The rectangular form of the house represents the celestial vault; thus, as in the astrological house, the *vintana* are placed in the four corners and on the walls.

Inside the center section one finds representations of astral elements. They include the sun *(masoandro*, left center west), the moon *(volana*, right center east), and a star *(kintana*, top center northeast). Constellations are symbolized by insects (bottom center south), including two poisonous spiders, *matahora* and *hala mena vody*, and a scorpion, *maingoka*.

Then there are the beings who have esoteric knowledge: *Komandiny*, the commandant of the guardians of destiny (large figure, left center) and the thirty-five guardians of destiny themselves, the *mpiandry alifo*, who are posted around the edges of the calendar.

The seven days of the week are represented by circles arranged in a vertical row in the center of the interior section. The days' names are of Arabic origin: *Alahady* (Sunday, second from top), *Alatsinainy* (Monday, first at top), *Talata* (Tuesday, seventh from top), *Alarobia* (Wednesday, sixth from top), *Alakamisy* (Thursday, fifth from top), *Zoma* (Friday, fourth from top), and *Asabotsy* (Saturday, third from top). The twelve months, also represented by circles, are located around

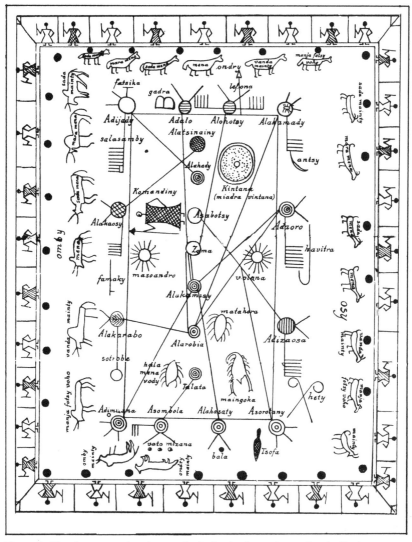

Figure 3. Sketch representing the astrological calendar and associated offerings as depicted on a house interior; north is at the top. *From Vig 1977; used by permission.*

the outside of the center section. Starting in the northeast corner and moving clockwise, they are *Alahamady, Adaoro, Adizaosa, Asorotany, Alahasaty, Asombola, Adimizana, Alakarabo, Alakaosy*, and *Adijady*.

Also located around the outside of the center section are objects necessary for an exorcism rite of *Ala-faditra*. Starting in the northeast and going clockwise, they are *antsy* (knife), *havitra* (iron hook), *hety* (scissors), *tsofa* (file), *bala* (musket ball), *vato mizana* (scale weights), *sotrobe* (large ladle), *famaky* (ax), *salasamby* (iron grill), *fantsika* (nail), *gadra* (prisoner's chains), and *lefona* (lance). Animals necessary for this rite are on the outer wall of the house, identified by the color of their coat and divided by direction. In the north are *ondry*—sheep of the colors *sada mainty* (mottled black and white), *mara mena* (mottled red), *sada mena* (mottled red and white), *mena* (red), *vanda mainty* (spotted), and *manja fetsy volo* (light brown with a white back); in the east, *osy*—goats with the same colors as the preceding sheep, plus *mainty* (black); in the south, *ondry mainty* (black sheep) and *omby mainty* (black cattle); and in the west, *omby*—cattle with the same colors as the sheep found in the north. And, finally, the black circles nearest the guardians of destiny represent the twenty-eight lunar days.

From this sketch we can see that the most critical work for the diviner is to situate the event in question temporally. This temporal orientation may be determined by the event itself (occurring on an auspicious or an inauspicious day) or by the individuals involved in the situation, as, for example, in the case of a husband and wife whose dates of birth revealed conflicting aspects in their destiny (*mifanohi-bintana*). But it is only through divination and the diagnosis of the *ombiasy* that the client may discover how to respond to the situation.

Vig (1977:14–24) and Ruud (1960:38–57) recorded the various situations which occur in the twenty-eight lunar houses or days, the *kitsary*.[14] These records give the results of a diviner's interpretation, with the days' advantages and disadvantages decoded; one can imagine which actions might be taken. But the charts Vig and Ruud constructed, remarkable as they are, constitute ethnological analyses; no *ombiasy* has such well-ordered charts at his disposal. The Arabico-Malagasy manuals are used by the *ombiasy* only for reference. The diviner's own interpretation, we must emphasize, remains very significant.

Berthier translated several texts containing interpretations of calendars concerning births and illnesses. For a child born in Alohotsy, we read this prediction: "(Boy) Maka, Soleiman, girl, Mary. Fridays are ominous for him. Azohora is contrary for him. Adalo compresses the nape of his neck. . . . There are three auspicious days: Thursday, Monday, Saturday" (Berthier 1933:63). Then comes a list of the auspicious days for those born in other astrological months. About a man who is ill in Alohotsy we read the following advice: "Do not let him be approached either by people coming from far away or by merchants; must refrain from eating red beef and the fruit from the 'badamier' tree" (64).

An Arabico-Malagasy manuscript from the Grandidier library, which is kept at the Musée de l'Homme in Paris, indicates that "illnesses are due to ominous actions (*mahakeo*), which vary according to the days of the month."[15] The course of destiny was disturbed and a blunder led to a negative balance. But for present and future actions, people know very well that they must pay attention to destiny and choose with the *ombiasy* the right time to perform an action or to prevent a situation from happening. In a way, a code on how to manage one's life is established under the control of destiny, which is what the Grandidiers called "the rules which guided the life of the Malagasy." Among those rules is the list of the auspicious days to start an action, to go on a trip, or to start building a house or a tomb. The Malagasy also have specific days to repudiate a contract, wash new clothes, remove their hairs, warp a cloth, or set up the bed of the mother of a newborn child. The manuscript at the Musée de l'Homme even includes predictions about different smells of unknown origin and about flies getting under someone's clothes (A. and G. Grandidier 1917:620).

Rajaonarimanana found these same predictions, together with many others, in the unpublished manuscript 10 of the Malagasy Academy.[16] The predictions are multiple, since they deal with events as different as animals visiting humans, atmospheric phenomena, and shivering. Yet they all have the same specificity; their significance varies according to the time when these events happen. By themselves they are neither good nor bad, and they may lead to opposite predictions if they happen at auspicious or inauspicious times.

This extract from manuscript 10 enumerates the probable events predicted by "the fly that gets under your robe when you are around people":

In Alamahaly, something good will happen.
In Asoro, something good will happen.
In Alizaoza, a disease is on its way but it won't last.
In Asaratan, you will get a new robe.
In Alahasady, something nasty will be said behind your back.
In Asombola, you will meet someone.
In Alimiza, the escaped prisoner will come back.
In Alakarabo, you will meet someone.
In Alakaosy, someone will come and visit you.
In Adalovy, there will be a separation.

Thus, from an apparently insignificant occurrence, happy or unhappy events are predicted according to the astrological month of the occurrence. When a rat has chewed on a piece of clothing, predictions are given for each half day in the week; but predictions vary according to the number of holes made by the rat. Here then one finds the notion of odd versus even, a distinction which is so essential in the *sikidy* geomancy.

The exploration of *vintana* by traditional astrological methods is not always possible. Such is the case, for example, when the consulting person does not know his date of birth. It may also happen that the *ombiasy* consulted will prefer to use the *sikidy* technique. *Sikidy* was described by Flacourt in the seventeenth century:

The Omptsiquili methods are generally used by Negroes and Anacandries; this is what is called Geomancy; the drawings are similar to those found in geomantic books, except that here they predict on a small wooden board, covered with sand, on which they draw with their fingers, while observing the day, the time, the month, the Planet, the sign representing the time when they make predictions, at which they are very good. However they rarely find the truth, and some of them, adding their own intuition to their prediction, are sometimes accurate, and are therefore admired and held in esteem by everybody. The ill ask for their advice in order to get better; some others ask them questions about their work; many of them do not leave their house without consulting them. In short, there is no nation which is more superstitious than this one. It is especially the case in Manghabai, where they do not do any business, buy, plant, build anything or travel without first consulting the diviner. (1661:172)

The technique has been described many times since then. Among more recent contributions are those by the Grandidiers (1917), Berthier (1933:89–100), Decary (1970), and Rabedimy (1976). Hébert (1961) compared Malagasy geomancy to that of the Comoro Islands and Africa. There are also some good regional analyses, including Linton (1933:203–10) on the Tanala and Deschemaeker (1969:208–12) on the Betsimisaraka. Lahady (1976:174–84) gathered some interesting data on the Betsimisaraka that Rahatoka (1985:55–60) completed. Other sources on *sikidy* are Callet (1974:82–104) for the Merina, Vig (1977:39–43) for the Vakinankaratra, and Dubois (1938:917–48) for the Betsileo. On Western Sakalava, Rabedimy (1976) is particularly up-to-date. Dandouau's article (1914), covering the northwestern part of the country, and Faublée's analysis (1954) of the divinatory techniques of the Bara are still useful.

A *sikidy* divination session has three phases. First comes the awakening of the *sikidy* (*mamoha sikidy*), during which the masters of *sikidy* and the great ancestors are invoked by incantations so that they will help the *ombiasy* interpret the data properly. Then the figures (*monoko sikidy*) are set up by interpreting even and odd piles of grain. Single or double dots are arranged by fours in sixteen columns, each of which has a name.(fig. 4)[17] In the third phase the figures are read, starting with the *tale*, the most important column. Several scholars, including Decary (1970), Rabedimy (1976), and Sussman and Sussman (1977), have attempted to describe this complex process of computing and reading the *sikidy* s, which vary by name, value, and association in different areas of Madagascar.

Ethnologist have been so anxious to describe the workings of *sikidy* divination that they often forget that divination with grain or seeds is just another way of approaching the *vintana* and that it is only used when the *vintana* is not clear. This last resort is all the more necessary when ordinary divination has not given the expected results and the *ombiasy* decides that something has to be done. The *mpanandro* diviner identifies the taboo (*fady*) that has been violated, but the *mpisikidy* diviner prescribes the sacrifices (*sadaka* or *ala-fatidra*) to offer and the medicines to take. That is why astrological predictions, *sikidy* figures, and recipes for medicines are sometimes presented together in the diviners' books. The names of figures (*volontsikidy*) sometimes correspond to days, sometimes to months of the *vintana* (see fig. 5), which further demonstrates that *sikidy* was built upon an existing system. With correlations provided for *sikidy* figures, it is then relatively easy to find the astrological date of an unlocated event and thereby reveal the appropriate *vintana*.

The book of the Ihosy *ombiasy*, given to Hébert (1961), consists mostly of prescriptions of this type: "If Alohomora [the figure formed by two, one, two, and two dots] is in the *tale* column, it means that he suffers from backache and that he needs a red or a white-necked ox." The *sikidy* here reveals the location

	4 bilady	3 fahatelo	2 maly	1 tale
5 fianaha	□	□ □	□ □	□
6 abily	□ □	□	□	□ □
7 alisay	□ □	□	□ □	□
8 fahavalo	□	□ □	□ □	□

9 fahasivy	11 ombiasa	10 hanina or haja	15 zanahary
□	□	□ □	□
□	□	□ □	□
□	□ □	□	□ □
□	□ □	□	□ □

12 sorotany	14 tovolahy	13 lalana or safary	16 kiba or trano
□	□ □	□	□ □
□	□ □	□	□
□	□ □	□	□
□	□ □	□	□

Figure 4. Names of the sixteen basic *sikidy* columns or positions with illustrative configurations. "Columns" 5 to 8 are established by reading from right to left the "rows" created by columns 1 to 4, which constitute the "mother of *sikidy*," the foundation of the casting. Then complex formulas are used to generate the other eight columns. *After Berthier 1933:97–99.*

of the pain and the nature of the sacrifice to perform. Farther down we read: "Here is the *Karija* figure in the *lalana* column; his trips won't be successful but he will have a long life." The client, though warned about the failure of his project, learns about his happy destiny. Lists of such prescriptions linked to the *sikidy* figures constitute most of the Ihosy book.

□   Taraiky   □ □   Alohotsy*
□   emaciation;   □   money;
□   path, road   □ □   unhappiness,
□   □   misfortune

□   Karija   □   Adalo*
□   slave;   □ □   chief or child;
□   cool speech   □   tears
□ □   □ □

□ □   Alakaosy*   □ □   Alatsimay
□   child;   □   slave;
□   evil thoughts   □   evil thoughts
□   □ □

□ □   Adabara   □   Alokola
□ □   Zanahary (High God);   □ □   house;
□   most sacred   □ □   food
□   □

□   Alikasajy   □ □   Alabiavo
□   charm;   □ □   water spirit;
□ □   mourning   □   joy
□   □ □

□   Alahijana   □ □   Alahamora
□ □   woman;   □   Ombiasa (diviner);
□ □   death   □ □   crowd, mob;
□ □   □ □   grief, trouble

□ □   Alikisy   □   Alahasady*
□ □   earth;   □   food;
□ □   auspicious   □ □   anger, wrath
□   □ □

□ □   Asombola*   □   Alakarabo*
□ □   abundance   □ □   robbers, rogues;
□ □   □   unhappiness,
□ □   □   misfortune

Figure 5. Names and most common meanings of the sixteen basic *sikidy* configurations. Several names are also names of lunar months (indicated by *), which suggests that when the *sikidy* system was introduced, correspondence might have been established for all the lunar months. *After Berthier 1933:97–99.*

One recipe is for a philtre to aid in seducing a woman:

> Take some *voarafitry*, take a few drops of water seeping from a rock, take some strong wind, take some *anatariky*, take some *hazomiady*, take some *masindrano* in which a woman bathed, some *vahifineno* creeping vine, bamboo thrown down by the cascade; take feathers from a brooding hen. Here are the association of geomantic figures. Ten *Asimbola* figures. *Asimbola* alone in the *lala* column, here they are. When you prepare them, take a little bit of the woman's sweat, get her under the spell, dedicate it while presenting it above the fire. Here it is. Here is its antidote. Take a little bit of the dirt on the door of the hen-house. Bathe it in it. Here it is.

The *sikidy* figure related to the problem is at the same time part of the medicine.

Part of the *ombiasy*'s book found by Vig (1977:35) illustrates the relation between the *sikidy* configurations and the animal sacrifice (*ala-fatidra*). Vig was the first to report this association, which previous scholars had missed. The animals for sacrifice, as noted earlier, are disposed around the interior of the astrological house (see fig. 3). The association with the *sikidy* is noticeable, since the disposition of the *sikidy* figures parallels the house's spatial orientation, being linked to the cardinal points.[18] These associations further demonstrate the strikingly intricate and comprehensive interrelationships of the Antemoro divination system, which has woven together the indigenous Malagasy belief with the Arab-influenced *sikidy* and astrology.

The ancestors' dominant role is reflected in the *sikidy* awakening invocations (Simon n.d.) and in prescriptions of all types. The *ombiasy* is not only an astrological seer but has become, in the Antemoro system, a mediator between the living and the ancestors. In a sense the Malagasy diviner is also a mediator of these distinct yet overlapping systems of knowledge as he dramatically manipulates the diagnostic means available to him in order to learn the ancestors' intentions. Our ongoing research reveals more and more about the complex code switching which the diviner manages in shifting from one system to the other as he refines the correct interpretation of the client's *vintana*.

The route taken is now known. The Muslims who came to the Antemoro many centuries ago brought an astrological system of divination at the same time that they brought Islam. Since astrology was not then a tenet of Malagasy culture (Hébert 1961), the Malagasy applied this system to their houses, which were rectangular like the Indian model of the zodiac, arranging it in the corners and on the walls. Evidence is now sufficient to assert that the Muslims who came to Madagascar were from the Persian Gulf and southward along the Gulf of Oman to the northwest corner of India. The Antemoro adapted this system and now, centuries later, continue to rely on it to ensure proper governance of the living by the ancestors.

Notes

This essay was translated by Martine Motard-Noar and Philip M. Peek. The translators sincerely thank the authors for reviewing the translation and Lee Haring and John Mack for their generous aid in clarifying citations and offering other editorial advice.

1. These procedures are found in the Republic of Malagasy Ordonnance no. 60–074, July 28, 1960.

2. Used by diviners in southeastern Malagasy for over three hundred years, the Arabico-Malagasy script records the Malagasy language in Arabic characters. Roman characters have been used in Antananarivo since 1820.

3. *Moasy* in the northwest; *mpimasy* in the central area.

4. The word *mpamintanana* comes from *vintana*, the general word for "destiny," a term of Austronesian origin (see Dempwolff 1938, vol. 3:31, under *bintan*, "star"; also Hébert 1965). The association with astrology is clear from the phrase *miandra vintana*, "to study the stars."

5. Specifically from the system called *ilm al-samb*, "the science of sand" (*kitab al-Fasl fi usul 'ilm al-rml* by Sheyk Muhamad al-Zanati); see Ferrand and Vérin (1985) and Ferrand (1891–1902).

6. See Bloch (1971, 1986), Mack (1986), and Vérin 1990:122–27 concerning the importance of the ancestors for the Malagasy people.

7. Providing our earliest record, Flacourt devotes two chapters to "ombiasses" (*ombiasy*) of the extreme south.

8. See Bloch (1968:280–83), Mack (1986:33–38), and Vérin (1986:79–89).

9. For further discussion of the role of Antemoro diviners in Madagascar's political history, see Bloch (1968:284–86), Mack (1986:38), and Rajaonarimanana (1990).

10. See Vig (1977:13), Délivré (1974:149), and Ruud (1960:29).

11. See Bloch (1968:288–89, 1986:52).

12. Ruud relied on Vig's work as well as Callet (1974; first published 1953–58) and materials collected among the Antanosy.

13. The causes of diseases are then listed (A. and G. Grandidier 1917:620):

> One falls ill on the first [day of the month] if three pieces of wood are planted on the eastern side of his house, on the second because one has made a rope with ravenal bark to tie up a young man or a quadruped, on the third because one has felled a tree in the shadow of which people used to protect themselves from the sun, etc. . . . If, when one is ill, one would like to avoid death or at least avoid worse sickness, one must not: during the three days of Alahamaly destiny, that is to say the first three days of the lunar month, allow a blacksmith to approach oneself nor eat skate, eel, turtle, or the heart of the *lafa*; during the two days of Adaoro destiny, that is to say during the fourth to fifth day of the month, allow strangers to enter into the house, nor eat honey, wild birds, and so on, each one of the twenty-eight days having its special prohibitions.

14. Many Arabico-Malagasy manuscripts of sacred esoteric knowledge have been collected, but few containing material on divination have been translated. One is Ferrand's partial translation (1905) of a manuscript from the Bibliothèque Nationale. The manuscript collected by Grandidier will appear in a forthcoming book on Malagasy divination by Rajaonarimanana.

15. The Antemoro call the sixteen columns *tale*, consulting person; *maly*, object or money given for the consultation; *fahatelo*, the third or the client's brother; *bilady*, residence; *fenaha*, child; *abidy*, mother; *betsimisay* or *alisay*, wife; *fahavalo*, enemy; *fahasivy*, spirit of the dead; *ombiasa*, the diviner; *haza*, food; *Haky*, God; *solotany*, king; *sely*, young people; *lala*, road; and *trano*, house. Regional variation may be seen by comparing this list with the terms in fig. 4.

16. These correlations, like others, vary by district, but among the peoples of southwestern Madagascar the following associations (using the names in fig. 5) are made: north —Karija, Alahijana, Adalo, and Alabiavo; east—Adabara, Alatsimay, and Alahamora; south —Taraiky, Alikasajy, Asombola, and Alahasady; west—Alakaosy, Alikisy, Alohotsy, Alokola, and Alakarabo (Sussman and Sussman 1977:281).

References

Berthier, Hugues. 1933. *Notes et impressions sur les moeurs et coutumes du peuple malgache.* Tananarive: Imprimerie Officielle.

Al-Biruni. 1964. *Alberuni's India* . . . (1888). English edition with notes and indices by Edward C. Sachau. Delhi: S. Chand.

Bloch, Maurice. 1968. "Astrology and Writing in Madagascar." In *Literacy in Traditional Society*, ed. J. Goody, 278–97. Cambridge: Cambridge University Press.

———. 1971. *Placing the Dead: Tombs, Ancestral Villages and Kinship Organization in Madagascar.* London: Seminar Press.

———. 1986. *From Blessing to Violence: History and Ideology in the Circumcision Ritual of the Merina of Madagascar.* Cambridge: Cambridge University Press.

Callet, R. P. 1974. *Tantaran'ny Andriana.* Trans. C. -S. Chapus and E. Ratsimba. Antananarivo: Librairie de Madagascar (reprint of 1953–58 edition, Tananarive: Academie Malgache).

Chapus, G. -S., and G. Mondain. 1953. *Un homme d'état Malgache: Rainilaiarivony.* Paris: Editions de l'Outre-mer.

Dahle, Lars. 1877a. *Madagaskar og dets Beboere.* Vol. 2. Christiania (Oslo).

———. 1877b. *Specimens of Malagasy Folklore.* Antananarivo: A. Kingdon.

———. 1886. "Sikidy and Vintana: Half-Hours with Malagasy Diviners." *Antananarivo Annual* 10:218–34.

Dandouau, André. 1914. "Le sikidy sakalava." *Anthropos* 9.

Decary, Raymond. 1970. "La divination malgache par le sikidy." *Publications du Centre Universitaire des Langues Orientales Vivantes.* Paris: Paul Geuthner.

Délivré, A. 1974. *L'histoire des rois d'Imerina—Interprétation d'une tradition orale.* Paris: Klinsieck.

Dempwolff, O. 1938. *Vergleichenden Lautlehre des Austronesischen Worterschatzes.* 3 vol. Berlin: Dietrich Reimer.

Deschemaeker, A. 1969. *Vocabulaire des betsimisaraka atsimo zafindriamanana (ny fomba fanaovany ny sikidy).* Ambositra (mimeo).

Dez, Jacques. 1983. "Le temps et le pouvoir: L'usage du calendrier divinatoire antemoro." In *Les souverains de Madagascar*, ed. F. Raison-Jourde, 108–23. Paris: Karthala.

———. 1984. "Essai sur le calendrier arabico-malgache." *Etudes sur l'Océan Indien*, 58–119. St. Denis: Université de Reunion.

Dubois, H. 1938. *Monographie des Betsileo.* Travaux et Mémoires, 34. Paris: Institut d'Ethnologie.

Fagereng, E. 1947–48. "Histoire des Maroserana du Menabe," *Bulletin de l'Academie Malgache* n.s. 28:115–35.

Faublée, J. 1954. *La cohésion des sociétés bara.* Paris: Presses Universitaires de France.

Ferrand, Gabriel. 1891–1902. *Les musulmans à Madagascar et aux Iles Comores.* 3 vols. (1891, 1893, 1902). Paris: Ernest Leroux.

———. 1905. "Un chapitre d'astrologie arabico-malgache." *Journal Asiatique*, Sept.-Oct., 193–273.

Ferrand, G., and P. Vérin. 1985. "Madagascar." In *Encyclopédie de l'Islam*, 943–48. Leiden: Brill.

Flacourt, E. de. 1661. *Histoire de l'isle de Madagascar*. Paris: Gervais Clouzier.

Grandidier, A. and G. 1905–57. *Bibliographie de Madagascar*. 3 vols. (1905, 1935, 1957). Paris: Societé d'Editions Geographiques, Maritimes et Coloniales.

———. 1917. "Ethnographie de Madagascar." In *Histoire physique, naturelle et politique de Madagascar*, bk. 3, vol. 4 (1892). Paris: Ed. Liliane Hachette.

Hébert, Jean-Claude. 1961. "Analyse structurale des géomancies comoriennes, malgaches et africaines." *Journal de la Société des Africanistes* 31(2): 115–208.

———. 1965. "La cosmographie ancienne Malgache suivie de l'énumération des points cardinaux et l'importance du nord-est." *Taloha* (Revue du Musée d'Art et d'Archéologie de l'Université de Madagascar) 1:83–195.

Lahady, P. 1976. *Le culte betsimisaraka et son systeme symbolique*. Fianarantsoa: Librairiel Ambozontany.

Linton, R. 1933. "The Tanala: A Hill Tribe of Madagascar." Field Museum of Natural History, Anthropology Series, vol. 21, pp. 1–334.

Mack, John. 1986. *Madagascar: Island of the Ancestors*. London: British Museum.

Rabedimy, J. F. 1976. "Pratique de divination à Madagascar: Technique du sikidy en pays sakalava-Menabe." Travaux et Documents de l'ORSTOM, no. 151. Paris: ORSTOM.

Rahatoka, S. 1985. "Pensée religieuse et rituel betsimisaraka." In *Ny rasana tsy mba maty: Cultures traditionnelles malgaches*. Antananarivo: Librairie de Madagascar.

Rajaonarimanana, Narivelo. 1990. "Sorabe, traités divinatoires et recettes médico-magiques de la tradition Malagache Antemoro." Thèse de doctorat nouveau régime soutenue à l'Institut National des Langues et Civilisations Orientales, Paris.

Ruud, Jorgen. 1960. *Taboo: A Study of Malagasy Customs and Belief*. Oslo: Oslo University Press.

Simon, Pierre. N.d. "Le reveil du Sikidy d'après un manuscrit de la Mahajamba." In *Etudes Océan Indien*. Paris: INALCO. (in press).

Sussman, Robert W., and Linda K. Sussman. 1977. "Divination among the Sakalava of Madagascar." In *Extrasensory Ecology*, ed. J. K. Long, 271–91. Metuchen, N.J.: Scarecrow Press.

Trautmann, René. 1939. "La divination à la côte des esclaves et à Madagascar." *Mémoire de l'IFAN*, no. 1. Dakar: IFAN.

Vérin, Pierre. 1986. *The History of Civilisation in North Madagascar*. Rotterdam: Balkema.

———. 1990. *Madagascar*. Paris: Editions Karthala.

Vig, Lars. 1977. *Croyances et moeurs des Malgaches*, fasc. 2. Trans. E. Fagereng. Antananarivo: Trano Printy Loterana.

PART THREE

Cultural Systems within Divination Systems

> Divination is not only a basic pattern in understanding the Lulua way of life, but it is also the most important institution in Lulua society.
>
> David A. McLean and Ted J. Solomon,
> "Divination among the Bena Lulua"

This section emphasizes divination's centrality in articulating culture and providing sufficient knowledge for orderly, meaningful human existence. Contrary to functionalist arguments that divination is merely supportive of kinship and political structures, closer examination reveals that these institutions depend on divination. While it intersects with religion, a divination system involves far more than religious belief. Divination is essential in providing a repository of cultural values as well as facilitating adjustments to a changing world.

Perhaps only for Ifa divination of the Yoruba is this fundamental role of divination in the maintenance of a society understood. That is a result of the work of Bascom (1969), Abimbola (1976, 1977), McClelland (1982), and others. Even Evans-Pritchard (1968) and Turner (1975) do not convey this perspective. The following chapters demonstrate the absolute dependency of cultures on divination in terms of health care (the Batammaliba of Togo), social authority (the Lobi of Burkina Faso), the life-sustaining hunt (the Pagabeti of Zaire), and social relations (the Yaka of Zaire). But most dramatic is the situation of the Lobi, whose sole source of social authority, the *thila* ("spirits"), are voiceless and can communicate only through divination. Similarly, Djimini Senufo diviners also "give voice" to the spirits, who have no mouths (Suthers 1987).

Just as divination materials reveal a "resume of [the] whole social order" (Junod 1927:571), so the diviner displays the behavioral ideals of the culture. With their reports of the selection, training, and practice of those unique Batammaliba and Yaka individuals with exceptional intelligence and sensory abilities who become diviners, Blier and Devisch complement the material in section II. Blier emphasizes the carefully balanced role of the Batammaliba diviner as alienist and annunciator, one who must be simultaneously outside and inside the society in order to properly serve the community. But a diviner does not act alone during consultation. The divinatory contingent, especially the representative of the afflicted, has not been treated in previous studies, but chapters here and in the next section demonstrate the critical role played by these individuals. The rich texts of divination sessions reveal not only the density of oracular speech but also the significance of the negotiated meaning which emerges from divination sessions.

Other significant issues emerge from the divination systems presented below, which, despite their differences, are basically mediumistic (although those of the Batammaliba and Pagibeti are better termed "oracular-interpretive" types [Devisch 1985]). Meyer argues that the deceptively simple Lobi technique has an extremely efficient "transmission capacity," and he suggests that certain divination types are technically better suited for certain types of oracular communication. Many African cultures have more than one divination technique and, occasionally, hierarchies are noted, as for the Azande (Evans-Pritchard 1968) and the Yoruba (Bascom 1969), who consider the Ifa palm nut form superior to the divining chain form. But what analytic reasons are there for these distinctions? Almquist's essay is one of the first to analyze criteria for choices among available divinatory mechanisms.

According to Devisch, mediumistic divination among the Yaka provides another arena for problem solving as opposed to adjudication in councils and courts. Paralleling the complementary uterine (matrilineal) and agnatic (patrilineal) descent groups are the realms of divinatory authority and customary law, each distinct yet both necessary for the full functioning of Yaka society. The Lugbara distinguish between male oracle operators who only deal with patrilineage affairs and female spirit mediums who are the sole means of coping with witches (Middleton 1964, 1973). Similarly for the Kaguru, only diviners can determine whether problems are due to ghosts, God, or witches (Beidelman 1986:114). There may be other correlations between systems of divination and kinship, just as there are correspondences between social structure and forms of divination (Park 1967) and spirit possession (Bourguignon 1976; Greenbaum 1973). In this regard, the Lobi are noteworthy because they have no alternatives; the *thila* are their authority on all matters.

Devisch's "praxeological approach" (1985), as developed below, raises the critical matter of differing concepts of causality. Devisch argues that strict linear causality is not to be found in the revelations of Yaka mediumistic divination, which relies on atemporal "structural causality." This distinction is similar to Young's concerning *awdungist* divination among the Ethiopian Amahara (1977) and anticipates the discussions on epistemology in the last section of this volume. For the Yaka, this structural causality revealed by divination brings forth the collective history of the client's uterine ascent group as well as the relevant traditional norms and values as the specific etiology of the afflicted person is diagnosed. This process recalls Lévi-Strauss's analysis of the therapeutic, abreactive function of the Cuna shaman's song, which relates the individual past to the group's common history (1967:181–201).

Devisch's query as to whether "Yaka society shorn of divination would still remain Yaka society" is not mere rhetoric but an essential statement of a society's dependence on divination. Indeed, Batammaliba society depends on divination for maintenance of its health system. The Pagibeti hunt—and thereby the whole society—relies on the suprahuman knowledge gained from the hunting oracles, which also restate basic values. As already noted, the Lobi totally depend on the guidance provided by the *thila*, who only communicate through divination. And as Yaka social fabric is repaired through the revelations of a divination session, that most important dimension of social harmony is restored.

Thus the practice of divination provides—indeed, requires—the reunification of social units through collective recounting of personal and group history and the reviewing of behavioral standards in light of a contemporary dilemma. In the end, not only has the community reunited to resolve a problem; it has revitalized its history and traditions as well.

References

See reference list at end of main introduction.

Rudolph Blier

Diviners as Alienists and Annunciators among the Batammaliba of Togo

At the center of the health care system of the Batammaliba (Tamberma, Somba) of northern Togo and Benin stands the diviner-consultant, *upon*, a figure who connects the individual, the family, and the community in providing answers to medical and social problems that arise. Such individuals are called on both to delimit the causes of physiological, psychological, and social problems and to indicate the means of resolution. *Upon*, from the root *pon*, "to give," means literally "the person who gives." The advice that these consultants give, called *tapananti* ("the words of the *upon*"), is the glue that holds the Batammaliba health care system together. These consultants provide the necessary formulas, principles, insights, and approaches both for understanding and for resolving problems.

The Batammaliba, the focus of this study, are a Gur-speaking people living in the Atacora mountains, which span the nations of Togo and Benin. My research among the Batammaliba centered on the social dimensions of their medical care and how residents view, define, categorize, and treat health-related crises. Diviner-consultants, it became clear to me in the course of this research, serve as important "pastoral guides" (according to Max Weber's definition), redefining, reexplaining, and reinterpreting the central cultural dimensions of their communities. Accordingly these consultants must be understood not only as spiritual guides for troubled individuals but also as interpreters and annunciators of the community's main cultural values.

Throughout the course of my research I resided with an elderly consultant, Yapita Tapoke. In my observations of Tapoke and other consultants, one of the first questions to emerge concerned the community's view of consultants. It soon became clear that such persons, while being at the heart of the community and having a central role in its major workings, were at the same time viewed as different. Such persons presented themselves and were perceived by others as often troubled and estranged. Frequently these consultants—women as well as men—were regarded as alienated from the very communities which they served. In the course of rethinking this seeming contradiction, and in reviewing related research in Africa and elsewhere, I was struck by the suggestive parallels to the phenomenon found in the English term *alienist*, a word used at the turn of the century to denote psychiatrists, i.e., the medical doctors who specialize in mental illness. This word, which derives from the Latin *alienus*, meaning "strange" or "insane," today finds use primarily in the field of medical jurisprudence.

The term *alienist*, in its reference to a group of specialists who treat the various problems of mental illness and in its parallel associations with alienation and strangeness in society, appears to have striking similarities with one of the key features of the Batammaliba view of the consultant. This essay accordingly examines the identity of the Batammaliba consultant as alienist. I suggest that by virtue of their distinct identity as outsiders, these persons are better able both to observe society and to serve as its annunciators. Stated another way, since these consultants are concerned with persons who are viewed as in some way troubled or estranged, they are themselves identified (both by the communities and by themselves) as outsiders. This in turn allows them greater freedom to view and treat the problems of illness and alienation in the community at large. Furthermore, it became clear that the alienist characteristics which are associated with these consultants are actively promoted by the Batammaliba through the means of their selection, training, modes of examination, and later patterns of life. This emphasis on alienation is often defined through the metaphor of a journey which the consultants take both within and outside themselves in the course of their consultation. The idea of alienation is also central in the terminologies which are applied to consultations and consultants.

Learning the Consultation Process

Children said to be born with the power to consult are believed to acquire this ability through two principal means, inheritance and the killing of an animal who had this power in the wilds. There are varying views on the relative importance of each means of acquisition.

Consultants say that they can feel related changes in their bodies when they are in the process of consultation. Some suggest that they feel a "high" similar to one derived from alcohol. As one consultant explained, "You begin to talk a lot. It is like you have had too much to drink and you are drunk" (12:494)[1] Others describe it as a swirling, whirlwindlike sensation, resembling a stream of air passing from one's head into one's chest and stomach. This "rushing" and often "dizzy" feeling is explained as being caused by the passage of the consultation deity, Kupon, into the consultant's body (via the fontanel at the top of the head) as one is about to consult. The weight and motion of Kupon are said to make one giddy. One consultant noted in this light that

Kupon, when it goes into your body, enters by way of the head, tormenting you with dizziness. It turns, and turns. Your head will react like it is crazy. Your mind will turn and turn like you want to fight with everyone. You fall down. When you fall like that it is like you are drunk. It is Kupon that makes you act like that. It is this that turns your mind. It is this that makes you crazy. (12:515)

This action of the deity is said to shift one's mind to the side. It is this misalignment that is said to make one feel dizzy.

Consultants often are distinguished from their peers even as children. Youngsters who eventually will become consultants are frequently described as being "tormented" or "dizzy" (5:18). Women who are pregnant with children who will become consultants say they can feel the difference while such babies are still in the womb. The considerable movement of these children is said to give a characteristic sensation (ache) during the pregnancy (6:229). The identity of these babies as future consultants is also observed at the time they are born. The midwife in particular is trained to observe their characteristics. As one person asserted emphatically, "When you give birth to this child, you *know* that he will be a consultant" (6:229).

It is said that such children, even as babies, have an overly active *bayama*, a word that means simultaneously "mind," "thought," and "bile." This *bayama* manifests itself most strongly as a form of energy that emerges in the course of both anger and intellectual reflection. Yafuata Tano explained accordingly that "the *bayama* is found in your forehead. It is your thought. It makes you not forget what you said. Bile is also called *bayama*. This is the thought of animals. It goes together with the head, and it is these together that give advice." (12:478).

Children with a very active *bayama* are said to display, from a very early age, the characteristic features of hyperactivity and manic behavior. They are said frequently to act with reckless abandon. They are constantly in motion. For this reason, they have trouble concentrating and considerable difficulty in adjusting to school (6:16). As one consultant stated, "This happens first when you are still young. It bothered me and made me act without thinking, like I was crazy. It was at this time that they gave me medication to take and I calmed down" (6: 72). The behavior of one young girl was described:

On the day when she became troubled with this, she grabbed a basket, calabash, and pipe from people attending a gathering and ran with them all the way to the river. She yelled as she ran that something was following her, when in fact it was we who were trying to catch up with her. At the river she threw the calabash and pipe into the water and stood there yelling. (12:494)

In such cases the person is treated by a consultant with various calming medications. If this works, then during subsequent crises the person will be given additional medication.

In addition to being distinguished by their bouts with manic behavior, children who will be consultants are also said to be characterized by their extraordinary brightness. Because their minds are said to be stronger and their intelligence greater than that of ordinary children, they are thought to be able to remember things with ease. This intelligence is actively promoted by their parents through ongoing tests of their memory. Outstanding memories are also identified with consultants as they get older. It was suggested accordingly that "consultants know all there is to know because they remember everything" (11:505). This gift is important both in the confirmation of a child as a potential consultant and in the later reaffirmation of his or her abilities in the course of consultation. Keen memories are necessary because the consultants must know not only the ailments of the spirit and body but also the past problems of the family and village. Thus one man, whose father had died before revealing his family history, said that when he himself became a family spokesman he had to turn to a consultant to reconstruct the family past.

Children who will be consultants, in addition to being extraordinarily active and bright, are also described as being accident prone. They are said to be careless, to have no sense of danger, and to recklessly explore anything and everything without fear. Such curiosity brings with it many potential problems. Most consultants had had a serious accident during their youths; many had fallen out of trees or off roofs, while others had suffered from serious cuts. Such children, explained one consultant, "If they see a knife, they will pick it up without knowing it" (11:618). Another consultant, when asked when he first knew that he would become a consultant, pointed to a long scar on his leg from an accident in his youth (6:72). Most such accidents come from carelessness, but some are acquired from quarrels, for persons who will be consultants are said to anger quickly. The children who are designated as future consultants are aware that they are different from their peers, and some say that they were frightened at this. One explained that as a child "I cried every night without sleeping. If I wanted to sleep, it frightened me" (11:614).

The first treatment which such children receive is intended to calm them. This treatment is given when the child is around six or seven years old, a time when he or she is particularly aware of the fact of being different. At the same time, these children are given a distinguishing haircut, a single line of hair along the top of the head. Such coiffures are said to offer a temporary place of rest for the deity so that it will leave the body in peace. "You shave the head to allow a place for Kupon to rest," explained one person (6:72). This coiffure, like the unusual behavior associated with (and to a certain extent expected of) these children, serves further to distinguish them from other children around them.

Later in life, still other features reinforce the identity of the consultants as being different from the norm. Most consultants are said to be clairvoyant. They are believed to have an additional set of eyes through which they can view the goings on of both the mind and the world beyond (6:75). Because the power of clairvoyance is also frequently associated with the potential for malice and discord when it is misused, the fact that consultants have this power is often seen as further reason for their identities as "outsiders." So important is this factor of extra vision for consultants that it is actively encouraged in children who will be consultants through the use of special medicated waters for bathing and drinking. The development of this deep vision is seen to be important not only for consultants but also for family advisers, certain health care practitioners, great hunters, and extraordinary singers.

Consultants use their extra "sight" in the course of their contact both with the deceased family members and with their animal companions during the course of consultation. It is these past elders and animal companions who provide background information on the problem that is being discussed. The animal companions are important because they are associated with in-depth knowledge of the natural world, in particular as it concerns medicine. The role of the deceased elders is also critical because these persons provide knowledge about the past. Thus the extra sight associated with consultants enables them to see more deeply into the problems that are brought for resolution. Such people in this way are believed to be able to view problems at the deepest level. They see things in a problem that the average person cannot see. This extra sight accordingly serves to further distinguish the consultants from other members of the community.

Another way that the consultants are distinguished is by the consultation materials, which they carry wherever they go. This equipment consists of a consultation club and cowries (traditional money) carried in a leather bag (today a cotton one may serve instead). This distinctiveness is reinforced further in the case of female consultants, for they wear the clothing of men—shorts rather than skirts. Furthermore, as Yafuata Tano noted,

> Only women who consult have head rests and stools. These women also carry axes, knives, and leather sacks. They need these things because they are consultants. If they do not carry these things, we will not know that they are consultants. They are women, how else would you know that they can do consultations? (12: 509)

Such women marry and have children. Ordinarily, however, they do not begin to have an active consultation practice until after they are past childbearing age.

Consultants are also distinguished from other men and women in the community by the series of interior journeys which they take in the course of acquiring the necessary knowledge of consultation. We recall that the consultation deity, when it first enters children who will be consultants, is thought to make them feel dizzy as it journeys inside them. Similarly, during a consultation, the consultant is said to take a journey within in the course of seeking a solution. This same idea of a journey is a central focus of the major actions performed during the transition that marks one's becoming a consultant. This journey takes place around the age of twenty, often in association with a period of increasingly bizarre behavior. Such behavior is said to be a signal to these persons that they are ready to become consultants. According to one consultant, this behavior is related to the fact that the mind is pushed to the side, causing the soul to become agitated and leave

the body (12:515). One woman I saw initiated as a consultant during this period
left her family and resided with others in the community (10:65–69). To the horror
of the community, she sang funeral songs in the course of her daily work.

When the person's unusual behavior becomes quite marked, he or she is taken
on a separate journey: induction into the society of consultants. This begins at
the house of the sponsoring consultant with in-depth lessons and tests concerning
both the medications used in particular illnesses and the symptoms of associated
problems. As a test at the end, the new consultant undertakes a practice consultation at the sponsoring consultant's house at which time she or he must answer
correctly the various questions that are asked by this sponsor. The consultation
runs through the night and terminates at dawn, when the new consultant is accompanied back to his or her house by the sponsor. Here a special stone serving
as an altar for the deity of consultation is set up in the new consultant's doorway.
The following evening, the test of the new consultant continues, as this person
is asked to demonstrate the necessary extra sight by locating objects hidden inside
and around the house. If this is done successfully, the final test takes place the
next morning at dawn. At this time, the person is asked to consult for the first
time at his or her home with a family adviser.

The Specialized Knowledge of Consultation

Like medical practitioners in many areas of the world, these consultants are
seen to draw on a large body of knowledge in the course of their consultations.
Each consultant, while being a specialist, thus must be a supergeneralist, for each
must have an understanding of a wide variety of factors—physiological, psychological, medical, social, political, historical, cultural, religious—that play a part in
the problems brought to them for resolution. Consultants represent in this way
a local form of documentation for many different types of knowledge. They are
both guardians of this knowledge for the future and active utilizers of it in the
present as they search for insight into the varying problems of their clients.

Much of their information on recurring problems, types of illnesses, and
available treatments is learned in the course of training. Once they have begun
to practice actively, their information is rapidly expanded, as problems of greater
and greater depth and variety are brought up for consideration. Since a number
of consultations are undertaken at public gatherings—at markets, funerals, feasts,
and large social events—the consultants have additional opportunities to examine
the work of other consultants and to hear what types of illnesses and treatments
have been done in various families. Outstanding consultants in addition will be
visited at their homes by people from outside communities.

Adding to their roles as guardians of community knowledge, these consultants
form a specialist group that can call on one another for aid in solving difficult
problems. For this reason, many consultants voluntarily seek out and pay for the
advice of other consultants in order to learn more about the history and circum-

stances of particular problems, types of illnesses, formulas, sources of medication, and affiliated practitioners.

The consultant is also aided in his or her work by the high god, Kuiye, and the earth deity, Butan, who are said to provide insight in the course of the consultation process. Accordingly, each consultant begins with an acknowledging gesture in the direction of the sun and the earth: one consultant noted at this time, "The consultants are not the ones who show what the problem is. God (Kuiye) is the one who does it. That is why during consultation we move the stick down towards the earth and then up in the direction of the sun. It is God who comes down to stay on the stick" (2:46). Another consultant began the session with "It is God that is in front of you and you follow. It is not you that provides the answers" (10:271). Reinforcing the importance of Kuiye in the consultation process is the tradition that all consultations must take place during daylight hours. Should a consultation last too long, the consultant will warn the adviser to "hurry up, the sun is ready to set" (4:81).

Each consultant also is aided by his or her sponsoring deceased family elders, particularly those who were consultants in their own lives. Their importance was noted frequently: "It is the deceased elder who allows the consultant to be able to indicate the response" (6:84); "it is both the deceased elder and God that gives one the ability to conduct consultations" (11:504–5); "a person gets the ability to consult from his deceased elders" (11:237).

Evaluating the Consultation Information

Despite the importance of these outside sources, the information that is given out by the consultant must be continually verified. Most family advisers thus will go to several consultants to reaffirm the advice that has been provided. This is particularly true in cases of serious problems or in cases which have multiple symptoms. "If I consult with someone from my own community, I will not be convinced," one person said. "I need to go to other communities to corroborate the consultants' advice" (1:72). Others shared these concerns: "I had to see many consultants before believing that this was the right combination" (4:159). Or, "When one needs to consult one does not stay in one place" (6:226). Thus the consultants' advice must be checked against that of other consultants, preferably with consultants from other communities. If the advice of one conflicts with that received from others, then the advice is considered probably to be erroneous and is not used.

Several methods are also employed during the course of a particular consultation to judge the efficacy of the advice being given. First, the family adviser comes into the consultation with certain knowledge about the problem, its history, and its potential causes. He in turn will ask the consultant details about the problem, such as who is sick and what the problem is. If the consultant does not answer correctly or if the solutions are not in line with the background that the family adviser knows, he may question the proposed solutions. Second, throughout the course of the consultation a number of trick questions (involving false problems or nonexistent persons) are put to the consultant to see how he or she will respond. If the consultant is wrong on these, it is thought that he or she could also be wrong on the real questions. As a final test, the consultant is asked to indicate what other consultants have suggested about the problem (see below).

The ultimate proof of the veracity of a given consultation, however, is defined in terms of whether or not the situation is ameliorated after the advice of the consultant has been accepted and carried out. A local saying reinforces this idea: "One thanks the blacksmith in front of him, but one thanks the consultant behind" (2:45). This saying, which is frequently repeated in the final phases of the consultation, refers to the fact that when one purchases something from a blacksmith, one can immediately evaluate the workmanship and praise the maker at this time. For the consultant, however, one must wait until after the advice has been followed ("behind" here meaning "following"). If the advice proves correct, i.e., if the treatment works and the person who is ill recovers, it is then that one will thank the consultant for his or her advice. As one person noted, "The consultant is thanked afterwards and not to his face. So I should now thank him and say that things have worked out" (6:217). In the words of another, "One accepts the peace of mind of the consultant, but one does not accept the advice of the consultant immediately. If the consultants really told me the truth then I should see my son go out today for a walk" (9:94).

The problem of consultants sometimes giving incorrect advice is also generally acknowledged. Not only do certain proposed solutions not alleviate the problem; many times, because of a lack of resources, some families are not able to do what the consultants have suggested and yet the person still recovers. In this light, it is interesting that consultants as a group are frequently called liars, a name which is seen in part to be based on their potential for stating falsities and making mistakes. More important, however, the consultants' identity as liars, as "persons who see only the surface of things," according to the Litammali literal translation of the term, is decidedly pejorative. This term acknowledges the problem posed by consultants who are not able to view the situation deeply enough or who are not able to get at the essential knowledge necessary for finding a solution (11: 508). The term *liar* is also used formally by the consultants themselves. As one consultant explained,

> The reason one ridicules consultants by calling them liars is that we do not consult with one person but with many people and we get certain lies in the process. Also, in the past after some consultations when the advice was followed, it did not work. Thus we ridicule the consultants saying they tricked us. (11: 508)

The term *liar* is also employed by consultants during the funerals of other consultants. Thus when a consultant dies, other consultants gather at his house and at a predetermined time walk around the house ringing a bell and singing, "It is the consultant who is the liar; he consults to eat." In this way the consultants acknowledge publicly the difficulties and potential problems in their profession.

Qualitative Differences between Consultants

While all consultants to a certain extent are seen as suspect, some are viewed as more accurate than others in the advice that they give. "There are consultants among the consultants," Yafuata Tano noted (11:483). The outstanding consultants are called *uponmwa*, "the real *upon*." Highly respected consultants are frequently honored with additional names, such as *utetantamwa*, "real practitioners" (11:483). Important consultants are, in addition, sometimes called *upononitiki*, "elder *upon*" (6:76). Because the credibility of the consultant is of such importance, people often walk for hours to see those who are highly regarded and after arriving are willing to wait for a long time for their turn. As Yafuata Tano noted, "The one that I call a great consultant, everyone comes to him or her for a consultation. People will say 'if I go to consult with that one I will be able to sleep.' They have consulted with this person before and they have seen that what they were told was true and the suggestions worked out" (11:483). It is these highly respected consultants who are approached to care for young children who may become consultants. They are also the ones who train and test those who are old enough to consult.

On the other hand, some consultants are seldom sought out, and those who are seen to continually offer poor advice—particularly when they send people to wrong specialists or misinterpret the severity of a problem—are heavily criticized or mocked and may eventually leave active practice. Some, particularly those who are young, may try again when they are older, but many others do not. Consultants who are known to give consultations after they have been drinking are strongly condemned as well. The is true of consultants who do not take their work seriously. Yafuata Tano identified the qualities of a poor consultant:

> The bad consultant even after dreaming of something important will stay without saying or doing anything. A good consultant will consult with other consultants. But a bad consultant will simply stay and wait saying, 'I will go tomorrow. I will go tomorrow to my friend's house to consult because there will be beer there. Today who should I go to?' The bad consultant will tell himself this and he will stay at home. The next morning when he goes, he will not even think about consulting but he will drink, and when he sees others consulting, then he will take the stick and say 'my friend I want to consult' and he will take hold of the cowries and throw them down. As he consults like this, he will do it without thinking. (11:563–64)

Consultants who are suffering from serious mental or physical illnesses likewise are viewed with skepticism and are not utilized. There are occasions accordingly when well-qualified and highly respected consultants will voluntarily retire for a time. This generally occurs if they have been sick or if they are troubled by other problems, such as a death in the family, which requires their attention. If the consultant has close relatives who are ill, consultations are also usually suspended. As one consultant explained, "If someone is really sick in your house such as your brother or your father or if your wife has just given birth, you cannot have consultations" (11:486–87). Thus, not only one's own health but also that of close family members is seen to impact on one's consulting ability.

When the problems are dissipated, these consultants may again begin practicing. I observed such a situation with an elderly consultant who had been seriously ill and therefore had stopped consulting. One night after treatment for an unrelated problem, he became energized and started singing, demonstrating the characteristic symptoms of Kupon craziness, the condition young people about to become consultants often manifest (9:143). At dawn the next morning, consultation medication was prepared for him and his hair was cut into a short circle. He then began to consult. The first adviser with whom he consulted explained: "It is the deity of consultation that did this to him. It is like he was crazy. It is like he wanted to run" (9:161).

The Role of Family Advisers

Each family, as suggested earlier, has an adviser who represents its members in the course of consultation. Such persons are generally family spokesmen who know the family history and have learned the specialized language of consultation. These advisers are called *uponcanta*, "receivers from *upon*." It was stated that when these advisers come to the consultation, "they receive from the consultant. The consultant gives and the adviser receives. If a member of his family is sick, he will go to the consultant and ask about this illness. The consultant tells him its source" (11:614).

In the consultation, the advisers play an important role, constantly checking the veracity of the information given and leading the discussion by asking questions. These advisers, who are always male, thus must have intimate knowledge of the history of each family, including its past achievements, discords, and problems, its members, their illnesses, and their affiliations. Frequently these advisers also must know the histories of other families and the illnesses and difficulties they have had. It was explained accordingly that "the adviser is someone who is serious and knows all about the family and community" (13:215). This knowledge is important, both because the consultation ranges widely in its coverage and because most problems are examined in the context of family history. Contemporary medical problems, in other words, are often seen to be continuations of problems that originated in the past. It is thought that such problems recur because each new generation is born with the sponsorship of past family members. It is assumed that if these problems are not resolved now, they will continue to bother members of the family, present and future. For this reason the consultation often concerns itself with the roots of the present problems so that these problems can be understood more deeply and thereby rectified.

Accordingly, the family adviser is selected both for his intelligence and for the seriousness of his attitude. The family adviser in addition must be fully knowledgeable about the meaning of the multiplicity of symbols used by the consultant in responding to his questions. For, although the adviser poses his questions orally, the consultant responds by indicating objects, directions, body parts, and the like (see below). This technique allows for private discussion in public places, but it also requires that an adviser be adept at interpreting the symbols given, especially considering the usual fast cadence of the consultation.

Because the consultation is often very tense, particularly when serious problems are being discussed, one sees occasional flareups between the consultant and the adviser. In one consultation, the adviser noted, "My friend, you lie" (6:22). In another consultation, the adviser exclaimed, "No, my friend, you are not a real consultant." The consultant responded, "This is not true. It is you who do not know how to do it. You drank. You should not think that I do not know how to conduct a consultation. The person you are advising did not know what to tell you before we began. If you think I lie, go ask him and return" (4:80). In this way, both the consultants and the advisers, while continually reaffirming the validity of the consultation process, acknowledge that inaccuracies occur.

The Consultation Process

The consultation process takes the form of a verbal and visual discourse carried out between two persons considered to have great acumen, the consultant and the family adviser. The process is an ordered give and take between them; the adviser verbally sets out a variety of possibilities that the consultant will accept or reject.

The structure of the consultation is relatively standard. The family adviser who has come to consult (most consultations take place at the house of the consultant) will ask the consultant's permission to sit down. He sits down across from the consultant and the consultation stone is placed between them. At this time the family adviser tosses two cowries on the ground. These serve both as payment and as a means of determining whether the day is propitious for the consultation. This is indicated by the cowries' falling one with its face up, the other with its face down. Several tries may be necessary, but if they continually fail to turn up in this way, then the consultation will be postponed.

If the day is propitious, the consultant takes hold of his or her consultation club, a carved branch about two and a half feet long with a thin shaft and a large bulbous knob at one end. The consultant holds the shaft in his right hand while the adviser clutches the knob in his right hand, helping to support it in the course of its movement during the fast-paced consultation process (see figure). Thus the reactions of the adviser to the club's movement, indicating particular signs during the course of consultation, may be noticed by a skillful consultant, although that possibility was denied by consultants with whom I discussed the process. They insisted that the process was carried out independently of both the adviser and the consultant through the direct intercession of God, the deceased elders, and the family animal companions.

At the outset of each consultation, the consultant points the knob end of the club toward the sun, then taps it on the flat, roughly circular stone that is placed on the ground between the two. In response to questions put by the adviser, the consultant points the knob end toward various parts of the adviser's body. He also draws patterns in the air or on the ground with this club. The designs drawn on the ground, the signs made in the air, and the parts of the body that are touched by this means form a coded language that is known to both the consultant and the adviser. This language refers to specific symptoms, illnesses, problems, persons, practitioners, courses of action, gatherings, payments, feast materials, deceased elders, deities, and animal companions that might be involved. Crucial questions are often asked several times. In addition, confirmation is usually sought by the adviser by whispering to the consultant the meaning that he has come to understand for a particular sign.

In principle, throughout this process the consultant is quiet, except for the whis-

A Batammaliba diviner, Mani of Koufitoukou (left) and a family adviser, Tifanmou of Koutalokou, holding the consultation club during a divination session in Koutalokou village, northern Togo, August 26, 1977. *Photo by Rudolph Blier.*

pering at the end. With this in mind, one consultant explained to another who was just learning, "You should only answer with the stick, not with your mouth" (12:728). At another test of a new consultant, she responded to a question directly and a family member in attendance exclaimed, "It is not you that speaks, it is God. Give your advice without speaking with your mouth. You must listen with your ears and let the stick speak for you" (10:270–71). A family adviser added, "You have to be quiet and show us only. There where your stick goes, you will follow it. You are not the one that knows. It is your stick that shows and we will know there where it shows" (10:271). Because this symbolic system is defined through motions of the consultant's club held by both the consultant and the adviser, persons who have hearing disabilities or are blind are able both to consult and to serve as family advisers. Elders, who play important roles in both situations, thus can continue their roles despite the infirmities of old age.

The language of this symbolic system is relatively straightforward. The use of these signs was observed at consultations throughout the year of research. Thirty-four such consultations were recorded and analyzed for content. A review of the related signs was discussed with local consultants and advisers. In general, illnesses are indicated by pointing with the knob end of the club to the part of the adviser's body where the most pronounced symptoms are found.

The seriousness of the problem is indicated later, when the consultant reveals the treatment that should be pursued. That too comes through a variety of signs. These signs refer to the implements that are used for a particular treatment, the therapy that is followed, the place in the house where this treatment is usually given, and the deity or sponsoring deceased elder that is associated with this treatment. After a particular treatment is suggested, further clarification is obtained through the designation of the time of day when this will take place, the types and amounts of food that will be prepared, whether beer should be prepared, and which practitioners, family members, and others should be invited.

The time of day for the treatment is indicated by pointing to where the sun will be in the sky. For work done at night, the time is conveyed by pointing to where the moon will be. If the stick points toward the east, the work should be done in the morning; if toward the west, the treatment gathering should be held in the afternoon. The time of month is described by an incomplete circle of varying size depending on the moon's shape. The payment form and the meats to be used at the gathering are indicated with a particular sign for each animal. The left hand refers to the chicken, the center of the head to the guinea fowl, and the upright stick on the ground to a goat; the drawing of the stick in a horizontal line toward the stone designates a sheep, and the pointing of the stick straight up in the air refers to a cow or bull. The preparation of beer is indicated by rubbing the stone with the club as if in the process of grinding the germinated millet used for beer.

The people involved in these gatherings are referred to in a number of ways. Usually this is done by pointing to those physical features or symbols that indicate the individual's characteristic "honors" and "injuries." The former include such positive attributes as numerous children, denoted by pointing either to the breast or to the thighs, where children sit. The left thumb denotes a good hunter, while pointing toward the consultant's house cattle room denotes a person rich in animals and food. Those who are clairvoyant are identified by two spots on the forehead designating the additional sight (eyes) of such persons.

The negative attributes usually include physiological abnormalities, malformations, or other distinguishing features—such things as a growth on the head, buck teeth, missing teeth, a large neck, a large navel, a lame leg, a hairy chest, a scar, a big nose, big ears, a hernia, leprosy, deafness, a body protrusion, blindness, and a beard. Each person is further singled out by identifying his or her gender (breast versus penis), age (one breast for an older woman, two for a young woman), generation (forehead for the father of your father), and place of birth in the family. The birth position is shown by the consultant's touching the stick to the finger of the adviser's hand, which indicates the appropriate birth order. The thumb indicates first son or daughter, the index finger second son or daughter, and so on.

Each deceased elder who is discussed is identified as having died of a particular illness. That is done by noting the predominating symptom that preceded his or her death. Death accompanied by fever and headache is noted by pointing to the head. Women who died in childbirth are indicated by pointing to the stomach. People who died of starvation or from internal problems accompanied by a swollen stomach are also noted by the stomach. Respiratory failure is indicated by pointing to the nose, leprosy by rubbing the stick across the fingers to suggest that they are missing, hernia by pointing to the groin, and snake bite by making an S-shaped sign in the air and indicating where the person was bitten. A serious infection that led to death is indicated by pointing to the site where the infection began. Suicide is noted by pointing to the area between the neck and the chin, since hanging is the most common means.

To identify or locate a person, a sacred area, or a practitioner or treatment center that should be used, the club is pointed in the appropriate direction. After a direction is given, the adviser may mention communities in that direction and then neighborhoods to narrow down the possibilities. If the treatments are to be given at the adviser's own house or in one of the houses of the extended family, that is indicated by making a line on the ground in front of the adviser or pointing to the adviser's solar plexus. Houses in other neighborhoods or communities that need to be visited are indicated both by pointing in the appropriate direction and by drawing a line on the ground away from the adviser. Thus, for example, if a medication container is required, a circle is drawn next to the adviser if the family's own medication container should be used, while it is drawn away from the adviser if he needs to seek it out elsewhere.

The consultant also specifies the exact spots in the house where treatments are to be done. The south side of the house is indicated with a counterclockwise motion around the stone, the north side with a clockwise motion, the main cattle room by pointing toward it, the upstairs by making a circular motion in the air over the stone, and the upstairs bedroom by drawing a line on the ground right next to the stone. If additions such as shrines need to be made to the house as part of the treatment, these are similarly indicated. The need to visit a sacred grove is conveyed by repeatedly hitting the stick on the ground, suggesting trees.

Major gathering types and treatment forms are also indicated through this sign system. Medication in general is suggested by pressing the stick into the open hand of the adviser. The open hand refers not only to applying an ointment or compress to an infected or swollen area of the body but also to taking oral medications. Root medications are denoted by a cross drawn on the ground; the cross is a common sign for a tree. The medication to be used is specified by identifying the place of residence of the specialist who is to treat the problem.

The need for a specialist to remove objects from the body is suggested by moving the stick on and off the painful area, an action similar to that taken by the specialist in the course of treatment. The need to suction off blood is defined by pointing to leather; this sign refers to the cattle horn used by the specialist as a suction cup. Passing the stick in circles around the adviser's face, which suggests the dizziness brought on by the consultation deity, shows that the problem is related to becoming a consultant.

As suggested above, the need for treatment with a medication container is noted by drawing a circle on the ground beside the stone, near or far from the adviser depending on where this container is found. This sign refers to the circular form of the vessel used for medication container treatments. Other signs indicate whose medication container should be used and whether it should be set up at the family home. The decorations for the container and the type of vessel needed are also indicated. A light tapping of the stick on the chest refers to spotted patterns. The use of cowries is indicated by touching the sticks to the thrown cowries. Various specialized medication containers are also indicated. Those for childbirth and infant care are indicated by pointing to the neck, where the necklace identified with this container is worn by patients. The sides of the neck refer to this type of container when it comes from a neighboring ethnic group. Two parallel lines drawn in the ground refer to a container used for the treatment of twins.

Gatherings for life passage crises are also noted with a variety of symbols. The most common sign for this treatment form is the rubbing of the stick on the adviser's head. This refers to the head shaving that is done for the first life passage gathering. Other signs include the touching of the forehead and the knee, which refers to later life passage actions of introducing the person to a particular animal. Other information indicated at this time includes the person's deceased elder sponsors and the animal companions. In addition, the consultant indicates the number and type of animals to be consumed and whether beer should be prepared. The placement of an abode for the person's soul is also noted. The building of associated altars for the deceased elder couple who are the sponsors of the person are suggested if necessary.

The gathering to rejuvenate the soul of an elderly person is indicated with a circular line drawn around the stone (rather than to the side as for a medication container). The circle represents the round form of the residence that is constructed for each person's soul. This sign is also given if there is need for a special gathering for the soul of one's wife. Such a sign would be followed by indicating the breast, which stands for one's maternal relatives, and the direction of her community. In addition, her deceased elder sponsors are identified. A gathering intended solely to renew the deceased elder's habitation is indicated by positioning the stick in the back of the stone (the back here referring to the past).

The need to visit a critical care practitioner is indicated by rubbing the stick up and down on the adviser's body, signifying the need for a special type of cleansing therapy. Pointing in the appropraite direction indicates the type of treatment suggested and its associated practitioner.

If deities are seen to be involved in problems or treatments, they too will be noted. Kuiye, a solar manifestation, is indicated by holding the stick up vertically, toward the sky. Butan is suggested by digging with the stick in the earth and tossing up some soil. Fawafa, the serpentine deity of men's initiation, is designated by using the stick to make dots around the stone, suggesting a serpent's mottled skin. Treatments associated with Litakon, the deity of fertility, twins, and infants, is noted by pointing to the area in front of the neck where related necklaces are placed. Critical care treatments associated with the god of war and death, Fayenfe, are designated by pointing to the adviser's middle finger, where an associated ring-bracelet is sometimes secured.

Grave cases that offer no hope of treatment through any means are indicated in several ways. Pushing the stick under the stone is one way, for the stone symbolizes the stone in the center of the house terrace that serves as the deceased elder's tombstone. Another such sign is made by touching both of the adviser's ears with the stick, which means that the adviser should no longer run around trying to find (hear) a solution but should stay at home and await the inevitable, since the person will soon die.

The Structure of Questions in the Consultation Format

The types of questions raised during the consultation frequently follow a set format and structure. Generally, the adviser begins by suggesting the most catastrophic possibilities, often that Kuiye and Butan have abandoned him: "Is it God that has rejected me? Has the earth deity rejected me? Is it this suffering that we are talking about?" (10:552). If this suggestion were accepted by the consultant, it would be a sign that the situation was hopeless, that death was near, for there can be no life without the solar and earth deities. But it almost always is rejected.

When the suggestion is refused, the adviser goes on to less grave but equally negative statements. Often he suggests that the whole family is dead or that the house will be destroyed: "Has the house fallen on us? You should know. If the house falls and kills all the people inside, would one be happy? . . . Has my house fallen and have my crosspieces been burnt? . . . There where I built should I leave there?" (4:62). These catastrophic suggestions are usually rejected as well by the consultant ("What are you saying my friend? No, no, never, impossible") as he vigorously beats on the stone with the knob end of the stick for emphasis. The adviser goes on to more general possibilities, suggesting that matters are confused and that he would like to understand why: "It is this that mixed everything up like this and I do not see it?" (7:490). "My friend, in my house it is as if the grains got all mixed up. I have come like this so that you will clear up this and I will be able to see" (12:36).

The adviser finally turns to more specific things by asking in various ways what the sources of the problem are: "This thing hurts me everyday. What did I say so that it hurts me so much?" (12:37). "What is not going well with me, my friend? What are you telling me to do?" (10:405–7). The consultant responds by indicating a particular problem through the signs discussed above. At this time the adviser may also ask about the symptoms that are bothering the person who is sick: "My friend, tell me if it is a stomach ache that she has?" (4:62). "What is the problem, my friend? You say it is her soul that attacks her like this and she falls. Is it her soul that did this?" (11:22–24). Throughout these discussions the adviser continually suggests alternatives to what the consultant is proposing, often rejecting the signs given by the consultant and offering new possibilities instead.

Finally, questions turn to the actual solutions indicated by the consultant and the various details concerning those who will do the work, those who will be there, where it will be done, what will be needed, what day it will take place, and at what time it will be held.

It is important to note here that if the problem or solution is not brought up by the adviser in his questions, the consultant usually takes it upon himself to indicate that there is another "road" that should be pursued. He often, in turn, offers clues (again pointing to certain body parts) concerning the direction the adviser should take in his questioning.

Once the problem and treatment have been defined, the adviser asks if there is anything else. The consultant may bring up a second ailment that should be cared for or may indicate that another family member should be treated at the same time. The adviser may ask what other consultants told him previously and what work he has done or is preparing to do. This serves as a test of the veracity of the consultant's answers. In the course of this latter part of the consultation, the adviser also reveals his optimism about breathing freely and sleeping well (10:575). Additional statements make reference to the fact that one will thank the consultant later when the veracity of the consultation is known. The consultation ends with a rhythmic tapping on the stone. Sometimes the consultant indicates verbally that the session has ended. Often he repeats: "I will leave the stick because I should not continue to pound in this way bothering the sun and the earth" (10: 417).

After the consultation, the adviser must decide whether to act on the advice given. At times the family does not have the ability to pay for a particular gathering. For this reason, in less than grave situations the adviser may simply keep an eye on things, hoping that the problem will clear up. In serious cases the consultation is often followed by a meeting at which the various family advisers who have consulted compare the results of their consultations.

The Diviner-Consultant as Alienist and Annunciator

The diviner-consultant is at the center of the Batammaliba health care system. He or she is the medical gatekeeper, designating the directions that must be traveled in one's search for treatment. As Tchanfa Atchana observed, "without the consultation you cannot know what you suffering from" (8:228). The position of these consultants as gatekeepers is clearly reinforced by their identity as outsiders, as people who are decidedly different from others in the community. Their childhood illnesses, their unusual behavior, their recklessness, their great intelligence, their curiosity, and their assumed extra sight all serve to separate them from the society of which they are observers. Furthermore, it is clear that these "alienist" characteristics are actively promoted by the Batammaliba through the means of selection, training, modes of examination, and later patterns of life. This emphasis on the consultants' identity as outsiders is also conveyed through the metaphor of the journey that they take both within and outside themselves in the course of their training and later consultation roles.

It is in part by virtue of their distinct position as outsiders or alienists that these persons are able both to observe the community and to serve as its annunciators. It is through the balancing of these two dimensions that their roles as consultants are made possible. Furthermore, it is frequently said that once one has become a consultant one must continually consult (i.e., serve as an annunciator) or else the overtly bizarre behavior (the alienist identity) will become too dominant. Similarly, if the consultant is viewed through his or her personal actions to be too much the outsider (too much the alien), this is seen as proof that it is not the deity of consultation but some other deity or power that is troubling the person. The consultant thus must continually balance his or her identities as societal alienist and annunciator. As both insiders and outsiders, consultants have greater freedom and viability in giving advice on problems in the community, but they also must walk a fine and difficult line in maintaining two conflicting identities. As both alienist and annunciator, the consultant stands at once at the center and the periphery of the society—the outsider who is the ultimate insider.

Note

1. Parenthetical notations refer to my field research journals. The first number indicates the month, from volume 1 (December 1976 and January 1977) to volume 13 (January 1978); the second indicates the page within that particular journal.

Piet Meyer

Divination among the Lobi of Burkina Faso

This essay discusses the Lobi diviner of Burkina Faso, his calling, practice, and position in Lobi society. After describing the divination method used almost exclusively by the Lobi, I discuss the most typical reasons for seeking out a diviner and the most important results of a consultation. The Lobi system, in the quantity and quality of information it conveys, may well be unique in Africa, but until now the only available description of it was a cursory treatment by Labouret (1931: 449–65).

The Lobi

Inhabiting the savannahs of the tri-country corner made up of Burkina Faso, Ivory Coast, and Ghana, the Lobi are hoe farmers, living primarily on millet and corn and carrying on small-scale breeding of cattle. The majority (57 percent) of the 160,000 Lobi live in the southwestern tip of Burkina Faso, while 40 percent live in neighboring Ivory Coast. As a result of repression by the French colonial government in the 1930s, five thousand Lobi fled to the Black Volta area in Ghana and settled there.

The Lobi speak a Voltaic language, Lobiri. It is similar to the language spoken to the west by the neighboring Dian but quite different from the languages of the Lobi's eastern neighbors, the Birifor, Dagara Lobr, and Dagara Wile, who belong to the Voltaic More group (Köhler 1975:187).[2] The Lobi are, however, culturally related to the Birifor, Dagara Lobr, and Dagara Wile, as well as to the Dian and the neighboring Tegessie. They all have a bilineal mode of descent, for example, and are politically acephalous. Nevertheless, cultural differences from area to area, even within linguistic groups, are very large and cannot be ignored. For this reason I will concentrate my remarks on a single Lobi subgroup, the one that speaks the Tyollo dialect and lives in the Wourbira area of Burkina Faso.

There, in 1976–77 and again in 1980, I spent a total of six months in field research. The religious system of the Wourbira Lobi is best viewed as a three-level pyramid. At the top is *thangba yu* (literally, "sky above"), the creator of the world and the force responsible for all life on earth ever since. In no way personified, this god is defined in a very abstract and general way as being behind all things. No shrines are built for *thangba yu*, and no sacrifices are made in this god's name. *Thangba yu* cannot, in the true sense of the word, be grasped.

Under this abstract god, on the second level of the pyramid, are the *thila* (singular, *thil*), invisible and bodiless beings endowed by *thangba yu* with superhuman powers and abilities. *Thila* fulfill various tasks in the human world that I will examine in detail later on. Unlike *thangba yu*, the *thila* can be communicated with through a medium, the diviner (*buor*), and one can, according to their instructions, build shrines, make sacrifices, or perform other services for them.

At the bottom of the pyramid are several kinds of bush beings (*kontuorse, krupaa*, and others), who are in principle visible and live in the bush just as people live in villages. The most humanlike beings of the Lobi pantheon, the bush beings even have their own *thila* and, like humans, must rely on a diviner to communicate with them.

The Task of the *Thila*

To help give an idea of the diviner's importance in Lobi culture, I will first discuss the meaning and function of the beings with which diviners communicate, the *thila*. I will start with a Lobi myth.

As Lobi elders still relate, in the beginning Man lived in a blissful state. God provided meat for him to eat; he did not have to work and knew neither strife and war nor sickness and death. He followed the norms of behavior, the "great interdictions" (*soser kotena*), which God had voiced: "You shall not steal, you shall not take away each other's wives, you shall not kill one another; always remain united!"[3] But as the population increased, the men began to steal each other's wives. As punishment, God ceased to provide the meat with which they had nourished themselves, gave them hoes so they could work, and beset them with sickness and death. Then God retreated forever to the sky (*thangba*) above (*yu*). That is how the Lobi came to know sadness, helplessness, and suffering. So that the people would not be completely alone, *thangba yu* gave them the *thila*, entrusting these invisible beings from then on with the task of attending to (*yaale*) the people's welfare (*bopha*) and saving (*taare*) their bodies (*tumber*) from hunger, sickness, and death.

Since that time the *thila* have carried out this important task. To ensure the Lobi's survival, the *thila* maintain the political, social, and moral order in the society, which knows no central political, administrative, or legal institutions. They do this by issuing interdictions similar to the great interdictions of *thangba yu*. These *soser* regulate the behavior of the people within the individual houses (*tyor*), the villages (*de*), the patri- and matrilineal descent groupings (*kuon* and *tyaar*), the markets (*yaa*), and the initiation camps (*dyoro*). If a behavioral rule is broken, the *thil* in charge of the social area involved punishes the guilty one by causing him or a member of his immediate surroundings to fall ill; by causing crop damage, accidents, or other such calamities; or even by killing the transgressor. It is worth noting that the Lobi are well aware of this law-making and law-enforcing function of their *thila* and explain it by reference to the command which *thangba yu* gave to the *thila*.

The *thila* also look out for the welfare of the community by forcing certain individuals to open markets in specified places or to organize collective hunts. In fact, a market cannot be opened in Lobi country without being ordered in this way. In addition, the *thila* help people overcome their manifold problems. Through the diviner they prescribe medicine to heal certain diseases, for example, or methods for a bachelor to find a wife or for a wife to have children. They suggest which sacrifice to make to protect oneself from sorcerers or from soul-eating witches. The *thila* seem to have a solution for virtually every problem, but they offer their solutions only under certain conditions. Finally, the *thila* also look out for the welfare of their owners by supplying them with the means to use sorcery against their enemies.

The Diviners

To help the Lobi in the ways I have described, the *thila* need diviners, for, as bodiless beings, they have no voice. The diviners communicate their instructions, which differ from case to case.

The diviners are usually men; only 2 percent of them are women. Usually they are forced to become diviners by a *thil*, whom they discover in the bush and then embody in a shrine at home (such *thila* are called *wathila*; singular, *wathil*). It is correct to speak of a *thil's* relationship with a human as coercive. A Lobi who learns through consulting a diviner that, besides his usual work, he must also advise his fellow man free of charge, tends at first to ignore the command, waiting for further signs from his *wathil* and hearing what five or six other diviners have to say before he answers his calling. Some hard (*kiere*) individuals even defy their *wathil* for years under heavy physical and material hardship. But the *thil* has no understanding of his stubborn owner's reasons for resisting and employs ever stronger methods, such as crop damage, sicknesses, and deaths, to bend his owner finally to his will.

We may ask ourselves why the Lobi exhibit such dogged resistance to the calling of a diviner. The Lobi give several reasons. Most important, a diviner is not allowed to refuse a client who wants a consultation; he risks sanctions from his *wathil* if he does. An exception may be made only when someone in the family is seriously ill or has died or if the diviner himself is sick or in the process of making a sacrifice. This impossibility of refusing a client weighs heavily: a Lobi diviner gets four or five clients a day and on heavy days up to twenty, even though every ninth man between the ages of twenty-five and seventy years generally is a diviner and even though diviners are fairly evenly distributed throughout Lobi country. Thus a diviner has less time for his work in the fields or for his other activities than a Lobi who is not a diviner. That the diviner earns practically nothing for his divinatory services makes the situation even worse. He receives five cowries (about half a cent) per consultation when he divines at home and twenty cowries at another location chosen by the client. Furthermore, a diviner enjoys neither high social status nor any particular privileges; he gains in prestige only if his divination is particularly good, just as any Lobi does who performs some activity better than the others, be it farming, carving, or dancing. Finally, a diviner very seldom divines for himself. Should he have some serious problem, he too must seek the help of a diviner. All this means that a diviner dedicates much time to other people without really benefiting from it himself. That is why a Lobi tries to avoid the call from his *thil*. Nonetheless, I have never heard of a Lobi successfully defying his *wathil*.

Partly responsible for the low status of the diviner and his lack of compensation is the fact that divining requires no special education. The future diviner has already sat in on numerous consultations as a client, has watched various diviners during their relatively simple rituals, and has even taken an active part in them. He knows how to greet the *thila*, how to question them, and how to verify the results of the questioning. He must pass only one test consultation with a senior diviner: finding out what this aged diviner is thinking about and what is the reason for the consultation. As soon as he has passed the test he is a diviner and may —must, in fact—receive clients.

Both diviner and client are called *buor* in Lobiri, a terminological equality that is in keeping with what has just been said. The diviner does not distinguish himself from his peers through a larger income, a higher social status, or a wider technical knowledge. Usually he becomes a diviner simply to avoid further retribution from his *wathil*.

Reasons for Consulting a Diviner

When does a Lobi seek out a diviner? The only general answer I received from the Lobi was that "we go to the diviner when we are so afraid of something that we just don't know what else to do." By slightly modifying a formula of Herskovits (1938, vol. 2:305), we can apply it here and say that such a fear is unleashed by events that are "counter to the most common-place routine of every-day behavior." Besides deaths, serious illnesses, injuries, and accidents, such events include any important and inexplicable disturbances of daily life. The Lobi turn to a diviner when, for example, their harvest is worse than a neighbor's, when a man tries in vain to capture a woman, when a woman cannot have children, when pots continually break during the firing, or even when a person is disturbed by a bad dream.

Not only can the behavior of people lead to a consultation; the unusual behavior of animals can, too. For example, domestic animals may die in great numbers for some inexplicable reason, or wild animals may speak with human voices to someone in the bush or transform themselves into a piece of iron. Even objects may behave strangely: something can suddenly fall at the feet of a person alone in the bush or appear in a special form at various places for days at a time. Like the wild animals, such objects are believed to be manifestations of *thila* who wish to communicate with a person; for this reason, a diviner must be consulted to enter into contact with the respective *thila*.

A Lobi never questions his diviner out of pure intellectual curiosity or just because he does not understand a certain phenomenon. Instead, he acts out a very real fear that a disturbing situation (sickness, bad luck, and so on) will continue or even worsen, or that a harmless event (such as a bad dream or an omen) is a sign of some danger yet to come. In both cases only the diviner, by contacting the *thila*, can find a way of alleviating the actual or potential problem.

Usually it is the male head of the family who goes to see a diviner. But first, with five cowries in his right hand, he approaches the most important shrines in his own house and in a low voice says, for example:

> Hear, *thil*, I do not know what to do. I am afraid. My youngest daughter is seriously ill. We have tried everything to make her well, but in vain. If you are responsible for her illness or if you know exactly why she is sick, follow these five cowries to the diviner and say what you have to say so she will be cured. Have you understood?[4]

Then he goes to see the diviner; only rarely does he have the diviner come to his house.

The Consultation

When the client arrives at the diviner's house, he greets him and tells him that he wants him to divine (*bore*). At no time does he mention the reason (*no*) for his visit, for the diviner must find that out for himself. The diviner takes the client to a special room, usually his first wife's room or his shrine room (*thil du*), and asks him to be seated. The diviner takes his divining bag (*buorlokaar*), sits down (*to bul*, "sit down without knowledge") to the right of his client on the smooth dung-covered floor, and brings forth from his leather bag the objects which the *thil* who forced him to become a diviner has ordered him to use: a piece of white or red limestone (*mele*), with which he makes a drawing of circles, lines, and waves on the floor; an iron bell (*giel*), with which he will later greet the "big ones" (*kontena*); one or more leather bottles (*tyusu*), which are closed with a piece of millet stock and which contain the cowries (*be*) for the questioning of the *thila*; wooden statues (*bateba*), which represent either people or animals in various stances; mussels (*khaa*); stones (*bikaar*); and, in some cases, other objects.

When everything is laid out in front of him, he begins by greeting (*fuore*) the *kontena*. Holding the bell in his left hand, he rings it in a quick, continuous rhythm. He first greets God (*thangba yu*), then the earth (*ti*), then his own *thila*, and then his client's *thila* and important *thila* from the area to which deceased diviners belong. At the same time he asks them all to help the consultation be successful. After several proverbs (*sokpar*) about the essence and meaning of divination, he abruptly stops the loud ringing and greeting. He then opens a leather bottle, shakes out a few cowries, and asks his *thila* one after the other if he may divine. If all answers are affirmative, he begins the questioning.

The first thing he must learn from his *thila* is the reason for the consultation. In a raised voice he asks the *thila* questions which they may answer with a yes or a no. They give their answers through the diviner's left hand. From this point until the end of the consultation, the diviner holds the client's right hand in his own left hand. First the diviner asks very general questions: "Has there been a death in the client's family?" "Is someone sick?" "Has there been an accident?" "Has blood been shed in some other way?" A no answer by the *thila* is signified when the fingers of the joined hands run lightly over the diviner's left thigh; the diviner's and client's arms rise together (fig. 1), only to fall; and the back of the diviner's left hand slaps against his thigh (fig. 2). There the two joined hands rest until the next answer comes. If the diviner asks a right question, the *thila* answer with a yes sign: the two joined hands rise up a bit and sink slowly to the floor, then quickly rise and slap the diviner's left thigh. By asking yes or no questions, the diviner is able to obtain from the *thila* a great amount of precise and detailed information in a relatively short time.

If the diviner receives only negative answers for too long and cannot find out the reason for his client's visit, he may ask the *thila* a question that cannot be answered with a yes or no: "What is it that I cannot find?" The *thila* answer such a question by having the joined hands make drawinglike movements in the air or on the floor, movements that give the diviner a clue for further yes or no inquiries. If the diviner is not successful after returning to yes or no questions, he repeats the same analogical question; otherwise, he continues with the digital questions which can be answered with yes or no.

In this way the diviner usually learns his client's reason for the consultation. He must also be able, however, to find out the most important details. It is not enough for him to know, for example, that someone had a bad dream; he must say who in the family dreamed what. That is the only way the client can be sure the diviner really has entered into contact with the *thil* who made the consultation necessary and who can for that reason give the diviner the necessary information. The client does not want to make sacrifices to one *thil* only to find out later that his problem is not solved because the wishes of the proper *thil* were not satisfied. The diviner's attempt to find the client's reason is, therefore, a test, the result of which can supply the client with valuable information. The client has the opportunity to decide whether he trusts the information he receives, whether he should accept the diviner's diagnosis and carry out his orders, or whether he should seek out another diviner.

Figure 1. Arms of diviner Banyela Hien (left, with divination paraphernalia) and client shown rising during divination session in Gbuntara, Wourbire region, Burkina Faso, April 1980. *Photo by Piet Meyer.*

Figure 2. Hien's and client's arms fall during same divination session in Burkina Faso. This session was held on rooftop to facilitate Meyer's photo-taking; sessions normally are held in diviner's house.

When the diviner has learned the precise reason, he can proceed to ask which *thil* is connected with the case (*thimiir*). The diviner again tries to learn as much as possible with yes or no questions; only afterward does he resort to more complex questions. The diviner verifies all findings of relative importance by tossing cowries, then summarizes the findings in one sentence and asks the *thila* to use the cowries to tell him whether he has divined correctly or is still missing some important information. He picks up two to five cowries in his right hand and, while speaking, tosses them on the floor in front of him. If just one cowry lands with its open side up while all other face down, the *thila* have answered yes. Any other formation of the cowries means no. A no answer can force the diviner to start the questioning process all over again.

After the diviner has gathered the most important information, he turns the questioning over to his client, who until then has remained silent. The client may now ask the *thila* yes or no questions on some aspect of the problem which particularly interests him in order to obtain more details. His questions are answered through the technique of the two joined hands.

The whole consultation may average a total of eight hundred to a thousand questions, which diviner and client ask within an astonishingly short time—about forty-five minutes. When all desired information has been received and confirmed several times over, the diviner summarizes the results for his client and asks the *thila* some last questions for a final reassurance. After the diviner tosses the cowries two or three last times, the consultation comes to an end. If no more clients are waiting, the diviner puts his instruments away and leaves the room with his client. The latter shows in no way whether or not he is satisfied with the session. He returns home, where he will carry out the *thila*'s prohibitions or commands, should he choose to do so.

The Instruction of the *Thila*

The prohibitions (*soser*) and commands (*bonoo*) which the *thila* communicate to their owners through the diviner are extraordinarily varied. This variety represents a principle characteristic of the Logi socioreligious system.

The variety of the prohibitions derives from the fact that they may touch practically every aspect of Lobi life. The prohibitions govern not only interpersonal relationships but also the relationships of people to certain animals, plants, and objects. For example, the inhabitants of the village of Korhogo (about twelve miles southeast of Gaoua in Burkina Faso) do not use millet stem mats in their territory because their *dithil* (literally, "village *thil*") forbade it. Unlike other Lobi, they sleep on short mats; they also roll their dead in short mats to be able to inquire about the causes of death.

Commands, in contrast to prohibitions, are positive, constructive instructions. They too vary greatly. They may, for example, concern the building of a shrine, in which case the *thil* determines exactly where, how, and by whom the shrine is to be built. Commands also may order an addition to a standing shrine. Some concern the making of new wooden or clay statuettes, iron or brass objects, or pots, detailing numerous possible variations. Wooden statuettes, for example, may show two dozen different gestures and have different facial expressions or hairdos, depending on the *thil's* command (see Meyer 1981:56–118).

Thila also demand sacrifices (*toopar*) and determine who makes them, how, and where (see Meyer 1981:47–49). The same is true for the two-day sacrificial feasts (*buur*), which the *thila* may entrust to one person or a group. The *thila's* instructions for these feasts are so vast that several consultations are necessary before all the information is gathered.

Finally, the *thila* may ask (if necessary, force) their owners to become diviners or healers (*bibiir*), to drive a witch's dart (*dudube*) from the body of a sick person, to open a market at a certain place and tend it every fifth day, to organize a hunt, or to become sculptors (*bateba thel*), iron smiths (*phuberdaar*), brass founders (*phusiedaar*), or hunters (*babaal*). In these cases, too, the Lobi who receives such a command from his *thil* also receives instructions about how he is to engage in the activity. For example, a *thil* shows his owner just how he should, as a diviner, make the drawing on the floor at the outset of a consultation.

A Need for Comparison

As we have seen, the prohibitions and commands issued in Lobi divination can be extremely varied. From a technical perspective, that gives a certain uniqueness to the communicative processes used in Lobi divination. It is probable that few other divination methods used in Africa are capable of conveying the quantity and quality of information brought forth by the Lobi system to describe a prohibition or a command in such a precise and exhaustive way. Different divination systems have varying transmission capacities. It is time to investigate these very different transmission potentials because divination techniques are first of all the means by which the exchange of information between dissimilar beings is made possible (as for the Lobi, between humans and the *thila*). Such a comparative examination could supply us with important clues to the entire phenomenon of divination.

Notes

This paper was presented at the 1981 African Studies Association meeting, Bloomington, Indiana.

1. Goody (1967:5) called the Dagara Lobr "the LoDagaba" and the Dagara Wile "the LoWiili."

2. "Thangba sure tebela wyaa, wa tekha kharaa, wa kukhaa, wa tyiu kha puuwaa; wu do byel!" These interdictions were told to me in 1980 by Kherhim Da in Korhogo.

3. According to Bindouthe Da of Wourbira.

References

Goody, J. R. 1967. *The Social Organization of the LoWiili* (1956). Oxford: Oxford University Press.
————. 1972. *The Myth of the Bagre*. Oxford: Oxford University Press.
Herskovits, M. J. 1938. *Dahomey, an Ancient African Kingdom*. 2 vols. New York: J. J. Augustin.
Köhler, O. 1975. "Geschichte und Probleme der Gliederung der Sprachen Afrikas." In *Völker Afrikas und ihre traditionallen Kulturen*, ed. H. Baumann. Wiesbaden: Steiner.
Labouret, H. 1931. *Les tribus du rameau Lobi*. Paris: Institue d'Ethnologie.
Meyer, P. 1981. *Kunst und Religion der Lobi*. Zurich: Museum Reitberg.

Alden Almquist

Divination and the Hunt in Pagibeti Ideology

Studies of divination have conventionally focused on ethnographic description (Bascom 1969), on the processes and symbolism of divination (Turner 1975), on the diviners themselves, or on the place of divination within a particular peoples' system of thought (Evans-Pritchard 1937). While variation in divinatory practice between ethnic groups has been noted, only rarely, if at all, has the significance of variation within one group's corpus of divinatory practices been made a conscious object of study.

Given the fruitfulness of recent studies of variation and of its significance in traditional ritual by Fernandez (1965), Ardner (1972), Barth (1975), Burton (1980), and others, this neglect is somewhat surprising. This study hopes to illustrate the usefulness of such an approach by first reviewing the full range of Pagibeti divinatory practice, noting the anomalous state of features of two among them, the *biseye boko*, or sending the antelope, and *mbolongo*, the bursting pot oracle; finally, we account in turn for the anomalous features of these two oracles by situating them among a series of nonoracular practices common to their use context, the practice of the communal hunt. Features common to oracular and nonoracular practices alike are then explained in terms of Pagibeti concepts of person, action, and knowledge, particularly as these relate to the practice of the hunt and of its central concern, *lekeye paye* or *wukeye paye*, wakening or opening the forest.

To understand the relationship of divination to the hunt in Pagibeti ideology, some ethnographic background might be helpful. The Apagibeti are hunters/horticulturalists who live in the rain forests of north central Zaire. Isolated from the nearest road by some thirty-five kilometers of forest and by the Dua River, they combine plantain, manioc, corn, and peanut horticulture, together with extensive individual and group hunting and trapping of antelope, monkey, pig, buffalo, elephant, and other forest fauna. During the dry season, from January to May, gardens are cut and planted, communal hunts are common, and village ceremonial life is most active. With the June rains, men move out one by one into the forest to set their traps and hunt. They remain in the forest for most of the following seven months, returning to the village with their loads of smoke-dried meat only when salt, oil, or garden food stores are depleted.

Besides hunting, Pagibeti men's work involves garden clearing, trail maintenance, and village house, garden house, and forest shelter construction and maintenance. Women's work consists of garden planting, weeding, and harvesting, cooking, child care, and water and firewood hauling.

The Apagibeti were a subject of classificatory confusion among early Belgian sources. Lying along the line separating what used to be termed Bantu from Sudanic language groups, the Apagibeti are speakers of a Libuale dialect and belong linguistically to the Bantu group but culturally to the Sudanic. Patrilineal and virilocal, all Monveda Apagibeti belong to one of two founder clans, brothers descended from the mythic Kulegenge, common ancestor both to them and to their northern "Sudanic" neighbors, the Ngbandi. Local authority in the chiefless, precolonial era was vested in the *some*, the oldest male of the senior lineage in each village. He heard disputes and mediated between the village and the ancestors at the ancestral spirit shrine. Birth order is of particular importance in Pagibeti social organization. It structures aspects of social life as various as order of seating, division of game, eating order, goods and wives inheritance, dancing order and officiation over and maintenance of the ancestral spirit shrine, or *tolo*.

Apagibeti live at the juncture of a number of beneficent and maleficent forces. The first is the creator god *Nyombo*, or *Njambe*, giver of life, to whom a brief morning prayer succeeded by the *pa nzeke*, or ritual spitting, is performed by the male head of the household unit. Group cult in honor of *Nyombo* is an innovation brought first by Catholic catechists in the early 1930s and by Protestant missionaries in 1976. Most Apagibeti are nominal converts to Catholicism, and tension between them and the small Protestant congregation runs high. Evaluations of *Nyombo*'s power also vary. A comment heard frequently among nonbelievers and among many Catholics is that "Nyombo a yoye" ("God has grown tired") or "Nyombo a de boko" ("God has become an old man").

Another force is that of the ancestors. They ensure fertility, food crops, and good hunting for the village, given that good social relations are maintained among village members and the ancestors' living village representatives, the lineage elders, receive their due respect. Due respect includes maintenance of the ancestral spirit shrine by the youngest male member of the village's senior lineage, periodic offerings of kola nuts and meat portions to the shrine, and acceptance of the authority of the senior lineage's senior male, as when he washes the village of misfortune (*soseye ngi*) or says words to end anger and discord between villagers at the shrine. It also entails the turning over of all forest animals designated as shrine animals to the lineage elder for butchering and distribution.

A number of persons are particularly dangerous to hunting, gardening, health, and reproductive success. Among them are twins, witches, *mangodo* (persons whose top teeth erupted before the lower teeth), *yingo* (forest spirits), and sorcerers. Sorcerers are by far the most feared, as virtually all villagers have private stores of medicines, *bebobe*, whose use may be for good or for ill. As is frequently said, "Nto na nto na eboke te ngake" ("To each man, his own medicine" or, in variants of the same expression, "his own leaf" or "his own tree"). Medicines from neighboring villages, ethnic groups, and dispensaries are sought out by traveling villagers and brought back to the village. They are individually owned by the person who brought them and may be exercised for the benefit of others, often for a fee. One may know the medicine for healing broken bones, another for relieving neck stiffness, another for making infants walk, another for curing spirit possession, another for giving an enemy sickness, and another for seizing thieves of garden crops or of domestic or trapped forest animals. Specific medicines for good fortune in hunting monkey, elephant, and buffalo are found among local villagers or among neighboring Bale, Bua, and Ngbandi ethnic groups, respectively.

Ownership of such power can be dangerous to its possessors. The greatly feared *pomoli*, for example, guarantees spectacular success in killing forest game to the individual hunter who employs it for private gain; but in exchange, members of the hunter's lineage will, one by one, die the slow wasting death of the trapped animals themselves for as long as the medicine is employed. In view of its prevalence and ambivalent valence, *bebobe* ("medicines") is a favorite one-word explanatory tool used to account for the unusual power of a chief, a witch, or a highly successful curer or hunter.

Given this wide range of potentially menacing powers in Pagibeti life, divination is a useful adjunct to prayer to Nyombo, filial piety, and the collection and use of powerful medicines in the successful negotiation of everyday life. There exists no cover term for what anthropologists label as the class of divinatory practices; each has its own name. And, while there is no specialized term for or role of diviner, there is a named role for those few individuals who have the reputation of being especially skillful and powerful users and possessors of medicines (*nganga nkisi*), some of whom may also divine.

Oracles are the characteristic form of Pagibeti divinatory practice. The simplest oracles are the involuntary ones. If, on departing for the hunt or for the garden, or on a trip to a neighboring village, one should sneeze, the bulk of the air is experienced as passing through one nostril or the other; if it passes through the right nostril, one's fortunes will be bad. Dissenters from this interpretation argue that it depends on the individual, that if after sneezing through the right nostril one has good fortune, then that nostril becomes the auspicious one for that individual.

Another involuntary oracle is that of stubbing one's toe as one sets off on an outing. Generally, the right foot is considered auspicious or neutral and the left inauspicious, with dissenters insisting that only experience can decide which foot is "good" for an individual. Outcomes are taken seriously; a hunter, for example, will defer a hunt until the next day should he stub his left toe before exiting the village/garden zone and entering the forest.

Dreams, too, may be oracular.[4] A dream in which one peers down into a deep hole may presage a death in the lineage. Dreaming of an animal while in the forest presages a successful kill the next day. In recognition of their power, oracular dreams are consciously sought out and conditions favoring them are created. The hunter should respect his fathers, should have no thoughts of the village, and should talk only of things of the forest.

A man may also decide to let the kind of dream he has, auspicious or inauspicious, determine for him whether to embark on a trip or hunt. Dreams are thought to be sent by the ancestors, and the ancestral spirit shrine serves as its medium. One informant described this shrine as a radio, a medium through which the living and their "fathers" communicated.

Of the consultative oracles, the rubbing-stick oracle *diwa* was most frequently employed. One afflicted with illness or with a lack of reproductive, hunting, or gardening success may consult the oracle owner, an elderly man famed for his powerful medicines, who will, for a fee, put the question as to the source of the affliction to the oracle. While he addresses the oracle, he rubs two flat, palm-sized, smooth-bottomed boards together with a water and medicine mix between them. Going from the general to the particular, he asks the oracle if the cause is the anger of the fathers. If the boards stick or seize (*gboke*) while he addresses them, he knows that he has identified the cause. He then asks the board who is angry with the afflicted. The recital of names accompanies the rubbing together of the two boards until they stick together, thereby identifying the particular source of affliction. A remedy may or may not be suggested. If in reply to his initial address the boards continue to slide effortlessly against one another, then he moves on to other causes of affliction, such as witchcraft or sorcery.

Other uses of the oracle include not only diagnosis of the cause of the affliction but also the selection of the appropriate remedy. In one case I watched as a dying woman's neighbors and kin brought their combined stores of curative medicines to be given to the patient. Each was carefully tested by grinding it in a pestle, mixing it with water, and rubbing the mixture between the boards with the accompanying address: "If the medicine is strong, show us; if the medicine is good, show us." Only those medicines which made the boards seize were judged powerful and given to the dying woman.

The verdicts of the rubbing-board oracle, owned as it is by a few old men, are suspect. In my village of residence, the character of its operator was frequently referred to as grounds for disbelieving its judgments. The man was a child of a Pagibeti mother seized in Pagibeti-Buan warfare; he had returned to his mother's village following her death. He was feared for his knowledge of Buan medicines and, though frequently consulted for his divining skills, was suspected of using his sorcerer's powers for personal gain. Many villagers stated that he had introduced diseases not previously known to the village, such as the drying up of the breasts of nursing mothers. Those seeking a cure commonly paid him twice, once for the divining of the disease and once for the purchase of the remedy.

The poison oracle, on the other hand, was widely respected though rarely used. Its judgment is final. The name of the poison, *benge*, is the same as that noted by the Tanghe among the Ngbandi to the north and by Evans-Pritchard among the Azande much farther east. During my eighteen-month field study among the

Apagibeti, I saw it consulted only twice, once during a standard inquest (*enduma*) to determine the identity of the lineage member responsible for the deceased's death and once in a case of witchcraft accusation. Unlike the rubbing board, the poison oracle is not controlled or managed by any one individual, though a village elder should be present during its preparation and execution. As recently as the 1940s a person accused of witchcraft would ingest the poison himself, being innocent if he survived and guilty if he died. These days the question of guilt or innocence is stated, a fowl is fed the poison, and on its survival hangs the guilt or innocence of the accused.

Cases of possession by spirits of the village or forest are treated by the local Protestant minister or by a local entrepreneur who learned the art and acquired the requisite medicines by being himself healed by a diviner/healer of a neighboring ethnic group. The healing of the spirit-possessed is his personal specialty. His art, called "pulling the rope" (*wuseyekuse*), involves seclusion of the afflicted, treatment with medicines, and the pulling out of the possessing spirit under conditions of trance for both patient and healer. The healer calls out names while drawing thumb and forefinger lightly down the length of a raffia string tied to the big toe of the possessed, always pulling away from the patient and toward himself. When he calls out the correct name, the reclining or prostrate victim jerks into an upright position and is considered cured. *Yingo*, or spirits of the forest, are considered easy to cure, while a long-lasting possession of many months is invariably referred to as possession by village spirits sent by medicine-using witches.

The local pastor exorcises spirits in somewhat the same manner, placing one hand on the Bible and another on the head of the afflicted, naming names until the spirit departs the individual. He addresses Nyombo as his source of power rather than a medicine, but his own power is viewed by many villagers as having come from the outside, learned in Bible school. The Lingala term used frequently by older villagers to refer to him is the same as that applied to his unconverted colleague in healing/divining, *ngnanga nkisi*.

Finally, there are *ntiseye mboko*, the antelope-sending oracle, and *mbolongo*, the bursting-pot oracle, both employed by hunters in the forest, primarily during the great dry season communal net hunts when the whole village may move into the forest to set up temporary shelters and engage in cooperative hunting. The antelope-sending oracle is the simpler of the two and may be used whenever two or three successive attempts to net game have failed. One hunter is selected by his peers on the basis of his possession of a particular kind of fortune called "a good back," *ngonga enza*. A good back—unlike another form of good fortune, inherited good blood (*banga enza*)—is attributed to one who has consistent good fortune in his enterprises, particularly the hunt. It is gained by social attribution and can be shared; two men who share the same hunting medicine, or who regularly share productive hunts together, may be said to have a good back. The elected hunter then speaks to the forest while beating the ground with a branch, reciting the reason for the hunt, telling its history, and citing the individual names of those animals the hunters hope to kill. He concludes, "Antelope, if we are to kill much, die male." After he repeats this several times, the hunt begins, and if the first antelope caught in the strung circle of nets is male, the subsequent day's hunting should be good.

The bursting-pot oracle is more elaborate than *ntiseye mboko* and is employed only when the assembled hunters have repeatedly strung their nets in a circle, loosed the dogs and beaters into the "head" of the circle, flushed the hidden game out in the open and into the nets, and yet found the catch insufficient. A twenty-odd animal kill is considered good; after two or three days of desultory kills, *mbolongo* is suggested.

No specialist controls the oracle. Rather, once again a man chosen by his fellow hunters for his good back is selected. He goes out in the evening and cuts red wood scrapings from the *mbolongo* tree. The next morning at dawn he combines this with water and places the mixture in a small clay pot over a fire. While he works, the assembled hunters may or may not dance a dance miming the movements of the animals they hope to kill. The operator covers the top of the pot with a large *ngongo* leaf, sealing it tight by wrapping a string around the lip. He then draws three or four trails out from the fire center radiating outward like spokes from the center of a wheel. As he draws each line he addresses the oracle, citing the name of a specific cause of misfortune and asking that it be identified and thus exorcised:

> *Mbolongo*, I cut like this, I go, I cook you. May the forest open, may the forest boil over all at once. May we kill many animals. . . . If it be a pregnancy, spill here; if it be *mangodo*, spill here; if it be a death, spill here. . . . I cut like this, I go, I cook, may the forest open, may we kill animals.

When the pot boils long enough, its leaf cover splits open and a water/foam/ *mbolongo* mixture bursts out onto one of the three or four radiating spokes, indicating which of the causes of misfortune was responsible and exorcising it in a single stroke.

Some of the water/*mbolongo* mixture is then taken from the pot and carried in a leaf cone either by the oracle operator or by a child to the site of each new raising of the nets during the day. The remaining mixture is taken to the path where the operator squats facing the forest, his back to the village; he then hurls the remainder of the mixture over his shoulder in the direction of the village, stands up, and walks toward the forest without looking back.

If we take Pagibeti divinatory practices as a uniform set of techniques for dealing with misfortune, two stand out as being somewhat anomalous relative to the others: *ntiseye mboko* and the *mbolongo* oracle. They differ from all the others in site, as both are performed exclusively in the forest and never in the village. *Mbolongo* differs in its selection of potential causes of misfortune, in its emphasis on unknown pregnancy, unknown death, and unknown eating of the first kill by "he whose top teeth erupted first." Both differ in that they are not owned or managed by any one party, unlike the rubbing-board oracle or string-pulling exorcism. Both differ in the criteria used for selecting the operator—not that he have special medicines or knowledge but that he have a good back, or, in the case of the second *mbolongo* handler, that he be a child.

These features which differentiate *mbolongo* from the rest of Pagibeti divinatory practice illuminate characteristics of the ideology of practice in which *mbolongo* is situated, namely that of the hunt. Nondivinatory practices common to the context of the communal hunt show the same features and encourage us to draw the conclusion that there exists a certain ideology of the communal hunt centered on the goals of *wukeye paye* (opening the forest) and *lekeye paye* (waking up the forest).

First, the contrast between village, *ngi*, and forest, *paye*, is significant in Pagibeti thought. Numerous structuralist studies of African peoples have given the impression that the bush is associated with the disorder and danger of nature and that culture is associated with the order and safety of the village. To the Apagibeti, whose men dwell in the forest half of every year, this is clearly not the case. They say that *paye awukise basu*, "the forest saves us." It serves as a food source and as a source for the only cash crops they have: trapped meat and occasional tusks and skins from elephant, leopard, and okapi. It serves as a refuge. When I asked one of many local tax evaders what he planned to do, as the government tax collector was coming through that day, he smiled and replied, "The forest is large" (*paye aliki edingi*). Old men, despite the grumbling of fellow villagers, not infrequently flee their exhausting dry-season role of dispute hearer for their quiet forest shelters, thus using the forest as a refuge much as road dwellers use the cities.

Forest spirits are little feared. Even if they seize one, they are relatively easy to exorcise; village-origin cases of spirit possession, by contrast, are difficult to exorcise and are greatly feared. Again, regarding medicines, I was told that the dispensary medicines could cure any illness the forest could give, but that there were many illnesses given by the village which no dispensary medicine could combat. Misfortune in the village is never blamed on the forest, while misfortune in the forest is almost always blamed on the village. Oracles are not usually consulted regarding forest spirits. While forest spirits might tangle up one's trap lines or frighten one with sounds, village spirits can kill.

The forest is good, but only if it is kept open, only if it is awakened. A key contrast is between that which can open the forest, and that which can *dikeye paye*, "close the forest." Not only are forest oracles such as *mbolongo* said to open the forest but also the anomalous aspects of those features which distinguish forest oracles from other Pagibeti divinatory practices cease to be anomalous. Rather, they appear to be ideologically consonant with the goal of *wukeye paye* as manifested in other nondivinatory practices such as dreaming, talking, meat sharing, and various forest rites common to the context of the practice of the communal hunt.

The very practice of the communal hunt itself wakes up the forest. One kind of communal hunt is in fact named *paye leka*, "the forest wakening." It is performed on the morning following the burial of a deceased villager. Apagibeti hold that a death closes the forest to hunters; it will yield up no more of its bounty to hunters until it is opened or reawakened. Just before burial a boy is sent to find a red leaf, which he brings to the body to be rubbed over the deceased's lips to collect his spit. The boy takes the leaf and places it under the *tolo*, or ancestral spirit shrine. The next morning the men assemble their nets, dogs, spears, and supplies and depart together for the two- to three-day *paye leka* hunt, carrying with them the leaf which will be cast inside the first-strung circle of nets.

Nets will be strung (*gbase kogo*, "raised") from five to twelve times in the course of the day, depending on hunting fortune and the size of the hunting group. At evening camp, men may discuss that or a previous day's hunt, or they and the camp's women and children may tell *mato*, or animal tales, to one another around the campfires. The talk is important; talking of animals brings dreams of animals. A frequent late-night conversational ending is "dream well," for dreaming of animals means killing those animals on the following day. Talk has power. As talk appropriate to the forest, *mato* are rarely told in the village and then, never before sundown (not even when the anthropologist asks for a special late-afternoon taping session). Conversely, youths talking about village affairs at the forest camp are frequently rebuked for speaking "village talk" (*njumbi we ngi*), deemed inappropriate to the hunting camp.

Awakening or opening the forest may require other practices. While medicine belts, customarily worn on private hunts, are not permitted and use of private medicines is eschewed, hunters whose nets are not attracting game may legitimately ask a neighbor to engage in reciprocal rubbing of skin with a particular leaf (*daleye*) or they may take a leafy branch and beat the forest floor with it until they cut through the earth (*nya zonga*), in either case addressing, while acting, the names of all those animals they wish to step into (*ta*) their nets.

Of particular interest is the rite of *maleye ekalo*, the splitting of *ekalo* tree sticks. After the stringing of the nets but before the driving of the game into the nets, children and strangers will be given pairs of partially split, foot-long *ekalo* sticks, sticks from the tree used to build the ancestral spirit shrine, and asked to knock them loudly together. After this has gone on for a minute or two, all are asked to tear their split sticks in half and to toss the pieces into the hunting circle, he with the "good back" going first.

The reference to a "good back" brings us full circle, for the forest oracles in Pagibeti divinatory practices stood out in our review of those practices by making that feature a requirement for oracle manipulation. Seen in the context of categories of persons relevant to nonoracular as well as to oracular practices employed in assuring a successful communal hunt, it loses its anomalous status.

If divinatory power in the village is frequently based on special knowledge and medicines or on initiation into a cult of affliction (diviner of the spirit-possessed or the rubbing-board oracle) then the opposite characteristics are valued in forest divination. In the practice of the hunt, children, strangers, and possessors of good backs are key actors. A child carries the leaf bearing the dead man's saliva into the forest to awaken it, a child may carry the *mbolongo* from site to site, and a child or stranger will beat and split the *ekalo* sticks to call animals into the nets. Strangers are given key roles in rites and local people are chosen to perform *mbolongo* not on the basis of the usual village authority principles of superior age, medicine, or power, but on whether or not they have a good back.

Part of the explanation for this may lie with the significance in the ideology of the practice of the hunt of a final contrast not yet explicitly cited, namely, that between private and public activity and knowledge. The former is suspect within the context of the communal hunt, while the latter is affirmed as good. Children are good for performing *maleye ekalo* because, it is said, children have no knowledge (*ndate*), or because they do not know sex, or because they do not yet know the affairs of witchcraft. Strangers, too, are devoid of special knowledge of local affairs. Private medicines for attracting game to one's net at the expense of one's fellows is banned, as is the wearing of private medicine belts. Only open and public means of improving one's fortunes, as by talking, dancing animal-mime dances, encouraging dreaming, performing *nya zonga*, or performing *daleye*, are approved.

The private/public contrast is particularly sharp when we compare the aims, conduct, and outcome of communal hunts to those of private hunts. The aim of the private hunt is the killing of the maximum number of animals possible for private household consumption and household sale.[5] The aim of the *paye leka* communal hunt is the wakening of the forest for the benefit of the whole village and the killing and public sharing of game among hunters, villagers, and guests.

Preparations for communal hunts are conducted publicly; for private hunts they are conducted in secret. The repair of nets and weapons, the feeding of hunting dogs, and the amassing of food stores are carried out openly in preparation for the communal hunt; efforts to camouflage these steps are routinely taken in preparation for private hunts, and weapons and stores may be secreted in hiding places beside forest trails a day or two before departure.

Departure protocols for public and private hunts conform to the same contrastive logic. The day of the *paye leka* communal hunt is announced publicly and all lineage households within the village unit are invited to participate. Hunters assemble and depart together by daylight at a publicly agreed on, prearranged time and place. By contrast, the day of "entering the forest" is a closely guarded secret for the private hunt. Private hunters leave separately, before dawn, by private paths from the backs of houses. They leave in secrecy; if a private hunter is seen leaving wearing a medicine belt, either by a woman or by another man, he turns back, that day's hunt annulled. The hostile eyes of a single villager spotting a hunter before he makes good his escape to the forest can potentially ruin the hunt.

Once in the forest, the publicly recognized voice of the huntmaster rather than the individual voices of the assembled hunters determines where the nets are to be raised and when they are to be lowered and rolled up for the resting period that precedes a new raising. Rules governing the conduct of the hunt explicitly and publicly mandate a state of unusual equality among participants. Rotation of hunters' positions along the circle of nets at each new raising ensures that no one hunter will gain a better position for capturing and killing game than his peers. Further, in the conduct of the public hunt, private medicine belts are banned, women may accompany men, and the specific form of *esuma* or bad air which can be given by village eyes (*ndeye*) and thus close the forest to the private hunter is said to be inoperative.

Finally, the disposition and distribution of meat contrasts sharply in private and public hunts. The private hunter downplays or conceals the number of game killed and largely limits the distribution of the meat to his household and lineage. Much of the meat is sold for household gain. Animals killed in the raised nets of *paye leka* communal hunters are not even kept by the individuals who killed them. Rather they are carried back to the camp where they are turned over to the huntmaster. He tallies them, displays them publicly to assembled hunters, and oversees the butchering and distribution of the day's kill. Small portions, including the head and neck, intestines, and limbs, are given to the individual killers of the animals in the order of their arrival at the scene of the kill, but the bulk of the meat is retained by the huntmaster and carried back to the village. None of it is sold. It is distributed among village households in proportion to the number being hosted by that household. The meat, in short, is publicly accounted for and publicly shared.

The salience of the open and public character of all aspects of the communal hunt accounts in part for the previously cited, anomalous pantheon of forces which Apagibeti most frequently name in the *mbolongo* oracle as responsible for closing the forest, namely unknown deaths, unknown pregnancies, and unknown eating of first kills by *mangodo*. A death which has occurred but is not yet publicly known by the hunters can close the forest. A pregnancy in the village, not yet publicly known by hunters, can close the forest. The unknown eating of any part of the hunters' first kill by a *mangodo* (he whose upper teeth erupted first) can close the forest.

Less frequently cited causes of misfortune, such as angry words, curses, or witchcraft, follow much the same logic. Once publicly identified by the *mbolongo* oracle, the *esuma*, or bad air, they created around the hunters is dispelled and the forest is opened again. Even witchcraft obeys the logic of differential evaluation depending on the distinction between public and private knowledge. Though their power when privately employed is uniformly destructive, witches are viewed positively in at least one context; namely, when a publicly known witch is enjoined to use his power to call animals near to the village to be killed by hunters and feed the village, ending a time of hunger.

This essay displays, I trust, the value of taking variation within the corpus of a peoples' divinatory practices seriously, as a conscious object of study. By situating apparently anomalous divinatory techniques such as the *ntiseye boko* or *mbolongo* within the context of the practice in which they are embedded, in this case that of the communal hunt and of its aim of wakening and opening the forest, such variation becomes intelligible. The significance of such variation when seen within the context of the larger daily practices of which they are a part, such as the communal hunt, can lead us to an understanding of the ideologies which both structure and are created by the practice itself.

Notes

1. In speaking of oracular dreams I follow Evans-Pritchard's usage (1937). I depart from his usage in referring to the two previously cited forms as oracular forms; he would term them omens. I would argue that the similarity of behavioral consequences for this grab bag of techniques for coping with misfortune favors their inclusion under one term.

2. This is somewhat overstated. While in the forest, hunters who have killed game habitually share meat with hunters who have killed no game. Once out of the forest and back in the village, however, the in-forest ethic of sharing is sharply restricted; while households of the same lineage will share meat between them, meat is commonly bought and sold between households of different lineages.

References

Ardener, Edwin. 1972. "Belief and the Problem of Women." In *The Interpretation of Ritual*, ed. J. S. La Fontaine, 135–58. London: Tavistock Press.

Barth, F. 1975. *Ritual and Knowledge among the Baktamun of New Guinea*. New Haven, Conn.: Yale University Press.

Bascom, William R. 1969. *Ifa Divination*. Bloomington: Indiana University Press.

Burton, John W. 1980. "The Village and Cattle Camp: Aspects of Atuot Religion." In *Explorations in African Systems of Thought*, ed. I. Karp and C. Bird, 268–97. Bloomington: Indiana University Press.

Evans-Pritchard, E. E. 1937. *Witchcraft, Oracles and Magic among the Azande*. Oxford: Clarendon Press.

Fernandez, James W. 1965. "Symbolic Consensus in a Reformative Cult." *American Anthropologist* 67(4):902–930.

Turner, V. W. 1975. *Revelation and Divination in Ndembu Ritual*. Ithaca, N.Y.: Cornell University Press.

René Devisch

Mediumistic Divination among the Northern Yaka of Zaire

Etiology and Ways of Knowing

Mediumistic divination among the Yaka of Zaire reveals significant congruences between organizations and acts of people, on one hand, and unusual events, misfortune, illness and death, on the other. In referring the problem situation to a higher-order system of values and norms, divination allows for a meaningful interpretation and outlines the conditions for effective intervention. The concern of divination among the Yaka must be placed in the context of kinship and particularly in that of uterine relations. (Yaka diviners may be male or female, so the following applies to both masculine and feminine diviners.) Problems arising along agnatic ties are related primarily to politics; as such they are dealt with in courts and councils. Because the role of the mediumistic diviner is transmitted only through uterine heredity, divinership is the privilege of certain matrikin. Whereas political power and customary law go together with agnatic descent and are concerned with judicial and economic affairs, divination concerns the diagnosis and meaning of existential problems with a view to their management. Jurisdiction draws on societal rules spelled out in proverbs and sayings, whereas divination implies an axiological grid in relation basically to uterine life-transmission. It is the role of the divinatory oracle to interpret symbolically the meaning of given forms of affliction and anomaly, or of the unavoidable conflicts that result from differences between individuals. While the political leader, in consensus with a council of elders or customary judges, can arbitrate in disputes where there is a common rule, the Yaka diviner draws on clairvoyance and can point with authority to the complex intertwinement of a social, moral, and physical onset of sickness, ill luck, or death. The divinatory oracle often discloses that the disease or other misfortune has been brought about by a curse pronounced in the matri- or patriline as a means of retaliation for a theft or another abuse. The curse thereby has invoked the support of a cult and its ancestral or spiritual agencies. Or the oracle may attribute the problem to sorcery by agnates and/or uterines.

Besides jurisdiction and mediumistic divination, there are more popular forms of etiology and arbitration. The more the etiology of the affliction relies on common sense, the more it brings into play a linear causalist way of thinking. The popular name attributed to some physical discomfort (e.g., *yivumu kiviimbiidi*, "the stomach is breeding [an egg]," i.e., a swollen stomach) and the symptomatic treatment evoke an immediate cause: what kind of illness is it, how did it come about, who or what is responsible for it? The popular etiologies, at least in their manifest content and as they are proceeding from common sense, attach great importance to accidents, contaminations, jealousies, sorcerers and fetishes, transgressions, and ancestral sanctions. Paradoxically, however, the more the patient and his/her kin try to act upon the illness's final cause to solve it, the more they will question themselves about the origin and the sense of what has been happening and the more this reflection will give way to a *structural causalist* way of reasoning instead of a linear one. Structuralist etiology is more hermeneutics than causal inquiry. This type of etiology makes no attempt to analyze the temporal axis of the causal chain but tries to relate the various dimensions, such as physical, social, axiological, and supernatural ones. It is on the basis of such semantic connections that clients, meeting with the whole family in council a few days after the oracle, arbitrate upon the source of the misfortune and interpret its meaning. The divinatory message can make for a complex redefining of the kin relations. It is then the aim of the ritual specialist called for, first, to reverse the process by lifting the curse or bewitchment and thereby the source of the illness, and then to treat the patient by means of the same cult.

Several minor divination procedures may be consulted in the case of bad dreams and certain material misfortunes, as in hunting, agriculture, or business, or the death and loss of animals and damage to or loss of tools. For such cases, a successful first rifle shot (*mbiimbi*), for example, might take on oracular value. In the past, ordeal by fire (*ngoombwa luufu*) has been used as well as the poison ordeal (*phutu*). Some people are specialized in a kind of inductive oracle using an adhering horn of a duiker (*ngoonbwa n-seengu*), or a rubbing stick or rubbing board (*ngoombwa n-ti*). Because it is thought that these oracle forms can be manipulated by those concerned, the Yaka do not accept their results without skepticism. On the other hand, the mediumistic diviner is consulted in cases of death, serious illness, deformity through birth or accident, lasting social failure of some kind, or failure in hunting and other crucial activities. Otherwise the problem may concern gynecological upsets, such as miscarriage, premature birth, sterility, debility, and so on. On average, an extended family may have to consult mediumistic divination once every two or three years. The divinatory protocol tends to become simpler in the capital of Kinshasa. In the urban context, the oracle is requested by many non-Yaka clients and for problems that are related to cash economy, urban jobs, school education, and outcome of biomedical health care. But the etiological approach seems not to differ in the rural and urban contexts. The Yaka diviner is mediumistic and oracular but not prophetic in the way some prophets and religious leaders of independent African churches are (Devisch and Vervaeck 1985).

There are about 250,000 Yaka, widely dispersed all over western Bandundu in the southern savannas, a region of Zaire bordering Angola and situated between the Kwaango and Waamba Rivers. The present-day Yaka reflect a sustained intermixture of cultural traditions in the borderland between the spheres of influence of Koongo and Luunda. Because the area has few natural riches and motorized access from Kinshasa across the sandy plateaus of northern Yaka land is difficult, the Yaka region has remained marginal to the mainstream of technoeconomic development in Zaire. There is very little production for commerce. Many young men migrate periodically to Kinshasa to earn some income from casual wage labor and petty commerce.

The Yaka organize in segmentary patrilineages. Each person is socially identified in relation to his patrilineal ascendants from whom he receives his position in the kin group, his rights, privileges and ancestral names, in short his social identity. Extended families live as corporate groups and make up hamlets formed according to patrilineal descent and patrilocal residence. A village numbers between one hundred and two hundred inhabitants who are divided over three to six extended families, each of which is headed by a family elder. The northern Yaka recognize uterine descent as well, thereby emphasizing the corporeality that characterizes the mother-child relation. It is believed that physical and innate characteristics, such as health, blood, inborn capacities, and the potency to develop and transmit life, are passed on to the individual primarily through maternity and the uterine line from a source of life that is conventionally associated with the individual's matrilateral great-grandmother (Devisch 1984). Siblings "coming from the one womb" share privileged bonds of warmth, trust, and mutual help in the household. Several major healing roles, as well as the clairvoyance and mediumistic role of the diviner, are also thought to be passed on through the uterine line.

The Mediumistic Diviner

Within the scope of this essay I deal with mediumistic divination only. The diviner can be man or woman: "his/her gift of divinatory clairvoyance" (*ngoombu*) is "innate and transmitted through the mothers" (*yibutukulu*). An individual's calling to become a diviner follows a given pattern. Diviners-to-be and young diviners commonly display hysteriform symptoms of depression. A few months before and after the death of a particular diviner, one of the uterine descendants begins to behave in a strange way, suffering from a persistent wasting illness. These candidates complain of chronic abdominal pains, nausea, anorexia, and/or dysmenorrhea. Some also suffer from headaches, suffocation, stiffening, cervical pains, and itching. They feel very irritable and go through periods of agitation that are of the depressive rather than the aggressive or euphoric type.

Compared to their peers, diviners and candidates excel in insight, imagination, fluency in language, and knowledge of traditions. They seem to consider themselves to be very vulnerable and show signs of restlessness and lack of self-assurance. They think they live under a menace of death when their oracle would turn out to be deceptive and the behavior would deny their ancestor or their initiation. During the divination process, the eyes of the diviner will become glazed, turned inward as if they mirror themselves. A man in his capacity as diviner usually speaks in a high-pitched voice. After the oracle, the diviner often shows clear signs of fatigue and great irritability.

Almost all of the eleven diviners interviewed, when asked about their states of epilepticlike crisis and the trance-possession (-*kaluka*) that proved their calling to divinership, said that they first felt themselves possessed by appearances of deceased diviners who frightened them. It seemed as if there was a "fire consuming their bodies with fever," like a death agony, like "a deep fear of being wounded or of losing a lot of blood." Two diviners mentioned that they felt an urge to throw themselves into the bush fire. Losing self-control, they felt an enormous power growing in them which enabled them to reach the roof of a hut in one bound.

According to eye witnesses, the trance always follows a particular transmitted pattern. In this state, the diviner-to-be jumps onto the roof of a hut without any help and proceeds to pull out some of the thatch. While twitching and jerking his head and body like a chicken's amid high-pitched cries of *koo koo koo*, in the esoteric language of the diviners, "he brings out" (*fula*, "foam," as if the indictment were a product of fermentation) his diviner name. He thus discloses the name of the deceased uterine ancestor who is leading him into trance as a proof of his calling. Other forms of trance behavior are exceptionally rapid tree climbing and amazingly fast digging in the ground with bare hands. The diviner-to-be is then secluded for initiation.

A narrow cylindrical wooden slit-gong with a carved human head on top and a stick inserted into the slit is commissioned from a local carver (Bourgeois 1983). It is considered to be "the very image" (*yidiimbu*) of the diviner. Its shape, both womblike and phalliclike, metaphorically gives form to his capacity to self-generate his new condition and to communicate or bring forth new meaning in a subverbal, bodily, manner. As a miniature and modified version of the heavy message slit-gong, it symbolizes the diviner's role as a message bearer to all people regardless of their sex or origin. He always takes it with him and uses it also as a container to drink, or as a stool to sit on; whenever he speaks in his capacity of diviner, he is rhythmically tapping it with a wooden stick (fig. 1).

According to the collective representations, a deep change takes place in the person of the diviner-to-be, in his knowing, in his awareness of reality. This change is brought about by his illness and by his condition of trance. To test the authenticity of this change, people ask him shortly after his trance what they

Figure 1. Yaka diviner Kyuulu tapping on his slit-gong *(n-kookwangoombu)* at onset of a divinatory consultation, village of Yibeengala, northern Kwaango region, southwest Zaire, August 23, 1974. *Photo by René Devisch.*

hold in their closed fists. When the genuineness of his calling to diviner-ship has been recognized by well-reputed senior diviners and elders and by his residential group, the diviner-to-be undergoes initiation. For nine months under the direction of a "senior diviner who is mothering him" *(ngula ngaanga)*, this initiation consolidates the diviner's heightened sensory capacity to perceive and penetrate the concealed. From the beginning of his initiation, people consult his oracle, since they are convinced that the capacity for divination is then at its most powerful. With his initiation, his illness practically disap-pears, and he becomes a member of a group apart, with its special ways of sitting, eating, washing, and speaking, standing outside all ordinary social categories. At the end of his initiation, he may travel in the neighborhood or from Yaka land to Kinshasa and back, in response to requests for oracular consultation.

At first glance the oracle of the Yaka diviner seems to be verbal discourse, but this aspect is really only an elaboration of the primary bodily and sensory dimension of this divination by way of clairvoyance. Through the initiatory trance-possession to which meaning is given by the metaphoric transference of the "chicken on the point of laying an egg" (*khoku yabutama*), the diviner-to-be generates himself in an androgynous way in his capacity and identity as diviner. During each divinatory session the diviner will draw on his paranormal capacities by reenacting his initial trance-possession.

The consultation process occurs near the diviner's house, in the open, and in the presence of the actual clients who represent the different patri- and matrikin groups and/or the allies of the afflicted individual. The afflicted, who is ill, has suffered from bad luck, or has died, is not present. A material "mediating or intermediary object" (*yiteendi*, conventionally a coin or a piece of kaolin or cloth which has been in physical contact with the afflicted) is given to the diviner without comment.

I will detail how, by making use of his keen talent for perceiving through olfactory means, his "listening with his heart to his dreamlike vision," and because of his clairvoyance, the diviner is able to describe and analyze the problem that has been referred to him. His clairvoyance enables him to "see," through dreamlike images, the problem that he first detects by his keen sense of smell and receptive listening. The clients who represent the different interested groups give credence to the oracle insofar as its divinatory or paranormal character is manifest. Furthermore, to make sure the oracle will bring out the concealed or unknown, the clients take care to remain anonymous and avoid informing the diviner. They check if the intermediary object presented to the diviner exclusively represents the afflicted. After arriving, they wait until the diviner spontaneously recognizes them as clients and determines the reason for the consultation. In the case of death, the intermediary object is handed over after laconic confirmation of this first revelation. During the oracle, confirmation or contradiction of the diviner's revelation is given tersely without any further information to make sure that nobody gives any help to him. For serious cases a diviner is consulted who is at least a day's march away in an area unconnected with the afflicted. To the clients the message of the oracle presents itself not only as something credible, but also as something self-evident and unassailable, when the diviner reveals facts that are unquestionably part of the particular problem situation.

The *keen sense of smell* (*fiimbu*) constitutes a first level of divinatory scrutiny. By smelling the intermediary object "like a hunting dog," the diviner develops an almost physical communication with the afflicted and the clients (fig. 2). The intermediary object has rested some time in contact with the afflicted, namely on top of the navel, the heart or the left shoulder blade "where the palpitations of the heart can be felt." These locations and signals express the afflicted individual's physical ties to his/her uterine life-source. The night before the oracle will be consulted, the afflicted rubs a coin or a piece of kaolin over his/her chest and between his/her palms while pronouncing the stereotyped wish that the diviner should cast light on the problem and unmask the evildoers. He/she then gives the intermediary object to the kinsman who is delegated to consult the oracle. In the event of a death, just before burial the uncle puts the intermediary object on the corpse and invites the deceased to make known the origin of his/her death through the mouth of the diviner (Devisch 1979:125–8). The night before the oracle, the widower or the deceased's elder puts this intermediary object on the grave at the head and takes it back next morning. He shields it from all external influence and confines himself. That same night, he abstains from sexual intercourse; on the way to the diviner he does not sit, speak to anybody, shake hands, or accept anything offered to him. The diviner observes the same rules from the time he receives the intermediary object till the end of the oracle.

The diviner's heightened sense of smell is symbolized by a twofold metonymic reference to the sniffing and smelling, also called *fiimbu*, of the hunting dog, who belongs to the wild forest as well as the domestic village. The diviner is able to unmask hidden sorcery, i.e., antisocial activities, in the same way as the dog is said to detect the spoor of nocturnal meetings of sorcerers. To preserve the effect of this metonymic reference, the diviner scrupulously avoids any ritually unprepared contact with a dog. To further give a metonymic form to his paranormal power of scrutiny the diviner will often sniff at a shell of scented plants during the oracle.

Receptive listening constitutes a second level of divinatory scrutiny. By putting the intermediary object in his ear, especially while sleeping, the diviner metonymically "incorporates" and learns the message of the afflicted with whom an olfactory fusion took place already. It is the heart "which sees the dreamlike images" (*-mona mundosi*, i.e., receives the sonoro-visual and dreamlike message and transforms it into a visual message). The dreamlike images enable the diviner to comprehend or "en-vision" in a contemplative way the problem first incorporated by the smelling and listening. The diviner's heart is the seat of his sensory and intellectual clairvoyant power.

The *clairvoyance* draws on dreamlike images. During the oracle, the diviner always uses such expressions as "see" or "dream." Questioned about this, the diviners say that the oracle consists in expressing what they have seen or were seeing at that moment in a dream, or what appeared suddenly to them from outside. They describe scenes crossing their vision. The people in these scenes appear vaguely, in a way the diviners describe as "people seen through an open door. You can see how tall they are, whether they are man or woman, what they carry with them, what they do, but you cannot recognize their faces." The diviner translates the "internal voices" that on such occasions may speak to him in a way that is hardly comprehensible. By contemplating these images and messages in his heart and by transposing them to the afflicted individual's problem the diviner establishes a metaphoric link between the problem situation and the initial divinatory interpretation. Many of these dreamlike images are concerned with avuncular

Figure 2. Yaka diviner Lusuungu relying on his olfactory scrutiny, village of Yibeengala, northern Kwaango region, southwest Zaire, July 10, 1974. *Photo by René Devisch.*

gestures (e.g., "I see the uncle who is approaching the bed, who is offering kaolin. . . ."); other images concern allies, sorcery, ritual care for the patient, initiation, illness, and so on. This connotation makes clear the importance and efficiency of the images, by the fact that they inscribe the given problem into the self-generative articulation of meaning in the oracle.

The diviner's extraordinary powers are also metonymically spoken of as "dreams," i.e., as a dreamlike form of understanding the hidden. The Yaka diviner defines himself in a song as "the one who crosses all divisions, limits, barriers, the one who can see into the deepest darknesses of the forest." That the oracle is founded on an extended consciousness which brings to light hidden forgotten meanings is also metonymically symbolized. Before the oracle, the diviner eats a piece of kola nut (a stimulant) mixed with wood that has been sucked into a whirlpool and has resurfaced.

Phases in the Oracle

The first stage of the consultation concerns the diviner's revealing of the reason for the visit. After the diviner has spontaneously welcomed the clients, he briefly mentions, speaking in his esoteric language, the reason for their visit. Then he applies horizontal stripes of kaolin to his temples at the edges of his eyes to widen his vision and squats in front of the clients. To reach an initial outline of the problem that is submitted without any information, the diviner works through an etiological list of questions which concern the range of different social relationships, afflictions and abuses, and subsequent curses and retaliation on the next generations. He enters into a trancelike state and reacts to his questions with an affirmative or negative answer. He examines them while singing in an esoteric language and tapping on his slit-gong (De Beir 1975:124–6). All diviners use a comparable etiological list. In this way, the particular problem is incipiently subsumed into the much wider context of the etiological and axiological tradition adopted by the society. By repeating together the end of each of the diviner's sentences, the clients become involved in the oracle. A solidarity grows among them, since they are all led in a similar way to a kind of self-scrutiny. Now squatted on the slit-gong, the diviner glances in a hand mirror that he holds in front of several shells "to awaken his capacity to bring the concealed into the open." Although he receives no information from the clients, the diviner must now "catch the problem submitted to the oracle" (-*kwaata ngoombu*). A skilled diviner can usually outline the problem at this initial stage. He proves his clairvoyance by revealing the nature of the case (a death, an illness, a lasting unproductive hunt, an act of sorcery) as well as the places where the events occurred, the family names, and the classificatory positions of the afflicted and individuals that are involved. Satisfied with a relevant revelation, the clients may confirm the first outline of the case, supply minor details, and make an initial payment.

The second stage of the consultation, which mainly offers a detailed etiological diagnosis, normally takes place the next morning to permit the diviner's "dreams" on the matter. This second stage first of all summarizes the first phase and then proceeds to complement the material provided by the dreamlike messages, "applying to it an etiological grid" (-*ta ngoombu*). According to the diviners, their main source of information is derived from their keen sense of smell, their listening as in dreaming, and their clairvoyance. As a matter of fact one has to distinguish between two processes at this stage. First the diviner describes the dreamlike messages by way of metaphoric transferences and metonymic associations rather than by way of causalist reasoning. In the act of contemplating these images "in his heart" and linking them to the afflicted individual's physical problem and his social and supernatural context, the diviner transmits factual elements of the illness or the case in question to the historical conjunction, the reconstitution of which makes intelligible the repetition of the affliction in the life of the afflicted and of the group of the concerned. Second, the diviner applies an etiological grid to the information that was obtained through clairvoyance (the manipulation of this grid is described below).

Putting an end to the oracular session is "cutting the *ngoombu*" (-*zeenga ngoombu*). On a social level the different groups that were involved in the conflict are now becoming disentangled. On the cosmological level the diviner reestablishes the norm. Through his clairvoyance's extreme breaking down or surpassing of ordinary forms of knowing, he calls for the reestablishing of boundaries between here and there, me and the other, present and past. His clairvoyance reactualizes the initiatory trance at each session. By confronting the problem situation and the norm and by dividing the groups into those who "receive charcoal" (-*kala mundiimba*) and those who "receive kaolin" (-*kala mupheemba*), i.e., into those who are most to be blamed and those who are less involved, the oracle links up the different groups concerned instead of exacerbating the discord.

For the oracle, the diviner is mainly drawing on his corporeal capacities, which are transmitted in the uterine line. Congruent with this, it is no surprise that the diviner inscribes the afflicted individual's problem in the history and axiology of the uterine line. The oracular interpretation finds its source through the intertwining of intellect and senses in the act of clairvoyance, as well as through the intertwining of body and language in the modulations of the voice during the initial phase of the oracle.

An Oracle: Summary and Text

Suuta is the afflicted individual, i.e., the main subject of the oracle. She died shortly after her father died and immediately after giving birth to her first child. The oracle interprets the meaning of her death in connection with sorcery in a collateral patriline and with curses. A curse has been uttered against sorcery by one of her father's uterine ascendants and it has acquired the force of a prohibition. When Suuta's father was fatally ill, his brother Mbela cursed all those who caused the illness. But Mbela's curse was hypocritical, because he himself was involved in the sorcery. Of its nature the curse is based on the utter hostility between, on one hand, the curser whose rights (or those of his primary kinsmen) are infringed and, on the other hand, the cursed who infringed those rights and who are consequently damned. Therefore, any collaboration between the hostile parties can lead to the destruction of the curser. By bewitching his brother, Mbela turned his curse back on himself and even on his classificatory daughter for having claimed her bridewealth. The oracle's interpretation of Suuta's death connected it with the hypocritical curse, with sorcery, and with the lack of required ritual compensation for her father's death and with the absence of familial reconciliation after his death.

> *Diviner* (very highly strung, his eyes starting from their sockets): Where are the sorcerers hiding who want to make so many difficulties for me? Where is Suuta? [He repeats the name five times.] Didn't she die because you used the bridewealth wrongly [i.e., took it yourself after a hypocritical curse]?[1] I see that Suuta went to Kinshasa. When she came back she was pregnant

and very sick and she had a suitcase with her. You haven't opened her suitcase.[2] Where are Koongu and Toonda? These are uterine forebears who transmitted prohibitions.[3] As if it wasn't true!

Answer (by one of his clients): Indeed!

Diviner: I have just seen a curse. Listen: it is Mbela who uttered this curse. How did he withdraw the curse? What do I see in connection with this cursing? What have you done with the bridewealth offered for your daughter Suuta? Have you thrown it away on the edge of the village, or what have you done with it?[4] I see a woman, called Meengi. How are you related to her? Has she a husband or not?

Answer: Meengi is one of father's sisters, she is not married.

Diviner: Meengi is a sorcerer. And I see that you, her brother Mbela [here present], went with Suuta to Kinshasa.

Answer: Yes, I alone went with her to Kinshasa, and came back with her to our village.

Diviner: I see her in front of me. On the same morning that she brought forth her child, she died, the same day, before evening. Deny that if you can.

Answer: It is true, I don't have to add anything. When I came to ask the oracle's advice [in connection with Suuta's sickness], there was talk of sorcery.

Diviner: Listen to the way in which Suuta's father who died shortly before Suuta uttered a curse: "We are killing ourselves with our own sorcery. There should be no more sorcery among us."[5] Who else had said, "let the sorcerers die," who else has uttered such a curse?

Answer: Yes, indeed, Suuta's father has spoken so.

Diviner: I see that the uterine forebears in this kin-group have uttered a curse: "If there is one of you involved in sorcery, then he should die." And who has infringed the prohibition [consequent to this curse]? Is it not true that in these circumstances you have killed one of your descendants [Suuta] as if she was a chicken [that men share in common meal]? Where have these sorcerers come from? I see that Mbela, the younger brother of Suuta's father, who has taken her bridewealth into his own house, uttered a curse against his paternal kingroup [i.e., a collateral patrilineage segment, to protect Suuta's fatally ill father]. Did he withdraw the curse before he took the bridewealth into his own house?[6]

Answer (given by the head of the family): Who would claim that there was no need to withdraw the curse acting as if he was innocent of his brother's illness, although he really bewitched him?

Diviner: Your uterine forebears have once uttered a curse against you all. I see that Suuta's father died first. Now, in what way did you offer the required compensation to his great-granduncle, after his death?[7] In what way did his uncle reunify the family and remove the hostility from your midst? What prohibitions did he remind you of? Moreover, who claimed that you don't have to look after Meengi, your father's sister, and that you don't have to share your income with her?

Answer: The head of the family offered no compensation for the first death [of Suuta's father] when his uncle came for it. We have been reunited sharing the same fire without having paid the required compensation for the deceased to his uncle.

Diviner: You [Mbela] took the bridewealth into your house, although you were

a sorcerer. Which fire united you? A quarrel arose among you when Suuta was ill. After another oracle, the head of the family here was asked to offer a chicken to Suuta.[8] He was angry, and there was strife between you both.
Mbela's answer: That's right; I went to ask the diviner's advice. There I heard that sorcery was involved [an explanation of Suuta's sickness]: "I as diviner tell you: go to the head of the family and tell him to give a chicken to the sick one." When I went to ask him for the chicken, he wouldn't hear of it, and so a quarrel arose between us. He refused to give a chicken.
Diviner: Concerning this young mother, Suuta, what do I see? A member of the family [Toonda] who came looking for her to kill her [by sorcery] stays in Kinshasa. Actually, I see three elders who consider themselves as heads of the family and who are competing for this position: there is a quarrel among you. I see that the sorcery prohibition left to you by your uterine forebears leads to the death of you who rule [as punishment for breaking this prohibition].

The man [Toonda] who cut the umbilical cord [i.e., the one who killed Suuta] and was staying in Kinshasa, I see he has returned. Notice that Meengi, Suuta's father's sister, is also involved as a sorcerer in Suuta's death, just as Toonda is. And you who consider yourselves heads of the family, what arrangement did you come to [to kill her]? The second head of the family is also involved as a sorcerer in Suuta's death; you were among the sorcerers who decided to kill Suuta. If you are not a sorcerer, when that child, Suuta, was ill, what kind of arrangement did you make? You are a sorcerer, I can see that. If you will deny it, tell me, so that I can offer you this water to drink: if you are not telling the truth you will kill yourself.[9]

Together with the second head of the family, you [Mbela, Toonda, and Meengi] have "eaten up" this young wife by compensation to her father's great-granduncle. I see that her father's great-granduncle is at odds with the other uncles. The following uncle [her father's primary uncle] joined the sorcery plot against one of those who call him uncle [namely against Suuta].

Listen, you second head of the family here before me, offer a chicken to the younger sister of the deceased[10] and invite the great-granduncles so as to offer compensation for the death [of Suuta and her father], so that after you have admitted your wrong and witnessed to your renewed disposition, the responsible uncle can remove the curse and unite you all in sharing the same fire [as a sign for the reconciliation and reunification of the family].[11] And you primary uncle, admit your wrong and bear witness to your new disposition by also making compensation to the great-granduncle of the deceased.

With regard to the cults, I see that the great-granduncle [of Suuta's father] uttered a curse proper to the institutions *n-luwa* and *n-tsa mutseki*. I see that the primary uncle is involved by the divination cult [hiding his real intentions behind the hereditary influence passed down in context of divination].

Divinatory Etiology

I propose to show that by considering the ongoing articulation process from a semantic-praxeological perspective concerned with the transformational and performative production of ritual praxis, it is evident that the Yaka divinatory oracle is to bring out a dimension of the problem not yet actualized. For example, the appropriation of someone's goods is said to be theft only when its illicit character has been established by the oracle's revealing that its harmful consequences are impermissible. By referring an event to a higher-order axiological principle or axiomatic etiological model, the oracle brings about the meanings of specific problem situations that are submitted to it. The symbolic articulation process in the oracle produces a meaning that surpasses conventional conceptualization and popular cause-effect reasoning. It gives way to a structural causality instead of a linear one. The diviner's oracle has compelling power over the clients inasmuch as it is performative, i.e., offers a self-validating, authoritative interpretation. It is as if the problem were self-revelatory and its meaning not fully to be grasped by conventional categorical thought. The meaning production in the oracle flows into an intervention which is not according to any predetermined strategies within the family and which therefore cannot, in advance, be politically manipulated.

The detailed oracular diagnosis, by applying a relatively uniform etiological grid, situates the afflicted individual in his family and network of matrimonial exchanges that connect him with the uterine source of life. It mentions the events leading up to or constituting the problem situation and then connects these events with past events (e.g., abuses) of a similar nature already repaired, and so enables the clients to intervene in the present problem situation in analogous ways.

The articulation process follows a pattern of assumptions which by their use in context reveal a structure rather than a content of meaning, and thus the oracle deals with submitted problems in a somewhat stereotyped way. These assumptions form a higher-order axiological system predefining, as it were, the different conditions under which social life is possible. A study of some twenty-six oracles (Devisch 1984:37ff.; 167–74). compared to the 180 others noted in the field, has revealed that the diviner employs the following etiological model in dealing with a particular case.

A *first* etiological assumption, applied in divination, concerns the uterine transmission of physical life. It is a basic assumption that life-giving and innate life-promoting or life-harming forces are inherited by the individual from the mother, the mother's mother, and the mother's mother's mother. The latter is said to connect with the uterine life source. These uterine ties "link the individual to the uterine source of life and well-being" (*m-mooyi kuyingudi myakala*) that he/she benefits from and will transmit when the time has come. Only offspring of the same mother share in the same life, but they can differ from each other by the selective (uterine) inheritance of different "innate characteristics" (*yibutukulu*). Physical handicaps and exceptional skills, such as clairvoyance and the capacity for divination, are attributed to this heredity. Agnates cannot pass on fatal hereditary characteristics to an individual, nor kill him/her through sorcery, without the complicity of the victim's matrikin.

For the Yaka, the tree, particularly its stem and branches, symbolizes the links with the source of life. Each branching reflects a matrimonial alliance by which a household cedes a woman to another lineage for transmitting life. One can say that each individual's uterine ascendance comprises as many networks of life transmission as there are descendants born of the same mother, matrilateral grand-mother, and great-grandmother. Each network founds a circuit of exchanges between givers and takers of a wife who transmits life. The task of each woman is to transmit life to her husband's group, and the individual owes his/her existence to this. Patri-virilocal residence being the rule, the in-married woman is expected to ensure the physical continuity of her husband's patridescent group through a fertility which is handed down to her matrilineally. Indeed, transmission of life becomes legitimately possible only after matrimonial alliance with the handing over of the bridewealth. The husband's patrikin gives a compensation to the wife's matrikin for each child born and for the services the chid is rendering; this takes place at the successive changes in the life and social identity of the descendant. Because of this, the uterine transmission of life is essentially spoken of in terms of exchange.

The corporeality that characterizes the mother-child relationship is the idiom in which the Yaka express their uterine descent relations. Only (semi-) siblings who "come from the one womb," together with their genitor, genitrix, wives, and unmarried children, share bonds of warmth, trust, and mutual help in the household. The domestic realm, as well as the seclusion in the rites of passage, and the relations between the diviner, the afflicted individual and/or clients, are based on maternal relations and, consequently, on bodily contact, food supply and cooking, commensality, and so on. Through these same bodily activities, uterines and co-initiates, diviner and clients may share their vital force and weaken or strengthen each other.

Socially speaking, uterine kin are represented by ego's uncle (mother's brother). great-uncle (mother's mother's brother) or great-granduncle (mother's mother's mother's brother). These avuncular relations are also figured in terms of this tree metaphor. The primary uncle is called "uncle from the top" (*leemba dyamathaandu*), the great-uncle is called "uncle from the middle" (*leemba dyamakati*), and finally the great-granduncle is the "uncle from the base or at the roots" (*leemba dyamasina*). Normally it is the primary uncle who actively assumes the avuncular role (*buleemba*), delegated to him by the uncles at the ascendant generations. This tree metaphor is transposed to the human body: the youngest descendants are the "buds" of the arm and the body. Referring to the brother of their mother, grandmother, or great-grandmother and her uterine ascent, people spontaneously point to their left wrist, elbow, shoulder, and over their shoulder to their back. For the Yaka, left is to right as uterine relations to agnatic ones. The maternal uncle is thus an instance of mediation and differentiation. Bonds through maternity (such as "male mother," "male wife," "male source," *ngwakhasi*) and alliance (as representative of the bride-givers) meet in his person.

Just as the divinatory capacity is transmitted by way of uterine heredity, so the relationships that the diviner establishes with his clients are predominantly of a uterine type. In this way he is the antipode of deadly sorcery, which needs to call on the fatal complicity of uterines and of the maternal uncle in particular. The diviner situates himself with regard to the subject of the oracle and the clients as a benevolent maternal uncle, through an almost physical bond.

The *second* etiological assumption regards the basic rules or prohibitions (*tsiku*) in Yaka society, also transmitted in the uterine line, as means of consolidating the uterine transmission of life. Any abuse, any infringement of rights, any act which seriously and for no justifiable reason hinders the transmission of life or its flowering is said "to kill the law" (*-hoonda tsiku*). Such an infringement calls for reparation, since life requires it in view of the exhange of fundamental reciprocity. Hence, any infringement is stereotyped as theft. Sorcery and illicit sexual relations, i.e., those relations that infringe the rights of the married couple or those relations that are considered to harm fertility, are called theft in ritual as well as in popular language. An event can be termed illicit if associated harm is considered, by the oracle or council, to be without reason. According to the divinatory diagnosis, a serious illness finds its origin in theft or an infringement committed by a uterine ancestor. But the oracle is very general about the reconstitution of the historical context, offering only broad indications as to the generation and the groups that are involved. If the oracle names an individual, it will only be by means of his title, e.g., the granduncle or the head of the family. The oracle's relevance is not measured by the empirical reality but by the significant value of the historical conjunction. Retracing the affliction in relation to the essential dimensions of the sociocultural order, the oracle will never ascribe an affliction to one factor only.

A *third* register of the divinatory etiology is related to the question of why the affliction strikes this particular individual instead of someone else, why this particular individual is the point of convergence of singular ill-bringing histories. The oracle considers the wronged party to have spoken by way of a curse (*n-sasu*) of the need for reparation and revenge. Such a curse invoked the support of a cult and its ancestral or spirtual agencies. This curse is used against kinsmen only and says that afflicition will befall the wrongdoer or one of his uterine ascendants by way of revenge. Curses are never resolved or ended but are "inherited"; although they are tied to uterine relations, they may cross lineages through marriage and birth. A curse threatens all of the uterine kinsmen of the wrongdoer and of the wronged, in fact, all of the kinsmen who might have committed such an infringement. The effects of the curse that are transmitted through uterine lines make up a matrilineal tradition. It is within this same tradition that the hereditary effects are ritually neutralized. The interlinking of infringement, curse, illness, affliction or death, and misfortune management or ritual intervention makes up a "ritual institution or cult" (*phoongu*).

Yaka people maintain ten major translineage cults considered to be capable of both transmitting affliction and offering initiatory treatment. The cults are of almost equal status and each is concerned with a particular syndrome and its social effects. The most important (whose names prove to be practically untranslatable) include *khita, mbwoolu, ngoombu, haamba, n-luwa, khosi*, and *mbaambi* (Devisch 1984:80–82). In every uterine line the curses that are uttered by the ascendants, as well as the wrong they revenge or the sad consequences they risk incurring, depend on one or another of these cults. In this almost negative way the cult protects and stimulates the flowering of life. The curses are the other side of a law, of a prohibition, the infringement of which is sanctioned. Therefore, not only are these cults a ritual frame in which these curses are articulated in a traditional form; in their sanctioning effects they also provide an etiological framework of the illness and consequently a therapeutic framework. Curing the victim from such a curse and sanction equals initiating him into the corresponding cult. Each cult links up, across lineage boundaries, all the individuals who have been cursed within this frame.

As for cursing, it is unthinkable for the Yaka that any individual should have the right in his own name to judge the acts of another, certainly not to wish his death. Rather a curse is based on evidence which exceeds any individual motivation. When wronged, the reciprocity between kinsmen seeks to repair itself and calls for revenge. Thus a curse which calls down self-evident unavoidable vengeance acquires the force of prohibition, since ill will come with its transgression. In the same way that the existential interdependence branches out through matrimonial alliance, so the curse threatens uterine descendants, prohibitions being transmitted in the same line. The following argument in the oracle could appear circular since it links ill with the infringement of a law/prohibition, and also with a curse which is the conditional formulation of the prohibition. But the circularity is only superficial because the curse by its conditional formulation includes a kind of oracle; the realization of the condition makes the effect unavoidable. "If it is true that a theft is punished" is the stereotyped opening of a curse; then, in applying this axiom to a concrete case ("If I myself have stolen, I should die"), the curse metaphorically refers to a general and higher-order rule going beyond the single case which the thief cannot avoid ("keep an eye on him/her" is the end of the curse). It is through this general rule that the elements of the structural triad law–infringement–sanction are hierarchically related in the etiological and axiological metasystem. One element evokes the other insofar as it is applicable in a given situation. More concretely, the curse presents the story of inevitable recurrence: it is the story of the existential interdependence of kinsmen which always will reassert itself, of life overcoming restraints, of evil calling for vengeance, of social order constantly restating itself. Parallel to the logic of the curse, the Yaka divinatory etiology not only expresses a structural causality but also actualizes a value system. The oracle draws on certain assumptions and evidence, as is shown by the association the oracle establishes between present and past affliction. In a performative and metaphoric way, the association provides the major signification of the affliction. Concretely, the oracle orders the facts according to the interlinking structural model: exchange–law/prohibition–infringement–curse–sanction–affliction or death.

There is no attempt within the oracle to give a causal interpretation of the "how" of events. Employing what I term a structural framework, it gives a semantic reading of the facts that characterizes the submitted problem, uncovers a meaning, and prepares an intervention to be efficacious. The meaning of the problem does not lie in the higher-order metasystem but in referring to it and in the unique semantic or metaphoric interconnecting of events, acts, and persons that were unconnected before, i.e., that belong to different semantic structures and patterns of social life (Devisch 1985a:70ff.). The oracle connects the submitted illness with some recent infringement or abuse, or some quarrel involving the sick person (e.g., arising from uncles failing to fulfil their duties) and also with an analogous situation in the history of the uterine descent. This connecting of present and historical situations is not causalist but metaphoric and brings to light an important dimension of the meaning of the problem. It is as if reference were made to the self-maintenance of social life and to a unifying, all-embracing, and axiological horizon of meaning and order. The oracle metonymically throws light on other phenomena, in linking them with the present family quarrel.

Among the clients and in *popular etiology*, this metaphoric reference is readily interpreted in a causal deterministic way: it is claimed either that the affliction is a direct retaliation for the wrong committed by some uterine ascendants threatened by a curse or that the family quarrel led the elders to reassert their status through sorcery. Jealousy, envy, offended honor and anger are seen as the motives for malevolent acts drawing on extrahuman avenging or bewitching powers. Any act of illicit sorcery is already threatened by the curse of an ascendant, so for popular interpretation it is unimportant whether affliction is the direct result of sorcery or is the retaliation of an act of sorcery committed by an ascendant of the victim. In all these cases, it is through the uterine ties that one is most vitally threatened with and suffers from misfortune.

The divinatory session is ended by a verdict and a prescription: one party (e.g., the agnates, or the uterines of the first generation) gets accused of sorcery or of the infringement that has reactivated the curse from the past. Blame may be put on the other party (e.g., the uterines of the second ascendant generation) as well for their having angered the first generation. The prescription will be about a sacrifice, a restitution, an uncle that one has to contact, or a cult that must be organized. The clients then organize a hunt to test the oracle's veracity. The same system of values underlies the divinatory and therapeutic approaches, so that the therapy will aim at the actualization of these values in the form of a rite of passage. Ritual form is then given to the patient's symbolic death and rebirth via cult-specific metaphors. But the case's singular history only particularizes the first stage of the therapeutic intervention during which the kin groups redefine or readjust their mutual relations and their relations vis-à-vis the afflicted person.

The oracle's approach to the relationships between persons, patridescent groups, uterines, and affines is schematic and general. It seldom accuses an individual as individual, but usually agnatic or uterine kin groups and their leaders. By connecting a current problem with some form of familial discord, or with an analogous problem situation in the uterine ascent, it leads to a general all-embracing dramatized redefinition of the basic kinship relations. Any ritual intervention in a problem situation reflects the divinatory interpretation of the problem. Since any problem, even sickness (whose somatic aspects are, however, not minimized), is seen as a neglect of the reciprocity between kin, the ritual unraveling of the problem always begins as follows: a ritual compensation is offered by the sufferer or by his residential elder to the representative of the uterine forebear who uttered the curse in the distant past. This means that the granduncle or the great-granduncle of the sufferer receives the compensation so that he might remove the threat of the curse, turn back its fatal effects, and realize reconciliation symbolically: the uterine link is no longer the source of ill, but is now life giving and life promoting. Now the conditions are fulfilled for efficacious ritual intervention which dramatizes good health, renewed fertility, successful hunting, and so on.

Who Is Speaking in the Oracle?

As Zempléni noted (1982:8), the diviner who pronounces the oracle's inspired words declares himself and is by definition declared not to be the subject of enunciation. It is not the diviner himself who speaks in his own name, unlike the diviner-prophet who mixes "inspired" messages and statements in his personal name (Devisch and Vervaeck 1985). But, while it is true that the oracle as etiological discourse removes the diviner as subjective source of the enunciation, as the one who discloses and informs all by himself, it seems that the diviner is the agent of the corporeal drama with its self-generating meaning. The oracle does not annihilate the psychic and metaphorizing subject.

It seems to me that the problem situation is voiced nonverbally through the diviner's body or corporeal drama before it is translated in the light of the axiological tradition and in function of the questions from the etiological registers and the clients. The subject of enunciation is constituted by the intertwining of anomaly and norm, of deficient and normal, of social, cosmological, and bodily domains, and actualized through the diviner's corporeality. The initiatory trance and the heightened sensory capacities of the diviner (the keen sense of smell and the receptive introvertive listening linked to the clairvoyance) are the agents of and the place in which the intertwining takes place. This intertwining is brought about by the diviner's extreme transcending of limits, thereby negatively affirming the necessity of such limits and norms congruently on the social, cosmological, and bodily domains.

On the social level the diviner outlines the relations that reconcile the afflicted, the clients, and the uterine forebears. The diviner's extreme transgression of the norm and the limits of the cosmological level reestablishes, with regard to the problem situation, the pertinency of the traditional values and norms. This trangression indirectly offers normative models that help to interpret the meaning of the problem situation and the solution to it. In other words, the diviner violates the norm or transgresses the limits in such an extreme way that he thereby embodies both the norm and the limits, and their transgression. He sets the measure of transgression, simultaneously evoking the necessity of limits and norms. By embodying both the extreme limit-transgression and the reference to the center (namely, the conventional order of norms and vlaues), the diviner is able to dialectically intertwine, in a hierarchical relationship, center and margin, the norm and its violation. He is thereby able to capture the creative potential at the margin by its extreme violation. Like the culture hero, the diviner both situates himself outside the culture and creates it. The diviner does not act as the defender of the norm, nor as the judge. For the diviner, the consultation is an achievement of spiritual transcendence.

On the bodily level, by discerning the submitted problem with the help of his divinatory capacities inherited in the uterine line, the diviner develops an almost physical or umbilical bond with the afflicted individual and the clients (recall that the intermediary object has rested on the afflicted individual's navel). He prefigures in this way the restructuring of the bonds with the uterine life source. Through these uterine life-giving bonds, as well as through the symbolism of "the chicken on the point of laying an egg," the divination affirms itself as self-generative of new life. By means of his clairvoyance, which reactualizes the initiatory trance-possession, that is to say through his corporeality, the diviner gives support to his being the subject of enunciation. But the process involves more than this.

In his corporeality the diviner appears as the agent and the locus, the author (the psychic subject) and the scene of an innovative meaning production. In all these aspects Yaka divination is a resource of identity and existence for the diviner as well as for the afflicted and/or the clients. The divination shows how the fundamental symbolic process of world construction among the Yaka operates and how the sociocultural order finds its origin in this process and profoundly imposes itself on the bodily experience in a mutual modeling of each other.

The internal approach I have adopted succeeds in showing how divination more than any other institution repeatedly reveals the conventional character of the Yaka culture and society and especially how, when challenged by misfortune, it renews itself.

The oracle and its corollaries (the curse and ritual intervention) are founded in a higher-order system of basic values from which they draw an axiomatic, etiological model. Neither oracles nor rites prove their veracity by discursive reasoning; rather this veracity stems from linking up the problem situation to an axiological metasystem that is beyond any doubt. The oracle brings about the meaning of the unknown by laying bare the hidden coordinates of the problem situation in reference to the relevant higher-order axiological system, and allows in this way for efficacious intervention. This axiomatic metasystem generates and maintains itself as a self-defining reality, and is also an implicit expression of the conditions for healthy societal and individual life. My internal approach does not invoke extrahuman referents to account for the authoritative veracity in the oracle's articulation of meaning.

Yaka divination includes an ethical approach to the conditions for social life and does not propose to the individual an ideal for behavior. The oracle does not consider a problem such as sickness, affliction, anomaly, or death as the effect of a failure to correspond to an ideal, nor as something which compromises an ideal of human life. The oracle, and even the jurisdiction, speak of omission when the meaning of the actual problem is seen in the light of a former similar problem situation where infringement was cursed. For the oracle, the final responsibility does not lie in the fault for which an individual in his free decision is held responsible. The oracle does not look for a guilty person but for those responsible for the social reciprocity that needs to be restored.

Divinatory oracles, like trials and cults, make clear that the Yaka do not see the human life and affliction as deterministic, inevitable, or unintelligible and meaningless. It is in divination that the Yaka seek the answers to crucial existential questions. Indeed, so critical is this system that we might ask if Yaka society shorn of divination would still remain Yaka society.

Notes

The research for this study was conducted from 1972 to 1974 in the Taanda territory, about 450 kilometers southeast of Kinshasa, encompassing thirteen Yaka villages. My data on divination stem from participant observation and numerous lengthy conversations with eleven diviners; more than two hundered oracles were noted in detail (some audio-recorded during the divination, others rendered faithfully by a diviner or one of the clients). I also witnessed the trance and subsequent seclusion of a diviner-to-be. The data I gathered confirm in detail the observations of Huber (1965) and of Father De Beir (1975:31–33, 111–38), who observed divinatory practices in the regional chiefdom of N-nene (Taanda territory) between 1938 and 1945. My annual sojourns, since 1986, of seven weeks among the Yaka in Kinshasa allow me to say that divination remains very crucial in town. The research among rural and urban Yaka has been financed by the Belgian National Fund for Scientific Research. A few sections of this paper previously appeared in Devisch (1985b). I gratefully acknowledge editorial help from Filip De Boeck.

1. At the very beginning of the oracle, the diviner discloses the core message of the oracle, i.e., he defines the reason for the consultation: the young woman died primarily because the younger brother of her father turned his curse against her by bringing up the bridewealth, a substitution of the woman herself, with the sphere of the effect of the curse.

2. According to the clients, this factual detail of the suitcase and the divining of proper names and residences of those involved proves the diviner's extraordinary insight.

3. The prohibitions mentioned here are the normative formulation of curses uttered against related sorcerers. Since the related forebears have handed down prohibitions, they are also in some way at the root of Suuta's death. Further on the oracle will reveal that Toonda is one of Suuta's classificatory fathers.

4. The oracle points to the fact that Suuta's bridewealth should not have been in the hands of those cursed, because this implies the danger of the curse being turned against Suuta.

5. By connecting Suuta's illness with sorcery, the oracle indirectly links the illness with a transgression of the sorcery prohibition which was transmitted in the maternal line to Suuta's classificatory fathers and to Suuta herself. By this curse, Suuta's father reinforces the prohibition, so that any transgression would of necessity have fatal consequences.

6. Such a removal of his curse was necessary in order to prevent Suuta's coming under the curse, on account of her being related to Mbela who by wronging his brother had turned the curse against himself and Suuta.

7. In the event of death, the deceased's residential group must offer compensation to the uterine ascent for the woman's services and fertility. The deceased is thereby handed back to the uncles who represent her uterine origin. When there has been murderous sorcery, the compensation is the equivalent of the bridewealth (Devisch 1979:140–46).

8. The oracle about Suuta's illness revealed the omission of reconciliation after the killing of Suuta's father by sorcery and the ignoring of the division within the group. This omission at the root of Suuta's illness could temporarily have been ritually neutralized by the head of the family. By being required to offer a chicken, the head of the family is being indirectly accused of malevolent omission, i.e, sorcery.

9. This diviner offers water, over which a spell has been uttered, to any doubter of the oracle. Such a test reveals the guilty and kills him.

10. To prevent the effect of the curse overtaking Suuta's younger sister and to prevent the second head of the family directing his malevolent acts against primary kinsmen of Suuta, he is asked as a sign of his reconciliation to offer a chicken to Suuta's sister.

11. See Devisch 1979:147–51.

References

Bourgeois, A. 1983. "*Mukoko Ngoombu*: Divination Paraphernalia of the Yaka." *African Arts* 15(3): 56–59, 80.

De Beir, L. 1975. *Religion et magie des Bayaka*. Augustin-Bonn: Anthropos-Institut.

Devisch, R. 1979. "Les Yaka du Nord." In *Mort, deuil et compensations mortuaires chez les Komo et les Yaka du Nord au Zaïre*, ed. R. Devisch and W. de Mahieu, 67–179. Tervuren: Annales du Musée Royal de l'Afrique Centrale.

———. 1984. *Se recréer femme: Manipulation d'une situation d'infécondité chez les Yaka du Zaïre*. Berlin: Reimer.

———. 1985a. "Perspectives on Divination in Contemporary Sub-Saharan Africa." In *Theoretical Explorations in African Religion*, ed. W. Van Binsbergen and M. Schoffeleers, 50–83. London: Kegan Paul.

———. 1985b. "Diagnostic divinatoire chez les Yaka du Zaïre: Les axes étiologiques et le sujet de l'énonciation." *L'Ethnographie* 81(96–97):197–216.

Devisch, R., and B. Vervaeck. 1985. "Autoproduction, production et reproduction: Divination et politique chez les Yaka du Zaïre." *Social Compass* 32:111–32.

Huber, H. 1965. "A Diviner's Apprenticeship and Work among the Bayaka." *Man* 66:46–48.

Zempléni, A. 1982. "Anciens et nouveaux usages sociaux de la maladie en Afrique." *Archives de sciences sociales des religions* 54:5–19.

PART FOUR

Divination, Epistemology, and Truth

> Any culture which admits the use of oracles and divination is committed to a distinction between appearances and reality. The oracle offers a way of reaching behind appearances to another source of knowledge.
>
> Mary Douglas, "If the Dogon . . ."

The essays in this section discuss the making of meaning, delineating how usable knowledge is socially and semantically constituted from oracular messages. Rosalind Shaw discusses the epistemological foundations of *an-bere* divination and other Temne ways of knowing. Developing several points raised in section III, Susan Reynolds Whyte analyzes how divination, as the Nyole's primary means of defining social identity, is used to investigate the pathologies of social relations of the afflicted person. From his scrutiny of diagnostic texts by three diviners, David Parkin demonstrates the dynamics and logic of Giriama and Swahili oracular speech.

Several new topics emerge in these essays. Both Shaw and Whyte comment on the relationship of women to divination. Whyte informs us that although there are female diviners and clients, Nyole divination is primarily situated within a male ethos with men consulting with other men, often on behalf of women. Nevertheless, women can manipulate the system, as can Temne women, who also face gender-based patterns of divinatory consultation (Shaw 1985). In the present essay, Shaw contrasts the relatively private female consultations and the more public male divination sessions. Along with Glaze's portrayal of the centrality of women diviners in Senufo society (1981) and Ngubane's analysis of male and female relations in her study of Zulu women diviners (1977), these essays serve to counter the argument that women become involved in mediumistic divination because other avenues of expression are denied to them (see Lewis 1970:302–4, Gussler 1973, and Beattie and Middleton 1969). Certainly "knowledge is power" and the recipient of oracular revelations is in a superior position to the afflicted individual being represented, but we need to go beyond previous analyses of the uses of divinatory revelations (see Mendonsa 1982) to the actual acquisition of that knowledge. Here the representative of the afflicted individual is the key figure, which recalls the Batammaliba "adviser" and the Yaka divinatory contingent.

These chapters also address culture change, in terms both of new or altered systems of divination and of the diviner's role as cultural innovator. Whyte suggests that Nyole women may be turning to Muslim diviners as a reflection of their growing independence or because these diviners appear more "scientific." The importance of divination as a context for culture change and the diviner as the innovating *bricoleur* are central points in Parkin's contribution. Whether change comes from internal or external agents, the basic epistemological paradigm will remain the same. This holds true where there are different types of divination within one culture, a frequent occurrence further illustrated here by the Temne, Nyole, Giriama, and Swahili. While one or two forms may dominate, there are nevertheless alternatives, and within each culture a "common logic," as Parkin terms it, continues to underpin each form.

To understand these shared premises we especially need to understand the speech of divination. Shaw's description of oracular messages' "cryptic potency" and Parkin's analysis of divination's "polysemic vocabulary" are helpful extensions of Werbner's discussion (1973) of the "super-abundance of understanding" revealed in divinatory rhetoric. Deliberating a theme common to all three essays of the movement from ambiguous to explicit knowledge, from chaotic simultaneity to sequential clarity, Parkin demonstrates that in both structure and content divination "straightens the paths from wilderness." The initial flood of verbal images is analogous to the chaos of visual symbols in a diviner's basket, both demanding the diviner's translations. Further, Shaw observes that Temne public divination is characterized by articulate speech while private divination utilizes enigmatic speech—a contrast similar to the Dogon distinction between legal and divinatory pronouncements (see Calame-Griaule 1965 and Douglas 1979).

References to psychology and psychiatry are found in this section as well as elsewhere in this volume. Seeking to clarify aspects of oracular speech and diagnoses, Parkin cites research on schizophrenia as well as Jung's concept of synchronicity. Although Jung himself encountered problems in linking divination with his theory of the acausal connecting principle of synchronicity (1973, 1974), it is an intriguing proposition which has received too little attention. In the final section of this volume, Peek considers work in the psychology of superstition and cognition as well as split-brain research and the issue of hemispherical lateralization and specialization. In his afterword, Fernandez notes that divination initially expresses primary processes of intuitive and condensed thought which is then synthesized with secondary processes of thinking based on common cultural knowledge. Collectively these observations strongly recommend further cross-disciplinary use of psychology, especially given the crucial role of perception and cognition, in divination systems.

A last point of comparison among this section's articles, which we might introduce via Shaw's phrase "the authorizing process," is critical. Steiner (1954) called attention to this issue long ago, but Park also understood the need to study divination in relation to all means of problem solving (1967:246). Certainly divination participates in general cultural norms, but as we saw in section III it is the articulator, not merely an articulation, of these norms. How divination validates cultural norms rather than simply corresponding to them is approached in this section. Horton (1967) and Jackson (1978) summarize how we have traditionally understood the maintenance of divination's credibility by the people involved, a matter still best illustrated by Evans-Pritchard's interrogation of the Zande poison oracle (1968). But as Shaw observes, previous analyses overemphasized the "facts" of divinatory diagnoses as a result of the positivist bias in anthropology. The processes of divination, not simply the product and its use, must be studied because "truth" may lie at different points in each divination system. It may depend on a fixed system of esoteric knowledge accessible only through divination, or it may be a function of social authority (which also determines who has access to the mechanism of knowing) or ancestral/spiritual validation, or it may result from the debate about the oracular message by the diviner and the client working in concert. In fact, it may simply be the efficacious result of the diagnosis for the client and/or afflicted individual. Whatever the actual system, there will be an authorizing process accepted by all concerned.

But these processes may not be easy for us to accept, especially if there are fundamental differences in cultural systems and cognitive approaches. For example, a radical difference from European and American individualism is the communal orientation inherent in African systems of divination, from the attribution of skill and insight to the ancestors to the goal of harmony for the group not just the afflicted individual. Indeed, throughout this volume we see that "truth" is in the action generated, the social reality reconstituted, and the resultant well-being of the people; it is not to be found in an abstract system or specific verifications of separate oracular pronouncements. As Jackson (1978) recommends, we should not perpetuate only idealized belief but should allow for the flexibility of interpretation and action which in reality we all exercise toward our own cultural systems.

References

See reference list at end of main introduction.

Rosalind Shaw

Splitting Truths from Darkness

Epistemological Aspects of Temne Divination

Divination and Rationality

It would be difficult to find an anthropologist who would agree with the following assertion:

> In reply to the question as to what useful purpose is served by recourse to magic and religion as fortifications against the elements and misfortune, one can only answer that lacking other means of control, such as is often afforded men in civilized societies, native peoples fall back on their oracles. (Lessa 1959:203)

Yet, as Devisch has argued recently (1985:62–68), one dominant perspective in anthropological studies of divination has been an intellectualist one in which this characterization of divination as "failed scientific explanation" could be said to have been to a certain extent perpetuated. This is because discussions of divination as systems of knowledge have revolved almost exclusively around questions of explanatory validity, and while I do not wish to deny the importance of divination's explanatory function, it is necessary to draw attention to other dimensions of knowledge and truth which may be at least as relevant.

As recent critics of rationalism in anthropology have observed (e.g., the contributors to Overing 1985), when we think of "truth" in Western intellectual discourse, the positivist preoccupation with knowledge as verifiable observation tends to obscure not only the existence of alternative conceptions of truth but also the authorizing process through which truth is created. Both the ideological dimension, in which control over the definition of certain types of knowedge and meaning as "truthful" is enacted (see Asad 1983), and the semantic issue of what these definitions actually consist of are of critical relevance to divination. Nonetheless, they have been accorded little attention.

The classic work from which intellectualist (and, of course, functionalist) approaches to divination have drawn their influence is Evans-Pritchard's *Witchcraft, Oracles and Magic among the Azande* (1937). His aim in this study was to challenge Lévy-Bruhl's characterization of "primitive" thought as "pre-logical" by demonstrating the internal logical consistency of Zande ideas about oracles and witchcraft, but he saw this logic as based upon false premises and was moved to exclaim: "And yet Azande do not see that their oracles tell them nothing" (337–38). He explained this by pointing to what he called "secondary elaborations of belief" in Zande thought, in which the failure of oracles is attributed to such additional mystical contingencies as the breach of a taboo, ghostly anger, or sorcery, thus forming protective explanatory layers which prevent the primary conviction of the inherent truthfulness of the poison oracle from being questioned (330).

The fact that he was concerned at all to provide an explanation for the Zande acceptance of oracular truth was, unsurprisingly, a function of the epistemological politics of Evans-Pritchard's own intellectual environment:

> I have described to many people in England the facts related in the last chapter and they have been, in the main, incredulous or contemptuous. In their questions to me they have sought to explain away Zande behaviour by rationalising it, that is to say, by interpreting it in terms of our culture. . . . They ask what happens when the result of one test contradicts the other which it ought to confirm if the verdict be valid; what happens when the findings of oracles are belied by experience; and what happens when two oracles give contrary answers to the same question.
>
> These same, and other, problems, naturally occurred to me in Zandeland, and I made enquiries into, and observations on, those points which struck me as important. (1937:313)

As the terms "incredulous" and "contemptuous" indicate, the premises from which these "common sense" assumptions derive carry an emotionally charged normative weight which protects them from critical scrutiny just as effectively as secondary elaborations protect Zande assumptions about oracles. Although Evans-Pritchard's intention was to challenge such unhelpful (and pejorative) oppositions as "rational" versus "mystical" mentalities, the fact that he did so in terms of the "internal logic" and "false premises" underlying Zande ideas allowed an unexamined positivist ideology to continue to frame comparisons of Western and non-Western modes of thought.

This rationalist aspect of Evans-Pritchard's writing was developed further in Horton's renowned comparison (1967) between African traditional thought and Western scientific thought in terms of the Popperian dichotomy between "closed" and "open" intellectual predicaments. Horton argued that while Western science is constructed upon choices between alternative theories, through each of which the world may be explained, predicted, and controlled with varying degrees of accuracy, African traditional thought is characterized by an absence of theoretical choices. Since there are no alternatives except conceptual chaos, the existing system of thought must remain unquestioned, and therefore requires the protection of such devices as secondary elaborations of belief. A further form of conceptual defense described by Horton is that of "converging causal sequences," in which any one of several possible causes (such as witchcraft, ancestral punishment, or spirit attack) may be responsible for an identical misfortune. If one causal connection proves to be invalid (for instance, if a sacrifice to a particular spirit fails to restore a sick person's health), the conclusion is merely that another causal connection must be the right one; the conceptual system from which these causal sequences derive is not itself doubted.

Like Evans-Pritchard, Horton approached divination as an exclusively *intellectual* explanatory activity. Furthermore, it was viewed as central to the maintenance of the "closed" intellectual predicament, firstly because it provides the only available means of "going over the head of the evidence" by selecting one out of several converging causal connections as the "right" explanation (1964:9; 1967:170). The second reason is that it permits considerable scope for secondary elaborations, since fruitless diagnoses can easily be attributed to the sensitivity of the divination apparatus or the incompetence or fraudulence of particular diviners without bringing the entire system of ideas behind such diagnoses into question (1964:15; 1967:171).

That such processes constitute a crucial aspect of divination is not in question. This kind of analysis is not inaccurate but partial, in that it represents divinatory procedure as a purely intellectual exercise as well as marginalizing the role of interests and power in the production of both Western scientists' and African diviners' explanations. In the case of Western science the strongly normative tendencies which make this conceptual framework itself a somewhat "closed" system are ignored (as Horton has recently acknowledged [1982:211]), while in the case of African divination the issue of the impact of individual or group interests is limited to the question of dishonest diviners and thereby reduced, via the "secondary elaboration" argument, to a mere mechanism in the defensive intellectual armory of the "closed" predicament. Evans-Pritchard, on the other hand, acknowledged that the truthfulness of the Zande poison oracle in local contexts derived from the defined infallibility of the oracle of the prince. And yet, despite his assertion that confidence in the poison oracle would not be maintained were it not underpinned in this way by centralized power (1937:343), he paid scant attention to this authorizing process.

Intellectualist analyses are, inevitably, "authorized" forms of knowledge in our own subcultural environment as academics, and it is intriguing, as Malcolm Crick has observed, that "anthropology here incarnates a Western philosophy of mind, and values highly those intellectual gifts which are useful in academic life" (1982: 290). So embedded is the template through which our own discourse acquires its truth value that we tend to allow definitions of "what is true" in terms of verification to eclipse questions of "what truth means" in other situations.

Truth as Performative Efficacy and Cryptic Potency

More than thirty years ago, Franz Steiner (1954) argued that if anthropologists addressing issues of truth and knowledge were to cease restricting themselves to the concerns of positivist logicians, they would find applications of "truth" connected with notions of "the binding word," such as the oath, the vow, swearing, and witnessing. Witnessing, for example, refers in many types of legal procedure not to verification by an eyewitness but to a person's sworn declaration of solidarity with one of the parties and of his or her statements. Such a declaration helps to establish truth not by virtue of any logical properties it may have, but by its power in this specific context to authorize a transformation in social reality.

With the reality-defining potential of these and other such "performative utterances" we are of course familiar in Africa from Finnegan's researches (1969). In a similar vein, Lienhardt (1961) has stressed the social creation of truth via ritual speech among the Dinka. The speeches made at Dinka sacrifices, for example, by redescribing past events as the participants *intend* them to have been, reshape the participants' experience of the past so as to affirm what the Dinka see as more fundamental truths, such as kinship unity and ascendancy of life over death. "In Dinka thought," Lienhardt wrote, "it is this kind of truth which is arrived at and stated by a *communal* intention" (1961:247).

Divination is clearly another such truth-constructing process in which, through the public reclassification of people and events, a particular interpretation emerges as the authorized version of "what really happened." Yet in many instances ethnographically, notions of divinatory truth embrace much more than this performative social efficacy. Another alternative sense of truth is implied by the close association in West Africa of systems of divination with a trickster figure, typically an anthropomorphized animal who flouts formal rules of social and cosmic order and often takes the role of a rival creator who, through his haphazard (and often purely accidental) transformations of the world in the time of myth, acts as an antithesis to the principal creator-deity, though in a humorous and entirely non-satanic manner (see Pelton 1980).

In Dogon myth (Griaule 1965; Griaule and Dieterlen 1954), for instance, the Pale Fox (Yurugu) upsets the harmonious universe of dualities set up by his father, Amma, the creator, and Amma's well-balanced twin children, the Nommo, by virtue of his birth as a single and therefore lonely being instead of a twin. The Pale Fox's loneliness tempts him to commit incest by raping his mother, the earth, but through this central breach of order he gains knowledge of the "second word" of Amma, which possesses *nyama*, creative power, but which precedes the "third word" through which Amma gives man the power of speech.

Whereas the Nommo twins embody light and verbal articulacy, and preside over legal judgments and formal ritual, the Pale Fox, through his knowledge of the second word, is the unwitting agent behind divination. Dogon diviners lure foxes to the margins of villages by leaving food for them there, having first marked out squares on the ground over which the foxes run at night, leaving cryptic patterns of footprints which the diviners decipher the following morning (Griaule 1937; Paulme 1937). Mary Douglas argued from this that the Dogon "situate real truth . . . in the shadowy realm of the Pale Fox," while formal appearances are placed "in the daylight world of Nommo" (1975:130).

Thus the figure of the Pale Fox, this delinquent son of God wandering alone in the wild but from time to time speechlessly revealing knowledge to people through tracks left just outside the village's civilized order, presents an image of truth as an enigmatic, extra-social potency complementing the more legalistic and verbally articulate truth of the Nommo, which can be compared to the formal social efficacy described by Steiner, Lienhardt, and Finnegan (see Douglas 1975: 127). Evans-Pritchard's and Horton's view of divination as intellectual explanation and the definition of truth that this implies as the verifiable accuracy of a verbal proposition thus bears practically no resemblance to this aspect of the divinatory truth of the Pale Fox. Given the importance of secret knowledge and the prominence of non-verbal forms of learning in much West African ritual (see, e.g., Bellman 1984 and Jackson 1983), I would argue that a conception of truth as potent paraverbal enigma is likely to be a constantly recurring alternative to the more public, legalistic truth of clear definitions. Divination procedures, accordingly, may embody and reproduce either or both of these alternatives.

Divisions of Oracular Labor

Like Evans-Pritchard's analysis of Zande witchcraft and Nuer lineages (see Crick 1976:117), the paradigmatic status which his study of the Zande poison oracle has been accorded has shaped subsequent anthropological interpretations of divination in a more constraining manner than he probably intended. His emphasis upon the *logic* of the Zande use of the poison oracle can be attributed not only to his critical views on Lévy-Bruhl's concept of "pre-logical" mentality but also to the fact that this technique happens to be characterized by the highly analytical, "either-or" selection of binary distinctions. Although the methodological procedure of the poison oracle is by no means universal among African divination systems, it has been used to authorize not only Zande social hierarchies but also an overemphasis upon intellectual aspects of divination in anthropological explanation. Its "logical" qualities have been seized upon by those who give primacy to "rules" or "rationality" (e.g., Ahern 1982 and the contributors to Hollis and Lukes 1982), while its legalistic nature has been seized upon by those who give primacy to "legitimation" (e.g., Park 1963). Common to both of these modes of analysis, as Devisch has observed, is a concern for "order," for "regulation" at the social and "regularity" at the cognitive levels, which "reflects the models used by the authors, a moralizing hermeneutic, a positivistic and pragmatic philosophy," and which fails to take account of the symbolic nature of divination (1985:64, 51).

Turner cannot be accused of ignoring divinatory symbolism but he too can be said to have overemphasized its univocal rationality in Ndembu divination, which he describes as "a mode of analysis and a taxonomic system," a dualistic, intellectual, and highly verbal ritual form which "proceeds by a sequence of binary oppositions, moving stepwise from classes to elements" (1975:15–16). He contrasted what he perceived as the fragmented and somewhat "paranoid" but nonetheless "rational" sifting of evidence in divinatory ritual (24) with the nonverbal experiential wholeness characterizing revelatory ritual, the latter beginning with "authoritative images or root metaphors, manifested as sets of connected symbols," and asserting "the fundamental power and health of society and nature grasped integrally" (15–16). This stress upon the dualistic, rational nature of Ndembu divination echoes Evans-Pritchard's account of the Zande poison oracle, yet in most other respects the two divination systems are dissimiliar: the fact that Ndembu "basket tossing" divination makes use of a collection of symbols which forms a microcosm of social reality implies that the revelation of the wider whole, at least to the diviner, is unlikely to be entirely absent.

Recently, the overemphasis upon divination as an analytical ritual has begun to be balanced, firstly by Devisch, who reverses Turner's dichotomy in giving revelation priority in his interpretation of Yaka divination (1979), and secondly by Werbner's argument that both revelation and analysis constitute different emphases within Tswapong divination rather than distinct modes of ritual (1989:25–26). Both Werbner and, in a study of Giriama and Swahili divinatory speech, Parkin (1979; see also Parkin's essay in this volume) describe shifts in divinatory ritual and speech within a single session between classificatory, "logical" analysis on the one hand and a unifying synthesis via the use of polysemous symbols and metaphors on the other hand. Divination, then, appears to be, perhaps unsurprisingly, as disparate a process as other forms of ritual, such as sacrifice: predominantly analytical in some contexts (such as the Zande poison oracle), while in others either predominantly revelatory (e.g., Yaka divination) or consisting of an interplay of both modes.

I would suggest that the stronger the legalistic purpose of divination, the more "analytical" the method used is likely to be, involving sharp "either-or" categorizations and a systematic sifting of evidence, the Zande poison oracle being a prime example. In such contexts, the constitution of performative, public "truth" rests upon the creation of clear definitions and classifications, for which analytical divinatory procedures are eminently suited. Where such legalistic requirements are less important, however, divinatory analysis may be more likely to be balanced by revelation, involving such phenomena as the use of microcosm, the simultaneous use of polysemous symbols and metaphors, the resolution of disparate meanings, the cultivation of ambiguity and paradox, and the kind of enigmatic truth which the Pale Fox embodies, in which an integrative function emerges.

In the remainder of this essay, I will explore this "division of oracular labor" and its implications with reference to Temne divination. Most of my research was carried out in southeastern Temneland, which is roughly in the north-central region of Sierra Leone.

The Hidden and the Open in Temne Divination

The Temne do not have as spectacular a divinatory patron as the Pale Fox, and Temne stories are so replete with different trickster figures that the fact that one of them is associated with divination may seem completely unsurprising. What is significant, however, is that the trickster animal who is assigned the role of diviner in Temne stories, Pa Lulu, the Senegalese Fire-Finch, is a bird which comes unusually close to people and appears equally at home in town and bush. This characteristic of being a go-between from wild to social space makes Pa Lulu a particularly fitting choice, not only because diviners are ritual mediators between human and non-human realms, but also because the truths which they mediate are viewed partially in spatial terms.

It is therefore appropriate to sketch an outline of Temne spatial regions in which truth is seen to be located particularly. In addition to the visible world of ordinary human beings, which is called *no-ru*, three worlds invisible to humans are usually distinguished by those in southeastern Temneland: *ro-soki*, the place of spirits, *ro-kerfi*, the place of ancestors, and *ro-seron*, the place of witches.[1] These non-human regions are said to be like large towns and to be spatially contiguous with *no-ru*, although some describe the place of the ancestors as being in the east (see Littlejohn 1963). They are "here" and all around us, but as it is usually expressed in Temne, there is a "darkness" (*an-sum*) which hides them from us; their inhabitants can see us, but we cannot see them.

In some contexts, however, this "darkness" is not merely a visual barrier between us and the non-human worlds, but can be entered by those who mediate between them. Certain categories of people can penetrate the darkness and can see and participate in these worlds by virtue of possessing "four-eyed" vision, in which the two visible eyes of ordinary people are supplemented by two invisible eyes. Such people are termed *an-soki*, a word derived from the root *sok*, which is associated with vision and visibility as well as knowledge and comprehension (see Littlejohn 1960b:68). The world of spirits, *ro-soki*, is accordingly a place of vision and understanding, revealing an epistemological classification of space which is also apparent in the description of the world of the ancestors, *ro-kerfi*, as the "place of truths," *ro-ten*. "Truths" are always spoken of in the plural; there is no term for "truth" in the singular as a generalized entity but rather a multiplicity of powerful externally revealed items of knowledge, such as the knowledge of particular medicines revealed to those who become *an-soki* by ascending the initiatory hierarchy of the *an-Poro* cult association. Diviners are another category of people who are *an-soki*, their power to divine deriving from their relationship with either a patron spirit or a recent diviner-ancestor who gives them revelations of hidden knowledge, initially through an initiatory dream, and under whose auspices they are sometime able to enter *ro-soki* and *ro-kerfi*. As among the Dogon, then, divinatory knowledge and truths have an extra-social origin and a cryptic quality, being obscured by "darkness" to all but the diviner.[2]

This knowledge of the truths of *ro-soki* and *ro-kerfi* is explicitly distinguished from the divinatory techniques themselves, and is often described in visual terms. A synonym for divination, *keli-keli*, meaning "to look-look," indicates the intense act of vision required of the diviner; it may be compared with the Kuranko term for diviner, *bolomafelne*, meaning "hand-on-looker" (Jackson 1978:118), the Krio term, *luk-gron man* ("look-ground man"), and the Mende term, *toto-gbe-moi*, "the man who sets in motion intensive seeing" (Harris and Sawyerr 1968:136). Yet, although Temne diviners' four-eyed vision is the source of their divinatory ability and their means of access to hidden truths, it is also regarded as a cause of suspicion by ordinary Temne because witches, the inhabitants of *ro-seron*, are *an-soki* as well. Not all *an-soki* are witches, but there is always the possibility that they might be secretly serving their own ends at the expense of other members of the community by becoming citizens of *ro-seron* and invisibly preying upon the children and rice crops of their families and neighbors. Witches use their hidden knowledge and vision covertly, for destructive purposes; some say that they eat their victims with their eyes (see Lamp 1978:41).

For this reason, powerful hidden knowledge tends to be given ambivalent ethical connotations by the Temne, as with the lawbreaking Pale Fox. Temne diviners are able to reconcile this tension between the high epistemological value and the dubious ethical value accorded hidden knowledge by revealing in public divination sessions the secrets of others who are defined as covertly attacking the community —witches, thieves, murderers, and adulterers. Having the hidden knowledge of *an-soki* oneself, then, is morally acceptable to the extent that one uses it publicly, serving the community's interests by bringing others' illicit secrets into the open. However, only some diviners achieve sufficient renown to be hired to divine publicly in this way; the majority are part-time diviners who are consulted by individuals over private problems and do not publicly expose hidden secrets for the benefit of the community. In the eyes of ordinary Temne, both these diviners and their (mostly female) private clients retain the ambivalence inherent in their own hidden knowledge.

Public divination takes place either in the open space in the middle of a town or village, or on the verandah at the front of the house. The verandah is a predominantly male zone in which men talk and "keep company"; it is complemented by the back yard, which in a small village usually faces the bush and is a predominantly female zone, the site of the domestic work of women. The space in the center of the village is also the site of *an-bare*, the chief's court house, which is an open structure with no walls in order to enable the community to view all that takes place within it. Thus both the accusation, confession, and consequent redefinition of individuals in public divination (which is a legally binding process in Temne customary law) and the chief's administration of justice can be seen as alternative ways of constituting publicly authorized, performative truth, and both are therefore carried out in space which is as open and socially central as possible.

Inside the house, the central parlor (*an-pala*) is a semi-public space, which contains seating but usually no personal possessions, while the side bedrooms (*e-konko*) are private. It is usually in one of these side rooms, behind a closed door, that private divination is carried out. A form of spirit mediumship called *an-yina Musa* is normally held in the parlor, the intermediate not-quite-public but not-quite-private room at the center of the house, and this method tends to be used when the client has a high status and when his or her problem is perceived as being relatively serious but not yet serious enough to concern the entire community. Thus issues of maximum social concern demand public resolution in open village space or on the almost equally open space of the front verandah of a house, while problems of the individual are diagnosed privately by divination in a closed room, and questions defined as being of intermediate social concern are investigated in the intermediate space of the parlor.

Temne diviners use a large repertoire of methods of public and private divination. Many of these methods are defined as Islamic. Even those which are not often include Islamic elements, since the Temne are semi-Islamized and diviners have been highly influential in defining Islamic knowledge as powerful and prestigious. Both private and public methods may involve the manipulation of objects, while some use more direct forms of mediation, such as spirit mediumship. In the following section, I will compare the ways in which hidden truths are made manifest in *an-bere*, a prominent form of private divination, and in the public witch-detecting technique, *ka-gbak,* of the male *ra-Gbenle* cult association.

An-bere and *Ka-gbak*: Splitting Truths from Darkness

In *an-bere* divination, small river pebbles are cast and then arranged in an interpretable pattern according to the sequence of odd and even numbers obtained. The "powers" which enable the diviner to interpret this pattern are river spirits, of which the most important is the diviner's patron spirit (a river spirit of the opposite sex), and the diviner-ancestor Konkomusa, the first diviner to have used *an-bere*. While *an-bere* diviners use recognizably similar techniques, there is considerable individual variation in the casting and interpretation of the pebbles. I will describe the technique of Pa Biyare of Mafonke village (Bombali Sebora chiefdom), who was temporarily resident in the town of Makeni when he taught me how to use *an-bere*.

A client consulting Pa Biyare first gave a small quantity of money as a "shake-hand" and then explained the problem. Pa Biyare, seated on a Muslim prayer mat on the floor, rubbed the pebbles together in his hands and spoke the Muslim prayer, *Bismillahi Rahmani Rahim*, under his breath.[3] He then instructed the pebbles to reveal (*tori*) truly, softly repeated the client's question to them, and cast the pebbles, throwing a handful upward with his left and and catching some in his right hand. Putting those caught down on the mat, he counted them off two at a time until either two or one remained. Finally, he arranged them from right to left, into a pattern which eventually consisted of a variable number of rows, each made up of a line of four single or paired pebbles, so that there were four columns.[4]

At the first casting, he placed the remaining pebble or pair of pebbles in the top right-hand position to begin the first row. If an even number larger than two remained from out of the pebbles caught in the right hand, he placed them in pairs along the row and replaced the last two in the original pile of pebbles. If, in this case, the row was completed before all the pebbles from one casting were arranged, all those which remained were put back in the original pile, since each row was begun with a fresh casting. When an odd number remained, only the last pebble counted was placed in the row. The number of rows arranged depended upon the context of the pattern's message. When the message seemed incomplete or inappropriate, Pa Biyare continued until he perceived a complete or satisfactorily modified message.

During this process, there was no dialogue between diviner and client. Even when interpreting the pattern of pebbles and indicating the sacrifice required, neither Pa Biyare nor other diviners put much beyond a bare minimum of explanation and prescription into words.

My own training similarly involved minimal verbal exegesis, consisting mostly of the practical demonstration of patterns and the reading of key elements within them in response to hypothetical cases. The patterns were, to use Werbner's term (1989:21), microdramatic, iconically exhibiting categories of people, encounters, events, sacrifices, and medicines within a microcosm. I will examine two hypothetical cases which Pa Biyare constructed during my instruction.

In the first case the pebbles were aligned in this way:

```
□ □     □ □     □ □     □ □

□ □     □ □     □ □     □ □

□ □     □ □     □ □     □ □

□ □     □ □     □ □     □   —  white stone indicating
                                a "white" sacrifice
```

This pattern of twos, Pa Biyare explained, resembles a crowd of people and indicated death, because a funeral is the most common reason for such a gathering. He noted, however, that the same pattern would indicate good fortune if a client were asking whether he should make his farm in a particular place, or if he would succeed in a chieftaincy election. Pa Biyare's daughter, who was also learning *an-bere* from him and was perhaps for this reason more able to verbally articulate the basis for particular interpretations, interjected this explanation: "*An-bere* are showing a crowd. If you farm and get plenty of rice, plenty of people will come. If you get the chieftaincy, a crowd will come. If there is a death, people will come for the funeral." Pa Biyare added that the single white stone at the bottom right of the pattern showed that a "white" sacrifice should be made; for example, a white sheep, chicken, kola nuts, cloth, or rice flour cake.

The second alignment was as follows:

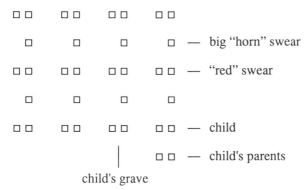

child's grave

Pa Biyare indicated the stones marked above, explaining that this pattern showed the imminent death of a person who had killed a child through witchcraft: "The person has eaten the child through witchcraft, and the child has died and been buried. The child's parents have sworn the man with the big 'horn' swear and a 'red' swear." A "swear" (*an-sasa* or *an-sena*) is a collection of harmful medicines which is sent to locate and afflict an unknown wrongdoer by ritualized verbal swearing (see Littlejohn 1960a), a "horn" swear being one which is contained in an animal horn and a "red" swear being one in which lethal "red" medicines are employed. Pa Biyare based his interpretations, as did many other *an-bere* diviners, upon stones located in the right-hand columns (which is consistent with the general Temne signification in which right is associated with openness to public view and left with concealment and obscurity; see Littlejohn 1973), and often upon those which are conspicuous in some way. A deeply reddish brown stone, for instance, was identified as showing the "red" swear.[5]

Pa Biyare said that his knowledge of how to interpret the patterns came from the spirits, and other *an-bere* diviners sometimes gaze into a small mirror in which they see spirits (especially their patron spirit) as an additional source of inspiration. Thus, although the pattern is built up by the methodical selection of odd and even numbers of stones, the crucial part of the divination is the inspired and holistic interpretation of this pattern. The diviner's perception of the relationship between the microcosm of stones and a wider reality, a perception which is attributed to the external agency of the spirits, is "revelatory" in Turner's terms, although this revelation is largely confined to the diviner. To the client, the diviner's barely audible prayers and cryptic manipulation of the pebbles underscore the "darkness" surrounding the source of the diviner's knowledge, but there is a movement toward clarity as the session progresses, when the diviner shows the client the correspondence between the stones' pattern and his or her own predicament and goes on to give more systematized verbal instructions concerning the ingredients and procedure of the sacrifice to be made.

But this explanatory clarity rarely extends to the naming of specific wrongdoers, such accusation being considered improper in private divination because it is said to cause social disruption. Private diviners who do reveal names are said to accrue *an-hake*, "sin," an Islamic-derived concept denoting an external force sent by God (*K-uru* or *Allah*) which will sooner or later bring about the exposure of the miscreant's wrongdoings. Rather than making specific accusations, private diviners use euphemistic language and veiled innuendos. If a diviner "sees" that a woman client's co-wife is a witch who is attacking her children, for instance, she may be told that "in your house, there is a woman who is a bad person," "bad person" (*o-wuni u les*) being a euphemism for "witch." She will usually be told to make a sacrifice which will cause the witch's *an-hake* to "fall upon her," bringing her witchcraft into the open by, for example, making her spontaneously confess her hidden deeds.

This is in marked contrast to the witch-finding procedure of *ka-gbak*, in which the calling of a public divination performance is itself an acknowledgment that social relations have already been disrupted. This may have been occasioned by a diagnosis of witchcraft given to a senior man consulting a private diviner, by some event, such as a sudden death, or by a dream involving a naked person, the cooking and eating of meat, or an attack by a wild animal, all of which indicate witchcraft. No *an-hake* falls upon those who divine publicly, since they are called in to restore peace by accusing individuals and making their guilt directly visible to the community.

Ka-gbak is conducted by the male *ra-Gbenle* cult association, which in eastern Temneland is primarily responsible for chieftaincy ritual, especially the coronation and funeral ceremonies of chiefs (see Dorjahn 1959; Dalby and Kamara 1964). The secret activities of witches can be seen by *ra-Gbenle*'s "masked" spirit embodiments, *ma-neke*, who in this instance are not masked by the covering of the face but by their concealment from view behind a mat hung over the doorway of the house in which witches are thought to be active. Being spirits, *ma-neke* are able to see into and enter the witch world, *ro-seron*, to investigate those suspected of witchcraft. While on this journey into *ro-seron* they can be heard singing songs in eerie nasal voices by those gathered outside the house.

On the verandah, the suspects are interrogated one at a time by *ma-neke* and by *o-Gbenle*, the head of *ra-Gbenle*, who holds the association's bowl of liquid medicine. This interrogation involves a highly elaborate and specific use of language, in which people and past events are redefined in detail. For example: "This boy is a friend of the other boy. Together, they have a witch-gun.[6] When they shoot, they never miss. These boys are only small in *no-ru* but they are very powerful, and both always work together." Suspects are directly accused of being witches ("You are a witch, not so?"), and if they deny this they are usually cursed with the words "your foreskin" or "your clitoris," indicating that, like the uncircumcised, they are not full human beings. If they continue to assert that they are not witches, they are challenged to pay a large sum of money[7] in order to take an ordeal which consists of touching the mat over the door, the barrier separating the human beings outside from *ma-neke* inside, after drinking the medicine; their witchcraft is made visible by involuntary defecation upon doing so. Most of these accused cannot afford this sum, however, and eventually confess to being witches, thereby contributing to the public redefinition of their identity by this performative statement.

This process is termed "splitting a divination," *ka-gbay ma-then*. *Ma-then*, which is only used of public divination, denotes all specific verbal accusations and manifestations of a person's guilt, and specific predictions about the future (usually involving sudden deaths or fires). The expression *ka-gbay ma-then* was explained to me as follows: "The divination is like a box that you split and reveal the truth." The image of the box here is significant. Boxes are used by lineage heads and by ordinary individuals to contain stones inhabited by lineage or personal spirits; they are also used by cult associations to house their most sacred objects. In southern and eastern Temneland the head of the former chief, for instance, is kept in one of the living chief's sacred boxes; likewise the spirit of *an-Poro*, the major male cult association, is carried through the town ceremonially by *an-Poro* officials in a gold box wrapped in white cloth (Lamp 1981).

Power, Truth, and Divination

In the complementary spheres of private and public divination, then, we find encapsulated the related contrasts of predominantly revelatory/predominantly analytical ritual and "truth as enigma"/legalistic, performative truth. Although not all methods of private divination involve the construction of a material microcosm, common to all of them is the spirit-inspiration, the minimal and euphemistic use of words and the location in a private room, behind a closed door, which characterize *an-bere* divination. Likewise, common to all forms of public divnation as well as *ka-gbak* is the strong "classificatory" element, the construction of sharp definitions. Through its sifting of evidence in its reconstruction of past events, as well as its performative use of specific verbal categorizations, *ka-gbak* is highly "analytical" in Turner's terms, despite its close resemblance to spirit mediumship, which is often assumed to be a less "rational" form of divination.

The contrasts outlined above are, furthermore, connected to the ways in which power and authority both constitute and are constituted by the two aspects of divinatory truth explored here. In a previous paper (Shaw 1985), I describe the interrelation of gender and divination. The majority of private diviners' clients are women, usually with sick children or reproductive problems, and are thereby regarded with suspicion by men, who see them as liable to make use of the negative ethical potential of diviners' knowledge. Moreover, just as the notion of *an-hake* makes the specific accusation of individuals ineffective and usually pointless in private divination, for a female client to use such an accusation in order to effect the redefinition of a co-wife would be impossible, not only because she has no authority to do so, but also because such a course of action would be unthinkable. Public divination, on the other hand, is monopolized mainly by senior men, since only a household head is entitled to call a public divination. It is consequently he who gives those who conduct the divination performance his own construction of events and individuals, which is usually in accord with his own interests, and which is then "objectified" through the public redefinition of the situation effected by the divination. Through his authority as household head, he thus has control over the "authorizing discourse" of public divination, through which performative, legalistic truth is constituted, and in which the use of the ethically ambivalent secret knowledge of the diviner is defined as acceptable and responsible.

Notes

Fieldwork in Sierra Leone was conducted over fifteen months in 1977 and 1978, in the village of Petbana Masimbo (Bombali Sebora Chiefdom) and the towns of Makeni, Magburaka, Matotoka, Freetown, and Koidu. Financial support was provided by the (then) Social Science Research Council of Great Britain, the Emslie Horniman Anthropological Research Fund, and the Central Research Fund of the University of London. I wish to thank Philip Peek for his encouragement and David Parkin for his comments on this paper.

1. Among many Temne Muslims, heaven and hell are added to these three invisible worlds.

2. Littlejohn explores this extrasocial origin in relation to lateral symbolism and concludes that "not-being-in-relation-with-others is for them [the Temne] a condition of perception of truth" (1973:298).

3. *An-bere* is not defined as an "Islamic" divination method, however.

4. Some diviners alternatively arranged the stones into four rows and a variable number of columns.

5. For a fuller account of *an-bere* divination, see Shaw 1978.

6. A witch-gun, *a-pinkar a seron*, is a small hollow object such as a groundnut shell or papaya stalk in which is placed a minute object such as a grain of sand or a seed of finger-millet. The witch whispers the name of the victim to the "gun," then "shoots" it by igniting a small amount of gunpowder-like substance (*a-popa*) next to it. The object will enter the victim's body and kill them if it is not removed.

7. Le40, approximately fifty dollars at the time of my research in 1978.

References

Ahern, Emily M. 1982. "Rules in Oracles and Games." *Man* n.s. 17(2): 302–12.

Asad, Talal. 1983. "Anthropological Conceptions of Religion: Reflections on Geertz." *Man* n.s. 18:237–59.

Bellman, Beryl. 1984. *The Language of Secrecy: Symbols and Metaphors in Poro Ritual.* New Brunswick, N.J.: Rutgers University Press.

Crick, Malcolm. 1976. *Explorations in Language and Meaning: Towards a Semantic Anthropology.* London: Malaby Press.

———. 1982. "Anthropology of Knowledge." *Annual Review of Anthropology* 11: 287–313.

Dalby, David, and Abdul Kamara. 1964. "Vocabulary of the Temne Ragbenle Society." *Sierra Leone Language Review* 3:35–42.

Devisch, René. 1979. "Perspectives on Mediumistic Divination in Contemporary Sub-Saharan Africa." Paper presented to the Conference on Recent African Religious Studies, Afrika Studie-Centrum, Leiden (cited in Werbner 1985).

————. 1985. "Perspectives on Divination in Contemporary Sub-Saharan Africa." In *Theoretical Explorations in African Religion*, ed. W. van Binsbergen and M. Schoffeleers. London: Kegan Paul.

Dorjahn, Vernon R. 1959. "The Organisation and Functions of the *Ragbenle* Society of the Temne." *Africa* 29:156–70.

Douglas, Mary. 1975. "If the Dogon . . ." *Implicit Meanings*. London: Routledge and Kegan Paul.

Evans-Pritchard, E. E. 1937. *Witchcraft, Oracles and Magic among the Azande*. Oxford: Clarendon Press.

Finnegan, Ruth. 1969. "How to Do Things with Words: Performative Utterances among the Limba of Sierra Leone." *Man* n.s. 4:537–52.

Griaule, Marcel. 1937. "Notes sur la divination par le chacal." *Bulletin du Comité d'Etudes Historiques et Scientifiques de l'Afrique Occidentale Française* 20(1–2):113–41.

————. 1965. *Conversations with Ogotemmeli: An Introduction to Dogon Religious Ideas.* London: International African Institute/Oxford University Press.

Griaule, Marcel, and Germaine Dieterlen. 1954. "The Dogon of the French Sudan." In *African Worlds*, ed. D. Forde. London: International African Institute /Oxford University Press.

Harris, W. T., and Harry Sawyerr. 1968. *The Springs of Mende Belief and Conduct*. Freetown: Sierra Leone University Press.

Hollis, M., and S. Lukes, eds., 1982. *Rationality and Relativism*. Oxford: Blackwell.

Horton, Robin. 1964. "Kalabari Diviners and Oracles." *Odu* 1:3–16.

————. 1967. "African Traditional Thought and Western Science, Part II." *Africa* 37: 155–87.

————. 1982. "Tradition and Modernity Revisited." In *Rationality and Relativism*, ed. M. Hollis and S. Lukes. Oxford: Blackwell.

Jackson, Michael. 1978. "An Approach to Kuranko Divination." *Human Relations* 31:117–38.

————. 1983. "Knowledge of the Body." *Man* n.s. 18:327–45.

Lamp, Frederick, 1978. "Frogs into Princes: The Temne Rabai Initiation." *African Arts* 11:38–49.

————. 1981. "The Poro House." Paper presented at the African Studies Association meeting, Bloomington, Ind.

Lessa, William A. 1959. "Divining by Knots in the Carolines." *Journal of the Polynesian Society* 68:188–204.

Lienhardt, R. G. 1969. *Divinity and Experience: The Religion of the Dinka*. Oxford: Clarendon Press.

Littlejohn, James. 1960a. "The Temne Ansasa." *Sierra Leone Studies* n.s. 14:32–35.

————. 1960b. "The Temne House." *Sierra Leone Studies* n.s. 14:63–79.

————. 1963. "Temne Space." *Anthropological Quarterly* 36:1–17.

————. 1973. "Temne Right and Left: An Essay on the Choreography of Everyday Life." In *Right and Left: Essays on Dual Symbolic Classification*, ed. R. Needham. Chicago: University of Chicago Press.

Overing, Joanna, ed., 1985. *Reason and Morality*. London: Tavistock.

Park, G. K. 1963. "Divination and Its Social Contexts." *Journal of the Royal Anthropological Institue* 93:195–209.

Parkin, David. 1979. "Straightening the Paths from Wilderness: The Case of Divinatory Speech." *Journal of the Anthropological Society of Oxford* 10:147–60.

Paulme, Denise. 1937. "La divination par les chacals chez les Dogon de Sanga." *Journal de la Société des Africanistes* 7:1–15.

Pelton, Robert D. 1980. *The Trickster in West Africa*. Berkeley: University of California Press.

Shaw, Rosalind. 1978. "*An-bere*: A Traditional Form of Temne Divination." *Africana Research Bulletin* 9:3–24.

———. 1985. "Gender and the Structuring of Reality in Temne Divination." *Africa* 55:286–303.

Steiner, Franz B. 1954. "Chagga Truth: A Note on Gutmann's Account of the Chagga Concept of Truth." *Africa* 24:364–69.

Turner, Victor. 1975. *Revelation and Divination in Ndembu Ritual*. Ithaca, N.Y.: Cornell University Press.

Werbner, Richard P. 1989. "Tswapong Wisdom Divination: Making the Hidden Seen." *Ritual Passage, Sacred Journey: The Process and Organization of Religous Movement*. Washington, D.C.: Smithsonian Institution Press and Manchester: Manchester University Press.

Susan Reynolds Whyte

Knowledge and Power in Nyole Divination

In his great work of ethnographic fiction, *Joseph and His Brothers*, Thomas Mann touches upon central problems in the anthropology of divination. Joseph has been summoned before Pharaoh, who, after conversing with the young "sooth-sayer," orders him to interpret the strange royal dreams whose meaning has eluded the "botchers from the book house." The way in which understanding emerges from their dialogue puzzles the god-king. "You have a way," he says, "of making it seem as though everything is all beautifully clear whereas so far you have only told me what I knew already." Mann makes Joseph reply, "Pharaoh errs . . . if he thinks he does not know. His servant can do no more than to prophesy to him what he already knows." And again after talk of fat cows and lean years, Joseph declares that it is Pharaoh who has prophesied. But Amenhotep contradicts him. "No, you are just saying that. . . . You made it seem as though I myself interpreted because you are a child of stratagems and descended from rogues. But why could I have not done it before you came? I only knew what was false but not what was true. For true is this interpretation, that I know in my very soul; my own dream knows itself again in the interpretation" (Mann 1968: 142–45). And true the divination did indeed prove to be; the knowledge allowed Pharaoh to consolidate and extend his power over Egypt and beyond.

In the drier prose of social science, we might say that Mann causes Joseph and Pharaoh to confront issues in the sociology of knowledge: who knows, how meaning emerges in a consultation to resolve uncertainty, and how divination fits into the dynamics of power.

The Nyole of Eastern Uganda, whose divination practices are examined here, did not have kings, were not particularly concerned to prophesy the future, and seldom consulted diviners about their dreams. Yet the problem of who knows the truth and how it is legitimately recognized in divination was raised by diviners and clients alike. Like Joseph, Nyole diviners had to establish an interpretation which the inquiring party recognized as true. And like Pharaoh, Nyole consulters very definitely knew what was false. Through divinatory dialogue between the two, an attempt was made to resolve uncertainty in favor of a specific interpretation of reality. This process of communication and construction is one important theme in the analysis that follows.

The other theme concerns relations and processes that are less amenable to direct observation. We want to know not only how communication proceeds but also what or whom it concerns. Joseph and the god-king were establishing a truth about all of Egypt. In the mundane Nyole world the object of divination was almost always the suffering of an individual. This victim of affliction might be the client, but often the sufferer was not present. The client consulted on behalf of someone, as Pharaoh asked about Egypt, over which he had authority and for which he was responsible. From the Nyole point of view, a person who "goes to ask" about the misfortune of another does so because he is concerned, because the affliction of "his person" is his misfortune too. I shall suggest that, at the same time, such a consulter exerts a kind of interpretive domination, proposing a social and moral identity for the suffering individual.

Nyole Knowledge about Misfortune and Personhood

Nyole divined almost exclusively concerning the causes and appropriate remedy of misfortune. Like the Ndembu (Turner 1975:209), Nyole sought retrospective knowledge in divination. Confronted by problems such as sickness, barrenness, death of livestock, and school failure, Nyole responded pragmatically—waiting to see if the trouble would pass, admonishing the child to study harder, or administering Western or "African" medicine to relieve symptoms. Such symptomatic treatment was sufficient unless troubles were prolonged, repetitive, or acutely dangerous. Then Nyole said, "there is a reason" (*erio esonga*) or "let us go to inquire" (*hwende ohwebusa*) or "let us take a divining fee" (*hung'ambe omuhemba*), indicating the need to divine about the cause of the problem in order to supplement symptomatic with etiological treatment.

Although Nyole might say that they were going to divine to find out whether or not there was a "reason" behind some problem, divination in fact always established a supernatural cause for misfortune. Of the hundreds of divinations of which I have records, only two concluded that there was "no cause" for a misfortune, that it was "just sickness" or death from old age.[1] In effect, the decision to divine was a decision that a misfortune had a deeper meaning.

That deeper meaning was determined through a process in which many possible meanings were confronted. The diviner's hut was a place where an abundance of interpretations pressed themselves upon the uncertain client: from this extraordinary and confusing excess of significance, some usable knowledge had to be selected so that the consulter could leave with a satisfying interpretation.

Nyole attributed misfortune to persons (living or dead) or to spirits. These agents were usually related to the victim of misfortune; they had motives for causing suffering, and there was a moral element in the relationship between victim and agent. As in many African cultures, the attribution of misfortune to a human or spirit agent was a statement about the victim's social and ritual relationships, and therefore about social identity.

Three categories of misfortune agents emphasized the moral universe of kinship. Senior relatives (both matrilateral and patrilateral) were thought able to curse (*ohulama, ohung'waba*) if their rights were not honored, if bridewealth was not paid and redistributed properly, if they were not treated respectfully. Ancestral ghosts (*emigu j'abafu*) were said to send misfortune to remind their descendants of their obligations to commemorate them through sacrifice and ceremonies. Similarly, clan spirits (*ekuni*) could make demands upon members of the clans with which they were associated (see Whyte and Whyte 1987). Attributing misfortune to these agents emphasized one's identity as a junior kinsman (related to a curser), as a member of a local descent group (descended from a particular forefather), or as a member of a patrilineal clan (associated with a specific clan spirit). The rituals prescribed to address these causes dramatized kinship identity by bringing kinsmen together for the common expression of moral ideals.

Opposed to these categories of moral, kin-related agents was the sorcerer (*omulogi*), who sent misfortune not as a punishment for failed obligations but out of such immoral motives as envy, jealousy, hatred, and vengefulness. Sorcery was the most dangerous cause of misfortune, and it was the cause to which death was most commonly attributed. (In illustration, one Nyole diviner remarked that even Jesus died by the malicious act of Judas, another human being.) Nyole suspected personal enemies of sorcery—not people who were irredeemably and totally evil and harmful toward everyone but persons who had specific motives for striking at the victim. Here too social relationships (albeit negative ones) were the mode of interpreting misfortune.

A final category of little spirits (*obusambwa*) and foreign spirits (*emisambwa miganda, miswahili*, etc.) were thought to have no preexisting relationships to their victims. These spirits were said to attack women and children primarily, with the significant exception of some foreign spirits which possessed both men and women in connection with divination. Elsewhere I have suggested that this aspect of the Nyole view of misfortune is a logical opposition to the emphasis on social relationship and serves as a counterpart to the dominant, male-oriented model of misfortune (Whyte 1981).

The Nyole view of misfortune is based on a relational concept of the person. To a large extent, a person is defined in terms of relations to external agents rather than in terms of internal psychological or biological states and processes. The difference between the Nyole concept and our own is very clear in the diagnosis of sickness. Western medicine subjects disease to what Foucault (1975) called "the medical gaze"; sick bodies are examined and compared in the clinic in order to identify pathological processes. Nyole were not unaware of pathological symptoms, but the diagnosis of serious sickness, the identification of what it *really* was, did not involve the clinical examination of the ailing individual. Diagnosis had to do primarily with social and ritual relations rather than the symptoms of the individual body and mind. Thus the diviner as diagnostician did not need to see the suffering individual at all. But he did need to examine the afflicted person's relations to spirits and people in consultation with someone who knew them intimately. Together they cast a "divinatory gaze" upon pathologies of relationship, defining a social identity for the suffering person.

Nyole regarded diviners as specialists who could tell them something they themselves did not know. Yet the specialist model of misfortune differed from the folk model only in that the specialist was aware of more detail. A diviner knew more techniques of sorcery, more names and characteristics of little spirits. But the basic structure of the explanatory models held by client and specialist was identical. This contrasts with the Fipa situation described by Willis (1973:370) in which the "scientific" theory of specialists elaborates more causal categories than the "lay" theory. And it is very different from the relation between biomedical expert and layman in that the former has knowledge and interpretations of pathologies which the latter does not share. With the intensification of the medical gaze made possible by X rays, CAT scans, and lab tests, a doctor can identify pathologies of which the patient is unaware, but a Nyole diviner must rely upon his client for knowledge about the state of a suffering person's relationships to spirits and other persons. In this matter of personhood, the specialist has no monopoly upon knowledge. As we shall see, this leads to a rich flow of communication during the divination seance.

Types of Diviners

Divination (*ohulagula*) was a distinct function performed by specialists (*abalagusi, abafumu*), who were paid a standard divination fee (*omuhemba*)— in 1970, two shillings. The divination (*endagu*) consisted of a diagnosis and a prescription for treatment. Most diviners specialized in some form of treatment as well. Some called themselves *abagangi* (from *ohuganga*, "to treat"), emphasizing their functions as healers in dealing with little and foreign spirits and administering herbal medicines. Some were also known as *abang'eng'a*, from the verb meaning "to protect"; through countermedicine they were thought able to guard people and homes against sorcery, and they were usually said to sell sorcery medicines too.

At the time of our fieldwork, there were two principal methods of divination in Bunyole: spirit possession and examination of Arabic books. "Those of the gourd rattles" (*ab'esaasi, ab'enyengo*) had a working relationship with teams of spirits who possessed them and spoke through them to reveal the causes of a client's misfortune (see figure). *Lamuli* performed calculations and consulted books of geomancy; although their technique was relatively new in Bunyole, they manipulated the same etiological model of misfortune used by the gourd rattle diviners. Both men and women could be diviners, but of the thirty-eight concerning whom I obtained information, fewer than one-third were women. Nearly half of the spirit diviners (ten of twenty-three) were women, but none of the twelve book diviners were women. This Arabic form of divination has become increasingly popular since the 1920s, and consequently divination as a whole has become a male-dominated specialty. Three of the thirty-eight diviners, including one woman, practiced forms of divination other than spirit possession and book examination.

Spirit Colleagues

Spirit diviners were thought to be chosen by spirit agents to take up divination. They may well have been familiar with the work through a close relative, but people did not think of becoming a spirit diviner in terms of apprenticeship. Rather some form of affliction, such as impotence, illness, and strange behavior, was attributed to spirits who wished to "settle" (*ohwihala*) and to work with the person they had chosen. Not everyone who received such an interpretation of misfortune became a diviner; it was possible to "say goodbye to" (*ohusebula*) divining spirits with a sacrifice, thus refusing the call. But those who accepted the call established a permanent relationship to their spirits.

A house called *amasawo*, the divining hut, was built in the compound for these spirits, and they were thought to stay there. Some diviners seemed to conceive

Heneriko Were, a Nyole diviner, in front of his divining hut with Emmanuel Mudoto, one of the author's field assistants, 1971. The diviner is holding his gourd rattles; the skin upon which he sits when divining is at his feet. Between the two men, near the hut, is a bundle of grass associated with the divining spirit. *Photo by Susan Reynolds Whyte.*

of their relationship to their spirits as similar to marriage. Two women mentioned that their spirits were like their husbands; they had to sleep in the *amasawo* with them.

Two experienced spirit diviners, a man and a woman, were called as "midwives" (*abalerwa*) to initiate the new diviner. They came first to plant a centerpole where the divining hut should be built, and later, when all was ready, they returned for the installation itself. This involved the sacrifice of chickens or goats for all the spirits involved and in some cases for the clan spirit of the initiate. Chickens were killed at a crossroads "to open the way" for the spirits to come in. All night long, beer was drunk and the "midwives" shook their gourd rattles. The spirits possessed the initiate, causing him or her to tremble (*ohusamira*), fall, speak strangely, and occasionally to run into the bush. One diviner told how his spirits had caused him to go into the bush and eat leaves like a goat, coming back with some in his mouth. In "settling" the spirits, Nyole seemed to be domesticating them, bringing them from outside, from the road or the bush to live in a home. They were straightening the paths from wilderness in the terms used by Parkin (1982; see also Parkin's essay in this volume).

The fact that the officiating diviners were not seen as teachers fits with the conception of gourd rattle diviners as mediums for their spirits. The spirits were the authorities, the active agents. When I asked one diviner what his "midwives" had taught him about divination when he was initiated, he replied, "Those people did not teach me anything, they just got drunk. The spirit is what taught me to divine."

What or who were these spirits which entered into such an active and useful relationship with human beings? The most important spirit of divination was Hing'ira or *ehifumu*, literally the "divination thing." Nyole said that *ehifumu* was composed of the spirits of people who died long ago. These spirits came from the brothers of the mothers of the diviner's mother and father—that is, from the diviner's great-uncles. Thus they were spirits to whom one was distantly related, but they were not named individuals. There was an androgynous quality about *ehifumu*: it came from both the maternal and paternal sides and was composed of the spirits of both men and women. Therefore, it had to be settled by both a male and a female diviner. Some diviners had two bundles of grass in the divining hut, one for the male and one for the female aspects of *ehifumu*.

In the old days, people said, diviners used only *ehifumu*. But in 1970 virtually all gourd rattle diviners had "foreign spirits" as well. One diviner told us that these spirits came to Bunyole on the roads built by the Europeans. Such spirits were sometimes called *emandwa* (c.f. Beattie 1967:222–23); they were named individuals whose provenance and sex were specified and who could even cause their medium to speak in appropriate foreign languages. Most of them were said to be Ganda; others were Soga, Swahili, Gwere, and Gisu.[2] They were settled in the divining hut at the same time or after *ehifumu*.

Divination sessions, which were private, took place in the divining hut with the diviner seated upon a skin (*ehyambi*), sometimes behind a partition. The clients, also seated, were always more clearly visible to the diviner than he or she was to them. The diviner began by shaking the gourd rattles rhythmically; in the small hut the sound was quite deafening. Sometimes he or she sang special songs to please the spirits. Then the diviner might begin to make strange noises —snorting, growling, belching, crying. The spirits would begin to speak then. One diviner explained that "the spirits come like a cold wind and stay in my throat and I don't know anything, I just speak."

Often the client could not understand what the spirits said; either their voices were indistinct or they spoke loudly and rapidly in incomprehensible words that were said to be other languages. The diviner had then to tell the client, in a more normal voice, what the spirits were saying. The spirits could speak through the diviner to the client or they could speak to the diviner who then passed the message on to the client. Some diviners apparently used ventriloquism; others seemed to be carrying on a conversation with other voices that were drowned out by the noise of the gourd rattles.

Sometimes the potential agents of misfortune themselves (sorcerers, cursers, spirits) seemed to speak to or through the diviner. In one session I recorded, the diviner kept speaking to indistinct voices and then saying to his clients, "the mother's brother is here quarreling," and later, "the father's sister has come to complain" and "now here is another one. . . ." In the cases which this same diviner recorded himself, he usually wrote that "Hing'ira said . . ."; that is, he wrote as if the divining spirit had spoken to the clients through him. But sometimes the diviner wrote as if the agent had spoken through him: "The mother's brother said, 'bring her so that I may pour water on her, bring her with 20 shillings, there is no one else but me.'"

In either case, the special quality of the spirit diviner was the ability to speak as another being. Listening to seances, one had the sense of at least three participants: the client, the diviner, and another being or beings (whether divining spirits or potential agents of misfortune), with the diviner mediating between the client and the unseen beings.

Examining Arabic Books

The system of divination by calculation and examination of Arabic books is widespread in East Africa.[3] The *lamuli* (from the Arabic *Khatt ar-raml*) were Muslim, but in Bunyole a majority of their clients were Christian. Of 101 persons seen for divination and/or treatment by a well-known *lamuli*, 37 were Roman Catholic, 34 Protestant (Anglican), and 16 Muslim. (Religion was not recorded for 14.) *Lamuli* seemed to attract clients from other ethnic groups, and this is in some sense a national or international technique.

This method of divination seems to have been introduced into Bunyole by an "Arab" trader who settled in Busolwe in 1902. He and other Swahili or Arab traders taught it to local Muslims. It is still a technique learned by apprenticeship, often to Muslims elsewhere. Of the two *lamuli* I knew well, one had studied with a Swahili man at a trading center in the next county and the other had learned in Mombasa where he lived for a time.

The *lamuli* saw their work as a science, based on calculation and reference to books of learning and wisdom. Numbers were an important input in their consultations, and they noted the time at which the client arrived. For this purpose, Yahaya, a well-known *lamuli*, had a fancy clock in the "office" where he received his clients. Each letter of the consulter's (and/or the sufferer's) name was said to represent a number, and the sum of these as well as the arrival time figured in calculations made upon a slate. Clients who came at a "bad" time were asked to return later. Time and its divisions were an important theme. Yahaya said: "My science is that of the seven days, I know how every hour is called and what can be done at that time."

After initial calculations, the *lamuli* referred to his books. Yahaya claimed to use books from Arabia; he mentioned *Sa'atili Habari*, "for examining the time," and *Abu Mashari Faraki*, for revealing the causes that operate in a particular time. He explained that this latter book helped him to know what kind of person had caused the client's troubles, where medicine was buried, and what type of sacrifice was needed.[4]

Book diviners proceeded by looking up appropriate passages and reading phrases aloud in Arabic. But since their clients did not understand, they had to translate for them and explain the relevance of the passages to the client's problem. As the client commented and conveyed more information, the *lamuli* might refer to other passages in his books. As in divination by spirit possession there was a three-way conversation, with the diviner mediating in this case between the client and the authoritative book.

Clients of *lamuli* diviners emphasized that these practitioners were able to find the truth without the help of spirits. "They do not deafen you with gourd rattles and strange noises," remarked one regular client, himself a pillar of the Catholic church. "They just examine their books quietly." A Muslim client said: "They do not lie while taking your money; they use only the book and the help of Allah."

The appeal of the book diviners seemed to lie in their "high technology" access to knowledge. The emphasis on measurement, counting, the division of time as measured by clocks, writing, reading, and books was part of what Nyole saw as a powerful way of ordering the world.[5] Considering the way in which the *lamuli* system with its books and writing has become established in Bunyole, one is reminded of the parallel which the Zande saw between their oracles and European ways of knowing. As Evans-Pritchard notes: "Azande often say: 'the poison oracle does not err, it is our paper. What your paper is to you the poison oracle is to us' for they see in the art of writing the source of a European's knowledge, accuracy, memory of events, and predictions of the future" (1937:263). Although writing came to be associated with mission education and the colonial regime in Uganda, it was in fact the Arabs who first introduced it, and it was Muslim *lamuli* who usefully applied it to the analysis of life's problems in Bunyole.

Two Systems or One?

The two forms of Nyole divination fit the opposition proposed by Zuesse (1979: 212) between "possession" and "wisdom" divination. In the former, ultimate reality is personalized and spirit agents communicate messages through and to human beings. In the latter, personal experience is subordinated to a profounder cosmic order which emphasizes atomistic, impersonal elements. Thus the *lamuli* make use of number, measuring, and writing as opposed to violent trance states. Zuesse notes the complexity of methods and long training periods of wisdom diviners, the authority gained by traveling far away for training, and the importance of these diviners as innovators.

This distinction between a personalized and an impersonal cosmic order was important at the level of technique rather than epistemology. A Nyole client returning from a divination by a *lamuli* said that at one point the diviner seemed about to mention a "reason" for his children's illness that had to do with his (the father's) side of the family. But then the diviner took up another explanation instead. The client commented: "The ancestral spirits were about to come, but they left." (This man had earlier been "reminded" by his dead grandfather to offer a goat.) Clearly for this man, the book diviner's methods gave access to a personalized spirit world. For him and most other Nyole there were two modes of divinatory approach to the same underlying reality.

In Bunyole, another more practical distinction seemed to be important for understanding the two types of divination. I mentioned earlier that most diviners also specialized in some type of treatment. Many gourd rattle diviners also performed ceremonies for getting rid of various bothersome little and foreign spirits or for settling divining spirits. Having spirit colleagues themselves, they seemed more aware of all types of spirit agencies, including ancestor and clan spirits, which were placated with rituals performed by kin. *Lamuli* diviners were often also *abang'eng'a,* "protectors" or medicine men who dealt with sorcery and even claimed to be able to "tie" curses by medicine, thus obviating the need for a family ritual of reconciliation. This use of medicine to obviate ritual and relational forms of therapy has potentially far-reaching implications in that it treats persons by the application of powerful substances, "liberating" therapy from the personal relations in which it would otherwise be embedded (see Whyte 1988).

Book diviners were very aware of human agency in their clients' misfortunes. In analyzing the records kept by two book diviners and one spirit diviner, I found that the spirit diviner diagnosed human agents (cursers or sorcerers) in 29 percent of his cases, while the two *lamuli* found human agency in 80 percent and 63 percent respectively. The relatively low proportion of sorcery (as opposed to cursing) diagnoses by the spirit diviner was particularly striking. Diviners differed in their diagnostic orientations and this fit with the different types of treatment which they carried out in addition to divination. The book diviners, who used modern technology and had learned their skills as medicine men from foreign sources, were more oriented toward sorcery as an explanation.

Yet these divergent patterns reflect more than differences between diviners; clients were aware of the differing skills and orientations of spirit and book diviners and they chose their specialist accordingly. Suspecting certain explanations for their troubles, clients selected a diviner who was particularly sensitive and competent in that area. Clients did not choose between two different systems of divination so much as between different alternatives within a single system of understanding.

A Grandfather's Case

In January 1971 I tape recorded a consultation between an older man and a gourd rattle diviner. As the consultation proceeds, it becomes clear that the man has come to divine the reason for the sickness of his baby granddaughter, his son's child. The problem is said to lie with his co-parents-in-law, that is, with his son's wife's father and father's brother. The bride's father's brother, appearing in the divination, claims he made a bridewealth loan to her father, who should have repaid it when his daughter married. When he failed to do so, the man cursed his niece to have a sick child. Later "little spirits" were also diagnosed. The session began with the deafening noise of the rattles, drowning out what the diviner was saying. When the rattles stopped, the diviner (D) spoke to his client (C).

> *D* (gourd rattles): Big Man . . . they are saying that the case is at home, it is in the home.
> *C*: That case, I do not know it. But if I were wise I would not [need to] come.
> *D* (interval of gourd rattles): They say we should send away the matter of moaning [sickness].
> *C*: Let the moaning come.
> *D* (gourd rattles): They are saying that the sickness is contesting with a child. Is it true?
> *C*: When it catches the child, it has caught you.
> *D*: Isn't it so that children are of many types. There is a real child which came from your body. There is also the child who came from the child you produced. Do you send this one away too?
> *C*: The child who is removed [the child of your child] is also your child.
> *D* (gourd rattles): Big man, messages are coming here too. They say that perhaps where there are dead people . . . Perhaps they will appear. But let us first speak with the living person; he also talks with the dead. That's who he talks with, it is not to say that he talks alone [implying that a living person invokes the ancestors in a curse]. So there are many types of living people. There is . . . the father of this person, the mothers of this person—perhaps the father's sister—perhaps the grandmother—perhaps the sister of the mother —perhaps the brother—so I want to know who first said 'thank you for asking.' He answered and said another thing on the side of women, except I am on the side of men. I said no you are his mother's brother. You may be his father, or his brother or his elder; no, on the side of uncles, leave it—and the side of grandmothers, leave it on the side of the brother also leave, but go where it says father.

C: Yee. He said that it is the parent himself who has caught the child.

D: Yee. When you go and get a child [bride for a son], you bring her, and she gives birth to a child, that is also yours. . . . This is a grandchild—and you also answered that when you go and produce a child and it also produces, that one is also your child.

C: And it is why I say that person [the curser] must not hide, he should come in public, he should not hide, a person who just comes to kill, that one always hides that he has come to kill.

D (gourd rattles): This case which this man is starting on, he says, thank you for bringing the case. But you are a Nyole. When you get a seed and give your friend, whether of cowpeas or of millet, you say, my friend, here is millet, go and sow. At planting time, he sows and that millet yields abundantly, and when he repays the loan, doesn't he repay extra [with interest]? That is where my case came from.

C: What I haven't yet learned is this—the person who has come to make a case with me here in this room—is it my co-parent-in-law or his brother?

D (gourd rattles): . . . let him know that I am the in-law who is called the brother of his real co-parent-in-law.

C: But how did that case come?

D (gourd rattles): Now I am going to tell him the facts. When you get a goat and you give to your brother—you get a cow and give to your brother—and he goes to buy a person and later with luck she produces a child for which bridewealth is paid—does he repay the goat or doesn't he? Does he repay that cow or doesn't he? And if he doesn't repay it, don't you quarrel? That is the millet which I have talked about saying I have given him millet seed to go and sow and it yielded abundantly and can't he repay with interest.

C: Ah, for me, I say let Gassani [here meaning the divining spirit] reconsider. They came, but I think they are deceiving me about that debt. Perhaps there is another case. If he is deceiving me in bringing this one, for me I still refuse.

D: You refuse this case?

C: Yes.

D (gourd rattles): This man is asking you—true you are saying that he should step aside. And yet, he says, were you there long ago? Did you know what happened in their home?

C: You people had sisters, and everyone was given his share from his sister— and everyone was assigned a sister.

D (gourd rattles): He says that it is true, we had our sisters, I'm not denying that. But if you have your sister and she goes to marry and the bridewealth they pay is little, and then when you go to marry and they negotiate a bridewealth that is greater than the one paid for your sister, and your brother sees that you fall short and he has something, doesn't he give to you?

C: He can give you . . . but the things of your home, I know them.

D (gourd rattles): This one is saying that you are lying. He says that he gave this person an animal for bridewealth. He is speaking for naught [that is, ground-lessly—he himself is lying].

C: Now you go away and if there are others, let them too come. I shall ask them. They themselves will be the ones to show me the way.

D (gourd rattles): These men might be telling falsehoods here. Maybe they have already done for us at home. The man called Namatango [little spirit], he is saying that they have not worked upon him, and the man called Nalulima [little spirit] has not been worked upon either. . . . Unless we are arguing for nothing—he should say so and send us away from here.

C: For me, why I argue with them, they bring lies for nothing. This is the firstborn. [The client does not believe that such little spirits attack a woman who has given birth for the first time and is still cooking together with her mother-in-law.]

D: You are dismissing these gentlemen, but they are refusing to go away from the divination. They are saying that we are with you. . . . [After a long discussion about the proper rituals demanded by these spirits, the client asks whether there are other reasons, that is other agents, as well. The spirits say no, and the client goes back to the matter of the bridewealth debt.]

C: I return to the man who came in the coat. Now I am just an in-law and you have come to kick in my divination. Now what do you want from your wife [granddaughter—Nyole observe the equivalence of alternate generations]? What can I do?

D (gourd rattles): This person says that you first argued a lot, and up to now you have not agreed that it's true. [The agent tells the client to go to his in-law, the father of his son's wife, and ask him if he owes his brother an animal.] Maybe he will say that I am deceiving and maybe he will immediately know that, ah, that's true. They will walk and reach where I am myself. I have the tongue which will answer. I know what I shall tell them. Let him first go and divine properly [together with his in-law]. If I have told untruths here, if I gave my brother nothing, neither a goat nor a cow, that will be the end of the matter. And so he may go and work upon the spirits alone.

C: You're a person who has just said he's tied someone with a rope. You came here and you say that you have a prisoner. I am the sick person. You want me to walk for nothing without telling me the final word?

D (gourd rattles): . . .the final word is, where there are three is where words are said. It is where they remove words [i.e., curses]—as for me, I shall pour water on the child [remove my curse]. . . . Where there is a child is where you can go and beg.

C: I want to leave here when I am all right. Your wife [granddaughter]. . . you have come to catch [her] but not to kill, so I like you . . . if you have a kind heart. I'll go and bring your wife to your home. If you will touch your wife, and if she gets well, then we shall know the difference. . . . Now if there are no other cases, let us take leave.

D (gourd rattles): Even if there are, go and finish these and leave the remaining cases for others.

Who Knows?

These selections from a longer consultation reveal fundamental characteristics of Nyole divination. The convention was that neither the diviner as an ordinary person nor the client knew the reasons behind the case being examined. Nyole said that to get the truth, one should not consult a diviner near home. A nearby diviner might be influenced by previous knowledge or local gossip, whereas a distant one would have to find things out using the power and authority of books or spirits. Because the diviner was not supposed to learn about the case in the ordinary way, he or she could not simply ask the consulter for the relevant details. The dialogue had to be carried on with the other voice; the diviner merely mediated. Likewise the client could not know the truth until it was revealed by the divination. In this case, the grandfather declared his ignorance: "if I were wise, I would not come." In two other recorded consultations, the clients also began by expressing their uncertainty. One consulter said that "thoughts fail us. . . that is what we want you to tell us, where it comes from and where its source is, where it ends and where it is going." Subsequently, this same person rejected all the suggestions made about the cause of the misfortune, pushing the divination in the direction of the curser she and her son suspected (see the case of the Dry Tree, Whyte 1990). Like Pharaoh, for whom Joseph divined, Nyole clients often had very definite preconceptions about what was false and even about what was true. But in principle the client could not know until the divination had created certainty.

Logically, it was divinatory authority, the spirits or Arabic book, which contained the truth about a case. But these sources were obscure and ambiguous; they had to be interpreted through the joint efforts of diviner and client. In Nyole divination, uncertainty was thus set up and emphasized so that it might be resolved. Obscurity took various forms. Book diviners read aloud in Arabic, which their clients did not understand. Gourd rattle diviners drowned out conversations with spirits by the noise of their pebble-filled calabashes. Sometimes they pronounced indistinct words in the growling or shrill voices of spirits; sometimes they seemed to be speaking strange languages. And even when they spoke in audible Lunyole, their meaning was often elusive. They used special idioms, circumlocutions, metaphors, and allusions. In the grandfather's case, the agent speaking to and through the diviner talked of millet seed to be repaid after the harvest; in case the client had misunderstood, he then explained that he was referring to a bridewealth loan which was to be returned when bridewealth was paid for the daughter of that marriage. Another common feature, which added to the confusion, was that the diviner regularly suggested that what he and the agents were saying might be untrue (cf. Werbner 1973:1421).

Parkin (1982; see also his essay in this volume) has shown how divination constructs simultaneities and then, through a process of sequencing, creates order out of confusion. In the grandfather's case, the diviner sometimes presents a number of possibilities at once, as when he says that "there are many types of living persons" and mentions a number of potential cursers. This confusion of possibilities must then be worked through, one by one, establishing causal chains of motivation, obligation, course of action, and result.

Sequencing was achieved through a dialogue in which diviners encouraged their clients to comment upon the suggestions made by the Arabic books or the spirits. One diviner confided to me that the most difficult clients were those who were not accustomed to divining and did not realize what role they had to play. In one of the consultations recorded, the client initially said little, remarking: "You are the one to speak to us; we have come so that you tell us." The diviner corrected this misapprehension, saying, "Don't you know that I speak to you and you also speak to me. I don't speak while you sit silent like one who can't talk. . . . Even if you go to a *lamuli*, he will ask you and you also answer." There had to be a dialogue, and the dialogue always included a metalevel of communication upon which information was sought and given concerning the quality of the other messages: is this true? am I right? do you believe it? shall we continue in this direction?

The diviner whose consultation was presented above used the rhetorical device that the agents appearing in the divination might be lying. They presented claims which had to be assessed and either accepted or rejected. The word *omusango*, which also means a court case, was often used. In another consultation, the client explicitly compared the seance to a legal proceeding, challenging the potential agents of misfortune to appear in the divination: "This a a court, come and we argue, he himself [referring to the diviner, perhaps] is the one to judge." It is clear in the grandfather's consultation that the diviner sought evidence, reminding the client of norms and expectations regarding relations with other people and spirits. But the client also weighed and judged, and decided which arguments had merit.

Thus one of the central mechanisms for establishing certainty was the phenomenon which Park called resistance. He explained that resistance to a client's proposals is inherent in chancelike mechanisms (such as the unpredictable effect of poison upon fowls or, in Bunyole, the number which determines the passage to be read from the Arabic book) and also in the professional independence of the diviner, who cannot simply label as truth every idea a client comes up with (Park 1967:238). The structure of Nyole divination provided a double resistance. The diviner resisted the client's proposals and opinions. And the client resisted some of the diviner's suggestions by denying their relevance or likelihood. The analogy of a court proceeding emphasizes the process of argument and counterargument; but unlike litigation, divination had to achieve consensus. The parties had ultimately to agree upon a conclusion.

A client once told me that in order to get the truth from a divination, one had to accuse the diviner of lying. The extent to which consulters actually resisted the proposals put forward by diviners seemed to depend upon their age and experience. The grandfather in the case above refused the diagnosis of cursing by his daughter-in-law's paternal uncle; but later, he returned to "the man in the coat" and seemed to accept the possibility. In the same way, he first rejected the idea of little spirits, but then allowed the diviner to convince him.

What is striking is that even when the consulter was less resistant, he always maintained a degree of autonomy. The diviner solicited and respected the client's opinion; he had to convince him; he could not just tell him what was the matter. The importance of the client's agreement to the diagnosis was clearly illustrated by the records kept in Lunyole by a gourd rattle diviner. He was asked to record basic information about number, provenance, and gender of his clients, the type of problems and what the divination revealed about the cause and treatment. No mention was made about the client's attitude, yet in nearly all of his entries, he noted the consulter's acceptance of the divinatory conclusion: "They replied, true, this is the second time we have divined [the agency of] the clan spirit," or "They replied, true that is how it is."

The autonomy of the client was brought home to me in discussing the causes of death with a spirit diviner. I asked him why sorcery was always said to be the cause, and whether spirits could kill people. He replied that they could indeed, but that his clients would not believe him if he found that their relative had been killed by spirits rather than human enemies. They would just go to a diviner elsewhere, he said. Apparently clients could be very stubborn. A man once told me how he had gone to consult a gourd rattle diviner on a certain matter. After two hours, she still had not found an explanation that seemed acceptable to him. So he left, refusing to pay the divination fee.

The knowledge and opinion of the client is essential inasmuch as the Nyole view of misfortune is based on a relational concept of the person. As long as relations to spirits and people must be examined and treated, the diviner must rely on the opinions and experiences of those involved.

Who Divines and Defines for Whom?

The diviner and client together work out an interpretation of misfortune and a plan for realizing it through appropriate thereapy. Suffering should be alleviated through appreciating and adjusting relations to senior kin, ancestral and clan spirits, enemies, and peripheral spirits. Divination is an arena for defining social identities which may later be enacted in ritual where representations are made real (Geertz 1966:28). Although uncertainty may not be completely resolved (see Whyte 1990) and the prescribed rituals may not actually be carried out, still the person who goes to divine potentially has a very important form of power: the ability to define reality for others. Because divination is the legitimate way of knowing, the consulter goes home with a privileged view of who the suffering person is and a strategy for enacting the vision of the sufferer's identity. From this perspective, the important questions about divination are not only what happens and how in the divining hut, but what implications divination has in the world outside it.

Knowledge is power, we say, and access to knowledge through divination is a means to maintain it. Evans-Pritchard (1937) states this explicitly in describing the monopoly of older men over the Zande poison oracle. This gave them power over younger men, but more especially over women. Evans-Pritchard declares the poison oracle to be a central mechanism of male control:

> When we consider to what extent social life is regulated by the poison oracle we shall at once appreciate how great an advantage men have over women in their ability to use it, and how being cut off from the main means of establishing contact with the mystical forces that so deeply affect human welfare degrades woman's

position in Zande society. I have little hesitation in affirming that the customary
exclusion of women from any dealings with the poison oracle is the most evident
symptom of their inferior social position and means of maintaining it. (284–285)

In another classic study of African religion, Middleton (1960) also emphasizes
that being able to interpret misfortune for others was a central aspect of authority.
Among the Lugbara, oracles were consulted by lineage elders "although a senior
man who is not an elder may consult them himself on behalf of his own dependents,
especially if the elder is away or if the patient is only a wife or child" (81).
In this perspective, women and children are pawns; they were extensions of their
husbands or fathers, and in oracular consultation their sicknesses were associated
with offenses committed by men. Since the outcome of oracle consultation was
determined by the consulter (84), he was able to produce knowledge that supported
his own political interests vis à vis other men. More recently Mendonsa has analyzed the politics of divination among the Sisala of northern Ghana. Here too
only elder men consult diviners, and the right to do so is the "keystone of lineage
authority" (1982:167).

The politics of Nyole divination are more complicated. Women could consult
diviners, although they did so less frequently than men. Records kept by three
diviners showed that men alone or accompanied by other men consulted in somewhat more than half of all the cases. In nearly a quarter of the cases, women
alone or together with other women came to divine. And in the rest of the cases,
a male and female client came together. Men were preponderant as clients of
the gourd rattle diviner, whereas women were more likely to be present at consultations with book diviners. In any case, women were present at divination seances
to a far greater extent than they were reported to be among Zande, Lugbara,
and Sisala. Given the part that the client plays in a divination seance, we must
conclude that Nyole women were able to influence the interpretation of misfortune.
Does this mean that divination does not support male dominance as has been
reported for the other societies?

To answer this question, we must ask several others, for the sexual politics
of divination have to do with more than whether diviners and their clients are
men or women. We need to know for whom consulters seek divination, what
sorts of political implications are contained in divinatory conclusions, and how
these conclusions are applied in practice.

Whereas men were more frequent consulters in Bunyole, women were far more
often objects of divination in the sense that the actual "events" whose causes
were being divined were usually the sicknesses and reproductive problems of
women. The sickness of children was also very common (see Whyte 1982:2058).
The afflictions of women were either more common or were better "to think with"
in divination.

These victims of misfortune were often not present at the divination session.
The records kept by three diviners show this to be an especially marked pattern
in divination by spirit possession. The victim was present at less than one-fifth
of the gourd rattle consultations, but at one-half and two-thirds respectively of

the book divinations. So if we can speak of a pattern on the basis of records from only three diviners, it is that in spirit divination, men tended to consult on behalf of women who were not there, whereas in book divination, the afflicted women were more likely to be present. I believe that this fits with the fact that the book diviners were also medicine men who gave treatment in connection with their divination practice. A woman who went to consult could get medicine at the same time. In addition, book diviners often suggested medicinal shortcuts to avoid ritual. Instead of having a curse removed or carrying out a clan spirit ceremony, one could take medicine. This sort of therapy does not support male authority in the way that ritual remedies do. It is a more individual treatment, in some ways more similar to that of biomedicine. This therapeutic perspective may account for the fact that afflicted women themselves were more likely to consult the examiners of Arabic books.

This situation is somewhat reminiscent of that described by Shaw in her analysis of the gender politics of Temne divination. She suggested that Temne women, who only consult private diviners, gain ontological assurance from a diagnosis which reaffirms their experience of reality, although they do not obtain the public validation that men achieve through public divination (1985:300). In Bunyole, all divination is private, but some forms of treatment are more public than others. As among the Temne, private forms allowed women to deal with misfortune in ways that more often reflected and reaffirmed their own experiences.

The dominant Nyole view of misfortune contains a male perspective. Whether suffering is attributed to cursing, ancestral ghosts, clan spirits, or sorcery, there is a tendency to define women in terms of their relations to men. There is a clear innocent victim pattern in which women's afflictions are associated with conflicts or offenses of their fathers or husbands. The curse discussed in the grandfather's case is typical of the way new brides are made to suffer because of the bridewealth dispositions of their fathers. The same diviner recorded the case of a husband who came to consult about his wife, who was very ill with a swollen arm. It was determined that she had touched a dead monitor lizard and bad medicine placed in her sweet potato garden by a neighbor with whom her husband was quarreling about land. In both these cases the consulters were interpreting women's afflictions in terms of their own relations with other men. In so doing they defined the suffering women as daughter and wives, as dependents and extensions of themselves whom other men (or spirits) might strike in order to hurt them. What I want to emphasize about this innocent victim pattern is the implications it has for women's perceptions of themselves. Divination creates such views in regard to situations where women are susceptible and in need of help. At such points they must be particularly receptive to definitions of who they are as social persons.

The tendency to define other people's problems from the consulter's own point of view can sometimes be seen where women are clients. In the case of the Dry Tree reported elsewhere (Whyte 1990), the consulting mother suspected her husband's mother of having caused the barrenness of her daughter, because she had often quarreled with her mother-in-law. The Dry Tree's affliction was interpreted in terms of the conflicts and interests of her mother; she was defined as her mother's daughter. But even here the more general problem was bridewealth, and one could say that the divinatory conclusion affirmed a general view of women as persons for whom bridewealth must be paid by some men to other men, who then redistribute some of it to women.

In spite of the fact that the knowledge of misfortune which is negotiated in divination has an androcentric tendency, we cannot simply say that divination affirms patrilineal values and male control. Women's misfortune can be attributed to the mischievous intervention of foreign and little spirits, and to sorcery directed against them as persons by jealous co-wives and rejected suitors. Perhaps this ability of representations to sometimes speak directly to women as individual subjects facilitates women's acceptance of those representations which define them as daughters and wives.

In terms of power, the essential point remains that whoever consults for someone else makes an assertion about who the other person is. This is potentially a form of domination, although many Nyole would see it as an expression of concern and responsibility. Very commonly, men consult on behalf of women and children. But power relationships also exist between older and younger women, between well and sick women, between fruitful and barren women. The power possibililty is there, so to speak, in the structure that allows a person to consult a diviner concerning someone else.

Why is divination such a special tool for shaping the power component in social relations? The diviner and the divination, which is seen as his work (although in fact it is a joint enterprise), have an authority deriving from access to a world of abundant significance—through books in which all possible meanings are written or through spirits which can represent all possible interpretations. Such authority can compel acceptance of the definition which is formulated in divination and brought home by the client. In a cultural system where people's views of their society and their place within it are so closely tied to the interpretation of misfortune, divination plays a key role in formulating and reformulating the understanding that is the basis for social action.

My purpose here has been to describe the creation of knowledge in Nyole divination and to draw attention to the structural relations of the parties involved. Between consuler and diviner, power is not at issue. They are jointly engaged in a process of discovery which moves from obscurity to certainty, with the diviner mediating between the overabundance of potential meaning in the divinatory world and the sure knowledge of the client that some interpretations are false. The authority of the diviner with his extraordinary access to ineffable reality, is balanced by the authority of the client, who knows the social and ritual details of the specific case under construction.

This distinction between consuler and diviner and all the wealth of communication between them is lost, as it were, when the client leaves the divining hut. Nyole ideology ignores the very considerable role played by the consuler in divination. What is significant is the result of their interaction, the divinatory conclusion, the *endagu*. It is this verdict which counts as far as the victim is concerned; the victim and the afflicition are defined by the authority of the diviner —at least that is how it appears. And insofar as this formulation is accepted and acted upon, an identity is proposed and perhaps accepted by the victim. The consulter's relation to the victim is potentially a dominant one. In this light, it is clear that going to consult concerning one's own affliction is a political act, an assertion of autonomy. It is no accident that this characterizes the clientele of the book diviners, who offer medicinal shortcuts to well-being.

The authority of senior relatives and of men can be challenged within the framework of divination, just at it can be asserted and maintained. What is more striking about Nyole divination is its vitality and flexibility as a mechanism for creating privileged definitions of persons and society.

Notes

The fieldwork on which this essay is based was carried out in Bunyole County, Bukedi District, Eastern Province of Uganda, between February 1968 and April 1971. Because nineteen years have passed, I have used the past tense in relating what I heard and saw then. The work was done together with my husband, Michael A. Whyte; I would like to thank him for his insightful suggestions concerning the present essay. We are both grateful for grants from the National Institute of Mental Health, which supported our research in Bunyole.

1. Two diviners kept records of their consultations for me, noting details of all the clients for whom they divined over specific periods of time. A field assistant made similar records for a third diviner who could not write in Lunyole. These journals contain information on about 350 cases in all. In addition to these data, I transcribed four divination seances, attended several more, and interviewed diviners and their clients as part of a more inclusive study of the interpretation and treatment of misfortune.

2. Diviners worked with sets of four to eight foreign spirits, of which the majority were said to be Ganda. No two diviners had exactly the same team of spirits, although Mukasa, a Ganda spirit, was mentioned by all six gourd rattle diviners whom I asked concerning the names of their spirit colleagues. Other Ganda spirits mentioned were Nabubi, Kiti, Kirongo, Kitambogwe, Kiwanuka, Jilaiya, Katema Muti, Musokiye, Omulalo Omulagusi (meaning Hima diviner!), Kidali, Luwanuka, and Musisi. Those named as Soga spirits were Musoke, Walumbe, and Gireya. Jilaiya was also mentioned as a Gwere spirit. Masaaba and Lugingo were named as Gisu spirits and Mukambi as a Swahili spirit.

3. Trimingham (1964:124) mentions Islamic systems of divination as being employed in towns; certainly they were employed in the countryside as well. Bloch (1968) describes the history and importance of written Arabic in Malagasy systems of astrology, geomancy, and medicine. He emphasizes the early recognition of "a feature which is still important today. That is, the power, religious, magical, astrological and medicinal, of the written word, both for those possessing the art and those without it. . . ." (283).

4. Trimingham (1964:124) mentions Abu Ma'shar al-Falaki as a book of astrology. In 1983 I found this book in use in Tanzania; a copy for sale in a shop in Moshi was printed in Delhi.

5. Young (1977) describes the somewhat similar system of *awdunigist* divination employed by Amhara ecclesiastics.

References

Beattie, John. 1967. "Divination in Bunyoro, Uganda." In *Magic, Witchcraft, and Curing*, ed. J. Middleton, 211–31. Garden City, N.Y.: Natural History Press.

Bloch, Maurice. 1968. "Astrology and Writing in Madagascar." In *Literacy in Traditional Societies*, ed. J. Goody, 277–97. Cambridge: Cambridge University Press.

Evans-Pritchard, E. E. 1937. *Witchcraft, Oracles and Magic among the Azande*. Oxford: Clarendon Press.

Foucault, Michel. 1975. *The Birth of the Clinic* (1963). New York: Vintage Books.

Geertz, Clifford. 1966. "Religion as a Cultural System." In *Anthropological Approaches to the Study of Religion*, ed. M. Banton, 1–46. London: Tavistock

Kleinman, Arthur. 1980. *Patients and Healers in the Context of Culture*. Berkeley: University of California Press.

Mann, Thomas, 1968. *Joseph the Provider* (1943). London: Sphere Books.

Mendonsa, Eugene L. 1982. *The Politics of Divination*. Berkeley: University of California Press.

Middleton, John. 1960. *Lugbara Religion: Ritual and Authority among an East African People*. London: Oxford University Press.

Park, George. 1967. "Divination and Its Social Context." In *Magic, Witchcraft, and Curing*, ed. J. Middleton, 233–54. Garden City, N.Y.: Natural History Press.

Parkin, David. 1982. "Straightening the Paths from Wilderness: Simultaneity and Sequencing in Divinatory Speech." *Paideuma* 28:71–83.

Shaw, Rosalind. 1985. "Gender and the Structuring of Reality in Temne Divination: An Interactive Study." *Africa* 55(3):286–303.

Trimingham, J. Spencer. 1964. *Islam in East Africa*. Oxford: Clarendon Press.

Turner, Victor. 1975 *Revelation and Divination in Ndembu Ritual*. Ithaca, N.Y.: Cornell University Press.

Werbner, Richard P. 1973. "The Superabundance of Understanding: Kalanga Rhetoric and Domestic Divination." *American Anthropologist* 75(5):1414–40.

Whyte, Susan Reynolds. 1981. "Men, Women and Misfortune in Bunyole." *Man* 16(3):350–66.

———. 1982. "Penicillin, Battery Acid and Sacrifice: Cures and Causes in Nyole Medicine." *Social Science and Medicine* 16:2055–64.

———. 1988. "The Power of Medicine in East Africa." In *The Context of Medicines in Developing Countries*, ed. S. van der Geest and S. R. Whyte. Dordrecht: Kluwer.

———. 1990. "Uncertain Persons in Nyole Divination." *Journal of Religion in Africa* 20(1):41-62.

Whyte, Susan Reynolds, and Michael A. Whyte. 1987. "Clans, Brides and Dancing Spirits." *Folk* 29:97–123.

Willis, R. G. 1973. "Pollution and Paradigms." *Man* 7(3):369–78.

Young, Allan. 1977. "Order, Analogy, and Efficacy in Ethiopian Medical Divination." *Culture, Medicine and Psychiatry* 1(2):183–99.

Zuesse, Evan M. 1979. *Ritual Cosmos: The Sanctification of Life in African Religions*. Athens: Ohio University Press.

David Parkin

Simultaneity and Sequencing in the Oracular Speech of Kenyan Diviners

A convergence of ideas that has occurred in linguistics and semantics has relevance also for social anthropology. In 1975 Marshall Durbin proposed formal models for distinguishing simultaneity and sequencing in human cognition. He noted the recent popular usage of this explanatory contrast in linguistics especially. Also in 1975, Paul Kay saw synchronic variability in basic color terms as generating a roughly linear evolution of more specialized terms. Kay's study demonstrated the more general hypothesis in lexical semantics that "all linguistic change has its roots in synchronic heterogeneity of the speech community" (1975:257). Finally, in a paper published in 1978 but delivered in 1973 at a conference I attended, Edwin Ardener distinguished between a simultaneity of events and their output as linear chains. A simultaneity is verbally unspecified, marked only by a "language shadow," while a causal sequence of events is distinguished more precisely in speech. Though they differ in other respects, these three views treat synchronicity or simultaneity as in some way generating sequential behavior, vocabulary, or events.

Sequentiality is, of course, the only logically possible alternative to simultaneity.[6] One "becomes" the other, though we tend to place the emphasis on sequenced events as emerging from a previously synchronic state and so as "produced" by that state. But the reverse direction is certainly possible, as when myths lump together events in overlapping and spatiotemporally contradictory ways. On the whole, though, the cases we present are of how "order" comes out of "disorder." We see this sequence as people at their most creative. A point I want to make is that this creativity consists not simply in answering the puzzles posed by cognitive simultaneity but also in setting up the simultaneity in the first place.

Jung clearly understood our fascination. His view of the synchronicity of events was that their coincidence in space and time meant much more to us than mere chance. Events occurring simultaneously showed a special interdependence both with each other and, through our psyches, with us as observers (Jung 1968:xxiv; cited in Jackson 1978:117). Indeed we do often ascribe a hidden causality to what we interpret as coincidence, which in that sense is taken as something prior to us. But when we look at certain social events, we see people actually creating a pool of meanings, first by speaking and thinking of different events as if they occur simultaneously, even in contradiction, and then by relating events to each other in causal sequence. That is to say, through an event initially evoking the idea of simultaneity, people reorder events and make the new combinations intelligible to a wider public.

The event I shall look at is that of divinatory speech among the people with whom I have worked. But first I shall suggest some more universal aspects of the contrast and relationship between simultaneity and sequencing.

An Archetypal Contrast

Let me begin with a biblical text, Mark 1:3 on John the Baptist: "The voice of one crying in the wilderness, Prepare ye the way of the Lord, and make his paths straight." The idea of confusion suggested by the crying in the wilderness and the implication that the confused paths of the Lord need to be straightened represent two common archetypal ideas which we conventionally associate with religion and ritual.

The first archetype can be seen in the many expressions of tangled, crossed, or confused states: the sins of incest and some forms of adultery; the ritualization of breech and other abnormal births; the dangers of improperly conducted rites of passage or of neglected relations between juniors and seniors; the use of key terms for witchcraft which relate to the idea of trapping and ensnaring and even the celebration of the Christian *Cross* (Easter) and the Jewish *Passover* as central events at about the same time of the year.

The second archetype may be thought of as an attribute of the broad contrast between nature and culture. It is the contrast between wilderness and wandering on one hand and fixed, secure, clearly and narrowly defined (often home) bases on the other. We have the biblical examples of Jesus and John the Baptist going off into the wilderness but returning new "straightened-out" men; the parable of the prodigal son forgiven and welcomed back from his aimless debauchery in the wastelands of the outside world; prophets coming into the small-scale society from a wider, alien, outside world; and, in at least some societies (including the Giriama[7] and Swahili of Kenya who are the subject of this essay), sick patients going off, sometimes in trances, to the forest or bush, impelled by an inner understanding, to gather the correct medicines required for their return to the now legitimate, i.e., "straight," role of diviner.

First then, tangled states become "objects of the ritual attitude." Like cases of boundary confusion, they may be thought of as sources of power, sometimes beneficial but sometimes so dangerous for the society and the transgressing individual that he has to withdraw from it. Second, victims are straightened out as a result of having wandered into the wilderness.

Linking the two archetypes, we can say that the geographical transition from wilderness to straight paths parallels the individual's movement from social or mental confusion to clarity. As a metaphor of change between personal states, this charcterizes divination among the Giriama and Swahili of Kenya. This movement is evident more from their speech than from their actions. By concentrating on the speech of diviners among the people I have studied, I am able to understand a little more about the thought processes associated with the two archetypes I have described.

Diagnosis of problems is arrived at through divination; treatment (i.e., attempted cure) takes place after the divination and at a set place and time. Diviners may be of either sex and are paid between two and five Kenya shillings for their diagnosis. They usually recommend that the patient be treated by a specialist doctor. This treatment is more expensive and is much more profitable than divination.

There is a hierarchy within these occupations, which include exorcism of spirits and reversal of witchcraft. It is based on the (sometimes cross-cutting) critieria of sex, age, and ethnic or religious group. Doctors who provide only therapy but not divination are always men. Diviners may be men or women among non-Muslims but only men among Muslims. "Arab" diviners and doctors (who are always men) are generally held to be the best, and are the most expensive; they are regarded as having mixed Arab-Swahili-Mijikenda ancestry. "Swahili" (i.e., Muslim Africans) are usually regarded as the next most efficacious, and "Giriama" (i.e., non-Muslim Mijikenda) as the least (see figure). Oracular techniques vary between these categories, and patients try a range of practitioners. Thus an individual Giriama may in fact achieve exceptional renown. Complicating the matter still further is the fact that non-Muslims say that all diviners must be Muslims, for the spirits that possess them will include "Arabic" (i.e., Muslim) ones. However, claims to Muslim status are graded in East Africa, and those who are most widely acknowledged as "full" Muslims do distinguish between Muslim and non-Muslim diviners. This practice of grading Muslim status and the inconsistency of the contrast between Muslim and non-Muslim is a result of shifts from partial to "full" Muslim status, which often take more than one generation; it is reflected in the loose hierarchy of divinatory and medical prowess. That is to say, the social is reflected in the ritual hierarchy.

Following this Durkheimian line, it might be possible to show how changes in judgments made about diviners in terms of their ethnic group, religion, sex, and age amount to statements about wider, changing social relations. But diviners of all kinds use the idea of moving from a boundless to a bounded realm of existence in their diagnoses. Such archetypal usage seems unaffected by difference of rank and status among diviners. By investigating the diagnoses of a social range of such diviners I think we are able to understand their thematic logic and its relative imperviousness to variations in the social circumstances of diviners.

Karisa Mulila, a "Giriama" diviner, near Chalani, Giriamaland, Kilifi district, Kenya, 1967. *Photo by David Parkin.*

Three Cases

I will reproduce in condensed form and comment on the diagnoses of three diviners: an "Arab," a "Swahili," and a "Giriama," as they are generally identified. First a few introductory remarks about them.

A client approaches a diviner without notice. The client is not necessarily the patient. Indeed it is often argued that he or she should not be. But some are.

The late middle-aged "Arab" diviner runs his profession like a true business; he uses a pocket watch as an oracle. Clients sit around in his ample, well-stocked homestead waiting to be seen, the humbler receiving shorter divinations than the more influential, though the fees are the same (five shillings). He presses clients to agree to his carrying out the therapy on an appointed day after the divination. The "Giriama" diviner, in this case a woman past childbearing age, differs in a number of respects. She divines through spirit possession. She may be found sitting in her mud and wattle hut, unseen from the outside, and apparently withdrawn from the world. The client enters the hut, makes his greeting, and responds to her polite, euphemistic requests for tobacco by placing the two-shilling fee in front of her. The divination begins slowly. Punctuated by sweet refrains, gasps, and whistling as the spirits pause in their reflections, it consists of dramatic use of voice tone and vocabulary. The third diviner, the Muslim Digo (referred to by his fellow African Muslims as "Swahili") is a little less dramatic. His divination is punctuated by the spirits speaking in other ethnic tongues rather than in refrains of song. He accepts the same fee as the Giriama woman, and like her, he puts time and efforts into the divination. The range in style from the least to the most dramatic among these three diviners does not alter certain common themes covered in their divinations.[8] The diviner is not expected to know anything of the victim's affliction nor indeed whether the person in front of him—the client—is himself the victim or a caring relative come to ask for a diagnosis on the victim's behalf.

The "Arab" Diviner

The "Arab" diviner speaks in Swahili. His client has come on behalf of his ten-year-old son, who talks to himself, whoops and yells as if possessed, plays by himself and not with other children, and is easily angered.

> The diviner's spirits first make these points:
> He [i.e., the victim] is troubled because of his trade—the trade carried out from his home—I mean the trade that results from a man marrying a wife and having a child by her. I mean that trade—for the wife is the investment and the child the profit. Women are the loads which we men trade with, feeding them, and hoping to trade further with.
> But the wife can't or won't get out of your body—she is the owner of it—it's your trade but she is the owner . . . and she can say I don't love you and she can leave you . . . but your child can't say that.
> That is why I say it is your business which is disturbing you [i.e., he refers to the victim by addressing the client].

By converting one metaphor into another (trade into domestic relations) and by using the metaphors inconsistently, the diviner simultaneously links a number of possible sources of distress: the victim's occupation or trade, the costs of running a family, a dominant and unloving wife, and the loss of a child through her desertion. Of particular note is the fact that the wife is locked in the victim's body, possessing it—perhaps even consuming it—and yet also leaving it. Bodily possession is also of course normally attributed to spirits, though as yet spirits have not been mentioned. The implicit proposition, therefore, is that the victim's wife is a controlling spirit. This is combined with another proposition, which states that the victim is troubled by his trade or occupation. Home and the outside are thus simultaneously linked as sources of distress. As yet, such propositions are only hinted at; they are not clear enough to be judged true or false by the client.

We see in the next section of paraphrase, however, that the diviner successfully locates a child as the victim. As usual, a positive response from the client has helped him. Clients do this by words of encouragement and agreement throughout the divination. The diviner says:

> I am looking at the [victim's] head, circling around, going now to the stomach, to the joints, circling all the time . . . and the child is suffering in all parts of the body—head, heart, stomach—but the stomach pain is ceasing, now it is the back which is troubling.
>
> And yet this child has been sent to hospital, but vomits. This is caused by the heart, for the disease is in the heart. And the head aches.
>
> He was given tablets but was sick on taking them. . . . He is constipated for two or three days. Isn't this so? [The client is asked, but courteously denies that the child is constipated.] He is constipated one day but not the next. He goes and then the stomach can be heard rumbling at his umbilicus. Where do you live? [The question is addressed to the client, who tells the diviner.]
>
> You saw something astonishing in his house, didn't you—like a wild animal from the forest going in? Now that animal came up to the child, who fell asleep and went "Haw haw" [the noise of an animal]. And even the next day, when he's about to recover, the sickness goes away a little but then comes right back. The disease then comes and goes every two days, with the child going "Haw haw" at its onset. For now there are spirits active there, which must be seen to quickly.

There is an interesting kind of two-part syllogism here, the first of which uses metonymy. First: the child is approached by the animal (which is understood to rasp); the child is approached by the sickness (initiated by a rasp); therefore the animal is the sickness. Second: the animal is from outside (i.e., the forest); spirits are from the outside; therefore the animal is the spirits (therefore to treat the spirits is to treat the sickness).

The diviner then follows up his admonition to treat the spirits with explicit instructions about the medicines needed for the treatment: "Get a cock, a hen of different colors, a white loin cloth, and materials for making an Arabic charm which can be drunk. The child has spirits, including the ape-spirit to which he is attracted. Get these spices: Ambari, Miski, Kafuri, Zafarani, Marashi, and also a sheep—a surrogate will do—even a sheep's hoof (literally, shoe)." After further instructions and then some open discussion, a date, time, and place are set for the treatment for which these items will be needed.

The first part of the divination links home and the outside world as simultaneously producing a number of sometimes conflicting sources of distress. The second repeatedly probes different areas of the body, then focuses on the home, which is entered by a wild animal from the forest (perhaps echoing the equation of home with wife in the first part). Merged ideas are broken down into separate ones through the idiom of following separate parts of the body. This is followed by a specific statement of the cause of sickness: outside spirits intruding and requiring appeasement. The final part of the divination carries still further the ordered sequencing of ideas and actually spells out the list of medical requirements and the time and place of their application. The shift is from conceptual simultaneity to sequencing.

The "Swahili" Diviner

The "Swahili" (Muslim Digo) diviner's client is a young unmarried man who has come on his own behalf. He seems to be suffering from venereal disease. This diviner also begins with a complex linking of concepts: man, woman, sadness, sympathy, lust and longing, including the supreme symbol of suffering, the shoe (*kirahu*). This word derives from the verb "to go here and there" (*ku-kira-kira*). The reflexive *ku-dzi-kirira* means "to walk about aimlessly" (see Deed 1964).[9]

> Why is there this need for sympathy my friend [addressing the client]? There is a woman loving a man. . . . The love is puzzled. The man loves the woman. The man loves with longing/lust [using the word *thamaa*, which can also stand for penis]. There is longing and there is the shoe. You [i.e., the client] have even followed the shoe [i.e. "you have really suffered"; suffering is implied by the notion of having wandered endlessly on foot.] Why is there sickness as well as longing here?

Here the interlinked notions of longing, lust, and the metonymic penis are denoted by the one word and merge into that of sickness. The use of the word *shoe* and the verb *followed* anticipates the more extensive treatment of the theme of wandering, as in the previous divination.

> He [i.e., the victim] is a man and is sick and wandering . . . this way and that. . . . He comes out quickly. . . . He can't cope [for which the verb *ku-kola* is used, which also means to penetrate]. . . . He runs about here and there . . . struggling, but to no avail. He goes to doctors but to no avail.
>
> Why has he this disease of the shoe? He can't stay in bed with the sickness. He wanders with it. Why is it a disease of the top [i.e., of the head]? It has gripped his head, but why the head, my friend? The head goes round and round and becomes dizzy. And because of the dizziness it becomes senseless and loses its memory. His [senseless] mind tells him to cry and produce tears.
>
> The disease is in the chest . . . in the stomach . . . in the solar plexus [*chembe cha moyo*] . . . and even his heart is bursting. . . . It is worn out from beating at great speed. The heart goes fast yet it wanders. It [the disease] is in the arteries and veins [*mishipa*] and his legs are lazy.
>
> Now the sickness is descending. It's in the middle. It is a male's sickness . . . to do with [sexual] satisfaction. . . . It's between the kidneys. Now we find it in the veins of the penis [for which an orthodox word, *kilume*, is used] . . .

and right beneath the umbilicus. Why is there fire burning there . . . like peppers
. . .? The disease makes one mindless. When you urinate it's a war, and even
injections have not helped.

Now the diviner, having located the distressing part of the body, proceeds to
itemize the causative agents:

You [i.e., the client, now identified as the victim] are caught by the [witchcraft]
trap [*tego*] which prevents you defecating [*ya zindika*], by the traps which prevents
you urinating [*tego ya mkufu*], by the trap which causes irritation [*ya lwambe*],
and by the traps called peppers [*pilipili*], laziness [*munyegero*], the needle [*sindano*],
black ants [*minyo*], and safari ants [*tsalafu*]. [Most of these traps indicate the sensa-
tions of itching, pricking, and stinging].

Have you entered someone's house? [The victim answers no.] I don't really
mean a house, I mean a human house [i.e., a woman, and this the victim does not
deny]. . . . You have had this sickness a long time, not a long time, yet a long
time, but you have been wandering around with this sickness, and you are sur-
prised that it has stayed with you. But you must cure the first causes [i.e., the
witchcraft traps which have physical effects].

Also, my friend, you have the following [other kinds of] witchcraft. [Here the
diviner uses the term *muhaso* but later *utsai*; both have mental rather than physical
effects.] These are: the witchcraft of self-hatred [*utsai wa dzimene*], of senseless
babbling [*mbayumbayu*], of indecisiveness and lack of concentration [*shulamoyo*],
and of restlessness [*mtango*]. These witchcrafts want to turn you into a perpetual
nomad, wandering unthinkingly around the world, never settling at home, with
your heart burning . . . and feeling numb in your head. You also have the witchcraft
[*nzaiko*] which makes you cry when combined with those that make you indecisive
and gibbering.

The disease comes from the west. . . . You had a job there. Maybe you were
learning there, but people are bad there and gave you these things.

The diviner next shifts from a focus on the causes of the affliction to a precise
statement of the items needed for the cure: "Find me seven loaves made out of
ashes, seven loaves of bread, seven sides of sand from a termite mound, a chain,
seven wild tomatoes [?] and with these we shall make you free." The diviner
shifts for a moment back to the focus on cause, then reverts to the medical prescription:

Your school absences and lack of concentration were due to bad people. You humans
really were bad to each other. . . . Do you hear, my friend?

Anyway, now also find a chicken [later called a cock] of mixed colors, and
a red hen; these are for the witchcraft traps. For reversing the mental effects of
the second kind of witchcraft and getting your memory back from God, you need
a chicken with frayed and tufted feathers [*kuku wa kidemu*], a newly hatched chick,
and an egg which never hatched.

I could mention the names of those who wanted you to become a vagrant and
who caused your apathy, while your friends forged ahead, but I [i.e., the spirit]
am asked only to "name" the sickness [i.e., to find its cause and remedy].

Don't think that by going off to another country you will resist them—you *must* be cured—your body must be treated . . . and then you will be somebody, settled with a job and money and able to face people. . . . The day for the treatment is next Tuesday, 10 A.M. to 3 P.M.

With this divination, we also have an initial amassing and overlapping of ideas: man and woman, loving and longing, following the shoe, getting sick. My translated abstract misses the polysemy of certain words used: *kimako* means sympathy, sorrow, astonishment; *thamaa* means hope, longing, lust, penis; *ku-kola* means to overcome or penetrate. The word used in divination for woman is *figa*, which normally refers to one of three stones making up a stand for cooking pots; the word used for man is the normal word for five (*tsano*), which admirably projects the five-limbed image of masculinity. The word for shoe (*kirahu*) carries the meaning also of wandering and therefore of random sickness. Conflicting innuendos are created through such polysemy, which heightens the ambivalence of concept. The listening client can try and judge for himself but may not be certain of what precisely is being proposed, while the diviner himself can always retreat from an unpromising lead and take up another through the use of the same words.

The theme of uncontrolled wandering follows on easily from such ambivalence. It occurs first in undefined outside space, then in pursuit through different parts of the body, eventually settling, in this case, on the genitals. But the young man is clearly mentally as well as physically distressed, and so his mind's wanderings are described. The physical and mental troubles are each explained by a different kind of witchcraft.

Finally, there is a well-ordered list of requisites for cure, interspersed with more direct admonitions not to wander. The subject of wandering may at any one time have been the sickness, the pain, the victim, the aggrieved relative of the victim, or even the agent causing the distress. The admonition not to wander places these phenomena (the subjects of wandering) in fixed rather than indeterminate relations to each other.

The "Giriama" Diviner

In the final case of divination, which I will summarize even more briefly, a Giriama woman about ten years past childbearing age treats a young man who has also come on his own behalf and who suffers from continual stomach pains, which, the diviner comes to assume, necessarily affect his sexuality.

The diviner opens with a short song in Giriama, which is mutually intelligible with Digo: "The spirits are coming with sympathy, and we are traveling along with that sympathy, and with our human hope." The spirit switches from song to speech.

We [i.e., the spirits—though perhaps the plural pronoun is used to denote respect for the client, who is a member of an adjacent generation and therefore a "father"] have stood with a female, but the sick person is a male. . . . Isn't that so? [The client agrees and the diviner responds with song.]

We are swaying like an eagle; Kayumba [name given to the client] has come, yes, and the sick person is asking. . . . I want to sleep, brothers. [The song ends.] We have gone with our male . . . he is small . . . and yet big . . . he can speak [i.e., is not a baby; the client assents to this]. He has a problem sent by God [i.e., not caused by witchcraft, *utsai*]. He has the shoe.

The diviner repeats the previous refrain and then speaks of the journey through the body.

We have tried the head and left it. Now we are down in the chest, and not the heart. My mind [i.e., that of the spirit, standing as the patient] is confused, isn't that true? [The client agrees and the diviner repeats the refrain.] Now we are down to the stomach. [To which the client assents readily: "The stomach, yes, the stomach, that's it!" And the diviner continues.] It is constipated and burning, and something in it gets up and stands erect and clings to the heart. . . . My heart is being pulled. And now we travel down to my back. [The client assents.] My back, my back. It is my loins/genitals [*thamaa*] isn't it father? It affects my legs, my hips, my *thamaa*.

The client asks what has caused the affliction and the diviner recounts a phase in the victim's childbirth when he was put in a lake and could not breathe, but he lived and has suffered ever since.

The diviner then suggests in detail three separate sets of causative agents: spirits, harmful exposure to a family tradition of the occult (the man's mother is also a diviner), and, as in the previous divination, witchcraft traps—which contradicts her earlier assertion that witchcraft was not involved. The diviner then spells out the curative plants, animals, and cloth that will be required, giving precise instructions as to the identification and whereabouts of the plants, indicating by which lake, in which area of bush, etc. A time for the exorcism of the spirits and reversal of the witchcraft is set for the same afternoon at the victim's home.

This Giriama diviner creates the same overlapping metaphors through use of the same polysemic vocabulary as does the Digo diviner. However, one expression used by the Giriama and not by the Digo is worth noting. It is a phrase for human being (*magulu mairi mudamu ludzere*), which literally means "a two-legged human with hair." The expression perhaps illustrates the underlying idea that though spirits are like humans in some aspects of their nature and in the forms some of them may assume, only "real" humans are of "real" flesh, blood, and hair.

The Giriama diviner also at first refers to the spirits she talks to by the term used for "ancestral spirit" (*koma*), but later uses the normal word for "possession spirit" (*pepo*). The Giriama people stress (patri-)lineage relationships and ancestry more than the Digo, and this initial reference to dead ancestors is therefore consistent. Otherwise, in both divinations there is the same idea of a wandering soul in distress who joins up with equally nomadic but undistressed spirits to search through the different parts of the body and locate the source of pain. Bodily and mental problems are eventually distinguished, as in the Digo's divination, but the bodily ones are emphasized. The final stage of the Giriama's diagnosis distinguishes three causative agents: spirits, having a diviner in the family, and witchcraft, which are further subdivided in some descriptive detail, whereas the Digo diviner confines himself to two kinds of witchcraft, one producing physical and the other mental distress.

A Common Logic

Such differences of detail in the diagnoses of the three diviners represent their individual creativity. It is, however, a creativity which operates within the successive frameworks I have suggested: jumbled ideas and metaphors that suggest various possible interpretations give way to their ordered sequencing and to more limited interpretations; they are finally superseded by an unambiguous classification of the causes of the sickness and the material needed to cure it.

This process of semantic disentanglement and clarification runs parallel with the idiom of movement from a wilderness to a set place and time. Taking the cases as a whole, this "spatial" idiom can be expressed as follows:

The victim, or perhaps we would say his soul, wanders aimlessly outside his body and home. The spirits wander too. They are always "unsettled," as diviners say. But it is part of their nature to be so. The human patient, whose nature it is not to be disembodied but rather to be settled in time and place, joins up with the spirits and with them frantically travels from one part of the body to another. Though the journey is frantic, it does at least exhibit a rough sequence. It always starts from the head and moves downward to the area of the genitals, and in the intermediary area of the trunk, alternates probingly between heart, stomach, chest, solar plexus, back, joints, hips and legs, usually linking up again with the mind.

Once the victim's source of pain has been located, the spirits, through the mouth of the diviner, can advise on its cure. In concentrating their advice on a fixed bodily area the spirits are themselves settled, at least while the remedy is effective.

In advising on the curative materials and methods to be used, the spirits order and classify, and so are turned from wanderers into busy *bricoleurs*. Indeed, the suggestion may now have become clear from my summaries of the divinations that the unraveling of ideas and their ordered reassembly as diagnosis and potential cure well fits the description of *bricolage* given by Lévi-Strauss (1966:16–22).

It is true that it is the diviner (or his spirits) rather than the patient who converts "debris" and "chaos" into "order," or we might properly say, jumbled thought into sequential thought. But the patient is not only figuratively carried along the paths from wilderness to settlement; he is also a point of reference and guidance along the way. That is to say, by his nods, cues, and statements of agreement, the patient helps the diviner, encouraging him to proceed from one possibility to another. So, while *we* may think of the patient as being led to a cure by the diviner, the patient also guides the diviner in this attempt to reach a satisfactory diagnosis, converting an unmanageably large number of interpretations into a more limited number.

This view, that the patient guides the diviner as well as being guided by him, suggests more than a mutual dependency of the two roles. It suggests that they may be seen as mirror images of each other. The further implicit idea that each person is both doctor and patient is reinforced by the process through which diviners achieve their position in the first place. They first suffer severely as a patient and then, as part of the cure, are instructed by a diviner's spirits to seek certain plants and medicines in the bush, thereby also coming to possess divinatory powers. Only a few patients become diviners, but all diviners were once patients. It is as if in order to become a psychotherapist, one would first need to be a schizophrenic patient and become a psychotherapist as part of one's "cure." Indeed, the parallel may be not without significance.

Just as divinatory diagnoses suggest *bricolage*, so also the idioms and language used to describe the patient's distressed state suggest at least some features of what we call schizophrenia: disembodiment, personal withdrawal into a "private" world of spirits, the creation of a "false self" which denies the diviner's "real" identity, and what I continue for the moment to call jumbled speech. Yet, once again, these are features which are as much, if not more, the creation of the diviner as they are attributable to the patient. Both the patient and the diviner participate willingly in this diagnosis, with the patient allowing himself into the "private' spirit world of the diviner. Also, both appear to be in control of the way in which the diagnosis proceeds. It may well be that cultures like those of the Swahili and the Giriama provide structured events and roles by which what we call schizophrenia is legitimized and thereby brought under the control of those who suffer from it. Be that as it may, it is not here my intent to claim that the diviner and patient are in some degree schizophrenic. What is interesting is that the diagnostic themes in the divinations appeal to thought and speech processes which, when very marked, we would label schizophrenic.

Does this mean, then, that divinatory diagnosis is both *bricolage* and schizophrenia? Or, to put the equation another way, that *bricolage* (or myth-making thought, as Lévi-Strauss alternatively calls it) and schizophrenic thought are basically the same thing? Schizophrenic thought has moreover been viewed by some scholars as resting on a basis similar to that of artistic thought (Wilson 1978:97); does this further mean that *bricolage* and schizophrenic *and* artistic thought are equivalent? This seems absurd and perhaps, in reaching this equation, I have merely allowed myself to be captured by the terms and have merged their respective referents.

On the other hand, absurd though the equation might seem, the fact that it can be reached at all suggests some further consideration of Lévi-Strauss's three-fold distinction between *bricolage*, art, and modern science as modes of thought. Art, it will be remembered, is placed halfway between *bricolage* and modern science. The artist is said to partake of both. He is a *bricoleur* in creating a model or structure, a recognizable painting for example, out of preexisting images. So does the myth maker. But he also works by design, like the modern scientist or engineer in producing, as well as reproducing, structures. That is to say, the picture only exists as a painting on canvas and remains under his technological control as creator. He can, if he wants to, alter it so as to signify new directions, as would an impressionist (Lévi-Strauss 1966:22, 25).

Likewise, we are told that intellectual *bricolage* in the form of myth making has a poetic quality and can achieve brilliant intellectual results (Lévi-Strauss 1966:17, 21). Much the same could be said of divination, which, as well as offering opportunities for dramatic and semantic creativity, solves the practical problem of mental as well as physical distress. The Digo and Giriama diviners, it will be remembered, elaborated to a greater extent than the "Arab" and in ways much more aesthetically pleasing. As well as being *bricolage*, and even touching on modern medical science in its diagnostic parallels with psychotherapy, the divination is also an art form.

Lévi-Strauss himself notes that the difference between the myth maker and the modern scientist, or the *bricoleur* and the engineer, with the artist in between, is not absolute, and the distinction remains an important general approach complementary to the recent discussion of whether "primitive" thought is based on two- or three-valued logic, and whether it may be said to exist at all (Cooper 1975; Salmon 1978; Hallpike 1976, 1977; Williams 1977; Warren 1978).

But there is another approach which, on the basis of my data, I would state as follows: analysis of the diviner's speech reveals two parallel patterns. One concerns the language used, the other the narrative theme. To take the linguistic dimension first, the diviner starts with what I called jumbled speech, or what we may now refer to as inconsistent and mixed use of metaphor, false syllogism, some reversals, and an apparent lack of path control, i.e., straying from one concept to another and back again inconsequentially. Though intended (we assume) rather than involuntary, these are features common to some degree to the speech of all of us, but in excess may characterize so-called schizophrenic speech (Werner and Levis-Matichek 1975). These features are rectified as the divination proceeds. The speech and argument become clearer and culminate in perfectly precise instructions based on a crisp classification of causative agents and remedial plants, animals, and other substances.

The narrative theme starts with the idea of aimless wandering in an unspecified and we may assume empty area, which is alien and remote. Within it, paths crisscross confusedly, but eventually, through the idiom of bodily exploration, lead to a settled point and prospective cure. We can see that the shifts from jumbled to sequential speech and from aimless wandering to purposeful direction "say" the same thing. But it would be difficult to conclude that one is an epiphenomenon of the other.

One view might be that the logic governing both may be said to lie in the contrast between deep-structure and surface semantics. Gerald Leech offers us a linguistic example with the sentence *I saw the girls crossing the street* (1974: 288). At a deep semantic level the crossing and the seeing occur at the same time; they are a "junction of two interacting events" (288). But the sentence orders them sequentially; the seeing comes before the crossing. It also subordinates the second clause (*crossing the street*) by embedding it in the main clause (*seeing the girls*). As Leech remarks, the truest "copy of the structure of events and circumstances we recognize in the reality around us" (288) is in fact the synchronous picture, or what he calls the orderless network of deep semantics. Sentence order "distorts" the "true" picture by separating events in time and ranking them. Events do of course occur which "in reality" are indeed sequentially ordered and may be ranked in utterances by entailment and presupposition. But even here, sentences used to describe them can never fully overcome syntactic and phonological restraints, and approach the semantic accuracy of personally rather than grammatically ordered words. Like the painter and the poet, the schizophrenic speaker can say things with a shocking but brilliant poignancy that conventional sentences rarely attain. As with the initial jumbled speech of diviners, they operate more freely at a level closer to the orderless networks of deep-structure semantics.

The shift from deep-structure to surface (sentence) semantics analytically parallels the shift in the diviner's speech style and narrative theme. We can recast what others call deep-structure semantics as the area of the most creative, artistic, poetic, and schizophrenic throught, and surface semantics as that of classification and taxonomy, i.e., of *bricolage*. To complete the model, modern science may be regarded as reflexive surface semantics, i.e., language used to refer to itself, including its deep-structure (which is what I have attempted in this essay).

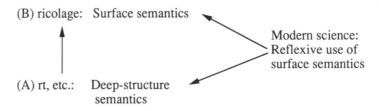

(B) ricolage: Surface semantics

Modern science:
Reflexive use of
surface semantics

(A) rt, etc.: Deep-structure
               semantics

The place of the two archetypes with which I began this essay can now be seen. Categorical overlap, crossing, or confusion (orderless networks) make up the area of deep-structure semantics and art. We are accustomed to the idea of this archetype being an object of the ritual attitude. More properly, we should say that it poses the intellectual puzzles which people seek to solve through aesthetically pleasing methods. The second archetype takes off from here and, in depicting the return from random wandering in the wilderness to straight and narrow paths, represents the movement from deep-structure to surface semantics (A)—(B), or, in the particular case of divination, from jumbled to clear speech.

We see, then, why the basic styles and themes of divination, at least in the society I have studied, are the same, regardless of the social circumstances of diviners. For they are part of a wider logic by which we solve problems as puzzles: by untangling them, and so clarifying and recognizing them. For that logic to operate we have to posit a simultaneity of confusion in the first place. This is the point at which I can bring the analysis to bear on the question in social anthropology of the innovative individual.

Innovating Individuals

To argue for a common logic in puzzle solving is not to deny the diviners choice in their proposed solutions. We have long known that many possibilities can emanate from a single logic (e.g., Leach 1961). It follows that diviners are perfectly able to comment socially. When they specify different kinds of witchcraft, or witchcraft rather than spirit possession, or whatever, as causes of misfortune, and when they hint at social relationships in which these differently valued acts may have arisen, they variously support, tear, or repair the social fabric. The many studies by Turner (1961) and others show this role of the diviner, and I could show the different ways in which Kenya coastal diviners do this. In this essay, however, I have tried to make the point that, however much such commentary may be viewed as sometimes reflecting social changes and continuities, the diviner and client together make up a cooperative enclave. Together they create a range of possible interpretations of cause and effect and then choose from within that range. They are in a good position, therefore, to articulate new ideas in the society which have not yet come into general currency.

This innovative power of the diviner-client relationship derives from the initial simultaneity of packed-in propositions which become progressively unpacked. That is to say, it is the initial tangled state or puzzle that inspires the discourse. This inspiration is commonly what we understand by events having become objects of the ritual attitude, and which I have glossed as incest, some kinds of adultery, breech births, badly performed rites of passage, crossing the generation gap, and the use of physical and verbal symbols which include the idea of crossing over. Such tangled states pose questions which demand answers.

This is a quite different view of the innovative individual from that held by Barth in his early work (1966). Even allowing for the fact that Barth was not specifically concerned with speech, he saw redefining roles by imparting to them new value or varying amounts of old value. The diviner and client clearly cooperate more than they compete, both inspired to disentangle a puzzle. Barth's view represents one dimension of individual innovation. Mine represents another. A tempting conclusion might be to locate Barth's innovative individual in the micropolitics of everyday life and mine in rituals dealing with tangled states. That is fine as far as it goes. But the phrasing is simplistic because it assumes a single definition of ritual and ignores the fact that what we call rituals may be conservative rather than innovative. Skorupski (1973) usefully redefined the contrast between the secular and the mystical as that between observable and hidden causality. This contrast may better illustrate the difference. Barth's individual innovates in the context of visible connections. For him the causality is already laid out before him: it is up to him to provide a new causal sequence of events or roles. My innovative individual is faced with a simultaneity of hidden causalities. He must straighten them out before he can see them and explain events through them. And to do this, he must cooperate with at least one other person.

For this reason tangled states generate social man, while straightened-out ones generate competitive man. Small wonder that so many leave for the wilderness.

But little surprise that those who wish to remain social must eventually return and compete, eventually creating further tangles.

Notes

Versions of this essay were presented in seminars at the Universities of California (Berkeley and San Diego), Sussex, Belfast (Queen's), and Oxford and appeared in the *Journal of the Anthropological Society of Oxford* 1979; 10(3):147–60 and *Paideuma* 1982; 28:71–83. Research was made possible by a grant from the SSRC. I thank this and the aforementioned institutions for their help and comments.

1. Two kinds of simultaneity and sequencing seem possible, a problem I shall deal with elsewhere. The present essay introduces the contrast and illuminates it.

2. The Giriama are a subgroup of the Mijikenda; they speak mutually intelligible dialects.

3. Technically, we should refer to the Giriama and Digo practitioners as shamans rather than simply diviners, for they speak through spirits which they also control. This is not, however, a distinction I wish to belabor here, though it is important for other analyses.

4. The root verb is in fact *ku-kira*, meaning "to cross" or "to go too far." From this is derived the noun *kirwa*, which refers to a disease arising from a breach of certain sexual prohibitions. Morphological variations of *kirwa* abound in Bantu and Nilotic cultures as key concepts (Parkin 1978:150–51, 327–30).

References

Ardener, E. 1978. "Some Outstanding Problems in the Analysis of Events." In *The Yearbook of Symbolic Anthropology*, vol. 1, ed. E. Schwimmer, 103–21. London: Hurst.

Barth, F. 1966. *Models of Social Organization*. London: Royal Anthropological Institute.

Cooper, D. E. 1975. "Alternative Logic in 'Primitive Thought.'" *Man* n.s. 10:238–56.

Deed, F. 1964. *Giryama-English Dictionary*. Nairobi: East African Literature Bureau.

Durbin, M. 1975. "Models of Simultaneity and Sequentiality in Human Cognition." In *Linguistics and Anthropology*, ed. M. Kinkade et al. Lisse: Reter de Ridder Press.

Hallpike, C. R. 1976. "Is There a Primitive Mentality?" *Man* n.s. 11:253–70.

———. 1977. "Is There A Primitive Mentality?" Correspondence in *Man* n.s. 12:530.

Jackson, M. 1978. "An Approach to Kuranko Divination." *Human Relations* 31(2): 117–38.

Jung, C. S. 1968. Foreword to *The I Ching or Book of Changes*, trans. R. Wilhelm. London: Routledge.

Kay, P. 1975. "Synchronic Variability and Diachronic Change in Basic Color Terms." *Language and Society* 4:257–70.

Leach, E. 1961. "Rethinking Anthropology." *Rethinking Anthropology*, 1–27 London: Athlone.

Leech, G. 1974. *Semantics*. Harmondsworth: Penguin Books.

Lévi-Strauss, C. 1966. *The Savage Mind*, London: Weidenfeld and Nicolson.

Lewis, I. M. 1971. *Ecstatic Religion*. Harmondsworth: Penguin Books.

Parkin, D. 1978. *The Cultural Definition of Poltical Response*. London: Academic Press.

Salmon, M. H. 1978. "Do Azande and Nuer Use a Non-standard Logic?" *Man* n.s. 13: 444–54.
Skorupski, J. 1978. *Symbol and Theory*. Oxford: Oxford University Press.
Turner, V. W. 1961. *Ndembu Divination*. Manchester: Manchester University Press.
Warren, N. 1978. "Is There a Primitive Mentality?" Correspondence in *Man* n.s. 13:477–78.
Werner, O., and G. Levis-Matichek, with M. Evans and B. Litowtiz. 1975. "An Ethnoscience View of Schizophrenic Speech." In *Sociocultural Dimensions of Language Use*, ed. M. Sanches and B. Blount, 349–78. New York: Academic Press.
Williams, R. 1977. "Is There a Primitive Mentality?" Correspondence in *Man* n.s. 12: 530.
Wilson, P. 1978. "The Outcast and the Prisoner: Models for Witchcraft and Schizophrenia." *Man* n.s. 13:88–99.

PART FIVE

Toward a New Approach to Divination

Philip M. Peek

African Divination Systems

Non-Normal Modes of Cognition

> The art of divination presents us with puzzling problems which I make no pretence to solve. A certain amount of communication goes on between diviners and non-human powers (whether living or otherwise or both). It is difficult to know exactly what this is: it might involve the diviner's extra-sensory ability, it may involve spiritual agents, it might be telepathy, it might be sharpened human perception, or a combination of these possibilities.
>
> John Mbiti, *African Religions and Philosophy*

The myriad techniques, mechanisms, and uses of divination in African cultures defy any easy categorizations. Certainly all aspects of divination must be understood in their cultural and performance contexts, but there is a striking commonality in most systems which might provide an answer for Mbiti's questions. Divination systems temporarily shift decision making into a liminal realm by emphatically participating in opposing cognitive modes; in fact, this may be the defining feature of divination. For example, no one could deny that the Ifa divination system of the Yoruba is based on an ancient epistemology or that the Odu verses it generates form literally a book of knowledge; yet the actual process of divination clearly operates in a contrary ("nonrational") mode. Why cast palm nuts to determine which verses to cite? Why not go directly to the verses themselves? And why with divination systems such as basket shaking and bone throwing, which appear so haphazard, do we find such careful "ratiocinating" and exacting analysis of the cast configurations by the diviners?

This essay will argue that it is just this opposition of modes that makes the divinatory enterprise unique and, ultimately, so effective. Drawing from different

African cultures, I will outline an interpretation of the cognitive processes involved in divination. All types of divination will be considered because comparable shifts to the non-normal occur irrespective of whether mechanical or mediumistic, interpretative or intuitive forms are being utilized. Also, similar processes are involved whether the divination type is a distinct system of esoteric knowledge on which interpretation of the oracular message is based or a diagnostic system which relies on symbolic use of common knowledge. As a means of acquiring normally inaccessible information, divination utilizes a non-normal mode of cognition which is then synthesized by the diviner and client(s) with everyday knowledge in order to allow the client(s) to make plans of action.

Risks are obviously involved at this level of generalization, but at some point ethnographic research must be taken beyond the culture specific to determine whether larger patterns are involved.[1] In fact, the degree of congruence found in African systems of divination suggests an explanation for divination's universality. After a brief review of the stereotypes of divination, we will consider aspects of the divination process, such as location, diviner, symbols, and sensory modes in order to demonstrate how the created liminality causes the necessary shift in cognitive processes.

Both the positivist functionalist bias in anthropology and the rigid European dichotomization between modes of thinking (magic versus science, intuitive versus rational, and so on) have served to perpetuate a portrayal of African peoples as gullible, resistant to change, seeking consulation in rituals empty of rational thought. Careful study of African systems of divination immediately contradicts these erroneous characterizations. Actually, divination practitioners exhibit an intense need to know the true reasons for events, a highly skeptical and pragmatic attitude toward all types of information, and a persistent concern with adjusting to change.

The search for knowledge so prominent in African cultures has a very distinctive character to it. According to Douglas, "Any culture which admits the use of oracles and divination is committed to a distinction between appearances and reality. The oracle offers a way of reaching behind appearances to another source of knowledge" (1979:129). There is truly a "thirst for objective knowledge," as Lévi-Strauss terms it (1966:3). Coincidence is never a sufficient explanation. Answers to all questions are available if, but only if, one uses the proper mode of communication in addressing the correct source of knowledge. Necessary information may only be available from suprahuman beings and powers, frequently because they have caused the problem which needs resolution but also because the suprahuman realm is the repository of true knowledge about our shared reality, as the Sisala of Ghana, among others, affirm (Mendonsa 1978:39).

The serious search for knowledge is never easily satisfied. It is not clear whether the skepticism about divination among some Africans that is sometimes recorded would be forthcoming without the ethnographer's persistent probing—the kind, for example, that Evans-Pritchard did (1968:313–51). But certainly there can be both an accepted philosophy and skepticism, as Hallen and Sodipo's study among the Yoruba shows (1986). The Kalabari Ijo, for example, are skeptical of diviners, travel far away for consultations, seek multiple sessions, loathe answering personal questions, and are generally secretive (Horton 1964:6–8, 12–14). Their attitudes find agreement throughout the continent. In eastern and southern Africa, diviners seldom know their clients because "foreign" diviners are intentionally sought to ensure objectivity (Colson 1966).[2] In other areas the diviner is never told (at least initially) what the client's problem is.[3] Among the Ndembu, the diviner is intentionally deceived as to the applicability of his diagnosis (Turner 1975:217). Thus, contrary to popular opinion, diviners often have no prior knowledge of their clients' problems.

Great care is taken to ensure the quality of divinatory communication. Attention is paid to the condition of the diviner as well as to the divination mechanisms, which are constantly tested. The proper type of divination must be chosen for the specific client and problem. Often multiple sessions are held to ensure that the same conditions remain operative. Finally, much debate characterizes the last stage of the session, when the diviner and client discuss the relationship of the oracular message to the matter under investigation. While the client may never have all the information necessary to make an immaculate decision, he or she strives to gain enough knowledge to take the best action possible. Clients are not simply "flipping a coin" to avoid personal responsibility for making difficult decisions. Divination is approached seriously and cautiously because the quality of the divination process determines the quality of the results and thereby the action taken.

Divination never results in a simple restatement of tradition to be followed blindly. It is a dynamic reassessment of customs and values in the face of an ever-changing world. Uchendu's concept of "moving equilibrium" as central to the Igbo world view (1965:12) well describes divination's function in providing the context in which old and new, secular and sacred, real and ideal may be contrasted and resolved. It is through divination that a harmonious balance can be maintained in which a culture's most cherished values are adapted to the real world of continual flux.[4] The increased use of divination in urban settings, especially in southern Africa, best illustrates this dimension.[5]

Although everything possible is done to ensure correct communication, all participants appreciate that there is a fundamental unknowability in the universe, even for suprahuman beings. Diviners can only report what they are told and that may not always be correct (Junod 1927:564; Mendonsa 1976:191). Some divination systems have the element of cosmic randomness built in, as represented by the "changeable man" image in Ndembu basket divination whose appearance can cancel a consultation (Turner 1975:221–25) or the presence of the face of Eshu (the Yoruba trickster) on the Ifa divination tray. The frequent association of tricksters, those representatives of disorder, in West African divination systems suggests they have a key role in the reordering of human behavior (Pelton 1980: 261).

The central figure in this enterprise is of course the diviner, whose ascribed and achieved characteristics contribute to the separation of divination from normal activities. In some societies, such as the Lobi of Burkina-Faso (see Meyer's essay in this volume), diviners are not emphatically distinguished from others, but for the most part diviners are considered unique (Peek 1985) and sometimes are greatly feared (Hammond-Tooke 1975:32). Often future diviners are determined at birth by auspicious signs (interpreted by divination), as for Zulu women (Ngubane 1977: 97), or by adolescent behavior, as among the Batammaliba (see Blier's essay above). Elsewhere, individuals are chosen by ancestors or spiritual powers, or they choose themselves to become diviners during adulthood, signaled again by specific omens or behavioral characteristics. Just as the manner by which one comes to begin divining differs widely, so do practices of initiation, training, testing, and recognition by the group (as discussed above in section II). We might simply recall at this point that whether or not there is a formal initiation and training period, there is usually a final examination (often public), after which the individual is officially recognized by the community as a diviner (see Abimbola 1977 and Turner 1967).

Certainly during divination diviners are acknowledged as special persons, but sometimes they are permanently marked off from others. For example, diviners may be distinguished by their clothing or regalia (Gebauer 1964:149, Vansina 1971). One of the most dramatic markers of diviners, especially in southern Africa, is cross-gender dressing, with women dressing as men because they have been possessed by male spirits (who are the actual divinatory agents).[6] Cross-gender identification is established in various ways throughout the continent. Middleton describes Lugbara diviners:

> The men are said occasionally to be impotent or homosexual, and those that are not, the elders and rainmakers, act when under the observance of sexual taboos which make them temporarily "like women" (*okule*). The women are either barren, or pre-pubertal, or post-menopausal, or temporarily not having intercourse with their husbands or other men; they are regarded as "like men" (*agule*). Among the Lugbara this permanent or temporary asexuality is an essential characteristic of their being able to act as a medium between the social and the Spirit spheres. It is a symbolic attribute, and has nothing to do with their other, normal, social roles. (1969:224).

While these practices may be rejections of normal sexuality in order to attain a sexless state (see Bjerke 1981:169), another interpretation seems more appropriate. Gender differences are accentuated by the highly visible reversals of dress and behavior; but as this is only temporary, the actual goal seems to be the symbolic synthesis of both sexes' features in one individual.[7] It is significant that diviners' spiritual aid is often by means of pairs of male and female spirits, as in Rjonga (Thonga) divination (Morris 1976:245; see also Tucker 1940:178, Kuukure 1985: 71, and Glaze 1981:67). Gola diviners are aided by opposite-sexed spirit helpers (d'Azevedo 1975:294), and among the Fipa, male diviners are referred to as "wives of the territorial spirits" (Willis 1968:142). Whyte's discussion (above) of Nyole diviners reflects similar imagery. Therefore, the common objective is a *combination* of male and female characteristics and we may better speak of diviners as seeking an androgynous state. Whatever our label for the resultant identity of the diviner, clearly the common process is the accentuated declaration of sexual identity by denial or reversal and then the melding of the two aspects. The dramatic marking of difference, which is then rejected by affirmation of complementarity and synthesis, is a key dynamic in divination. This is also demonstrated by those divination systems which depend on the interaction of male and female halves of the divining apparatus.[8]

Additional practices may be described to demonstrate how diviners are distinguished from others, all of which contribute to marking the diviner's liminality. As communicators between worlds, they do not fully belong to either realm, as Blier (above) observes about Batammaliba diviners, who are simultaneously inside and outside the society. Many have commented on diviners' marginality, but Middleton's label of "liminaries" is the strongest affirmation of this often permanent stateless status.[9] Even more important than the diviner's appearance is the diviner's mental state. This is most obvious when diviners use spirit possession or trance states (see Beattie and Middleton 1969), but any type of divination necessitates a heightening of the diviner's state of consciousness.

The location of the divination event in time and space also serves to establish and maintain its liminality. The time of divination is often restricted. The Azande never divine in the heat of day (Evans-Pritchard 1968:281), while in Madagascar divination never occurs at night (Sussman and Sussman 1977:282). The Dagaaba only divine in early morning (Kuukure 1985:106). Both Evans-Pritchard (1968) and Turner (1975) describe the importance of the preparation and placement of the divination session to prevent interference by antagonistic agents. By its very nature, divination participates in liminality because in order to permit transworld communication, it becomes a portal between different realms (Erivwo 1979). Spider divination in Cameroon occurs at the burrow of the ground-dwelling spider, the literal pathway between worlds (Gebauer 1964). Elsewhere divination is situated at the edge of a village or cultivated field, as among the Nuer and Dogon; thus it is neither of the wilderness nor of cultured human space. The ambiguity of attitudes toward divination is reflected in varying restrictions as to whether it occurs in public or in private.

Although divination practices vary throughout Africa, we see a significant number of commonalities. The association of negative characteristics (and femaleness) with the left hand and the left side of things (Hertz 1960) has long been considered one of the most intriguing of cultural universals. Because use of the left hand is prohibited absolutely in most cultures, its conscious utilization in some African divination systems is thus significant and obviously contributes to the establishment of divination's liminality. For example, Needham (1973:334, 301 n.24) comments on the use of the left hand by diviners among the LoDagaa of Ghana and the Nyoro of Uganda.

Further evidence of divination's creation of difference, which is then mediated, is found in the conscious integration of left and right sides of divinatory configurations. Among some southern Nigerians, the divining chain's right and left sides must corroborate each other by falling in reverse order (Talbot 1926:188); and for the Yoruba, even though the right side is considered more important, the diviner must "read" both sides for a complete understanding (Bascom 1969:40; see also Peek 1982). What is most common is not simply the distinction of left and right but the concentrated mediation of the two sides of the divinatory cast.[10] This is also true of *sikidy* divination (Sussman and Sussman 1977). Kaguru practice under-scores the symmetrical meld desired: "In divination . . . it is said that the signs must appear on both the right and left before the prognostication may be regarded as complete" (Beidelman 1986:32).

While divination creates, through its use of liminality and norm reversals, a shift to nonordinary cognitive processes, it also insists on bringing these opposi-tions together. It might be said that divination creates a dialectic in order to accom-plish the necessary synthesis which is the solution to the problem brought to the diviner. Just as divination stands between worlds, so it centers itself in other sym-bolic ways. The use of left/right duality in divination has as its goal a resolution in complementarity; both sides are necessary for completeness. We will pursue this mediation of right and left momentarily when we consider the split-brain phenomenon.

The choices of animal imagery in African expressive behavior are highly inform-ative of different world views. The creatures affiliated with divination appear to be selected for their anomolous characteristics (another reference to liminality), their exceptional sensory abilities, and/or their associations with the other world and thus their ability to facilitate transworld communications. Among the Lele, the bush pig is "the Diviner's animal" because it frequents the marshy sources of streams where spirits reside (Douglas 1984a:28). Creatures, whole or in part, in symbolic or in actual physical form, contribute to the diviner's regalia and divinatory paraphernalia, and may serve as the agents of divination. A well-known example is the ground-dwelling spider used for divination by the Kaka Tikar in Cameroon because of its proximity to the ancestors living below the earth. After the spider has crawled through the specially marked wooden cards placed next to its burrow, their positions are interpreted by the diviner (Gebauer 1964).[11] The Dogon, in like fashion, interpret the tracks of the pale fox after it has moved through the diviner's symbolic grid prepared on the ground at the edge of the village (Griaule and Dieterlen 1986). The fact that the fox is also the Dogon trick-ster figure further intensifies the ambiguous, liminal nature of divination.[12]

Divination apparatus often incorporate elements of creatures, possibly primor-dial, which have special sensory abilities or are somehow extraordinarily endowed. Tortoises are associated with divination in southern Nigeria because of their wis-dom (Peek 1982; Cole and Aniakor 1984:73). In Zaire, dogs are linked to divination because of their powers of detection (Huber 1965). Kongo rubbing oracles have dogs' heads facing opposite directions; because the village of dogs lies between the villages of the dead and the living, they can inform each village/world of the other (Thompson 1985:12). Zoomorphic Kuba divination instruments represent deep forest dwelling creatures who are emissaries for the *ngesh*, forest spirits with whom diviners must communicate (Mack 1981). Powers of detection and memory are heightened for southern African diviners by use of vultures' hearts in their medicines (Junod 1927:566; Gelfand 1959:115; Marwick 1965:91).

Diviners' diets reflect similar associations.[13] Myriad creatures are employed in African divination systems and close inspection of each cultural system will reveal that very exacting choices have been made.

We now see that there are numerous elements which come together in the act of divination to ensure that a non-normal mode of cognition is established and maintained. All these factors aid in the creation of a state of non-normal consciousness for the diviner and clients, and all contribute to the main activity of divination, which is communication. To ensure that accurate communication between worlds occurs during divination, all of the diviner's senses must operate in supersensitive fashion. Because divination deals with non-normal sources of knowledge, not only must the correct question be addressed properly to the correct source, but the diviner must also be able to receive and recognize the correct information.

Perhaps the most obvious instance of non-normal sensory activity is when the diviner functions through spirit possession, or altered states of consciousness (Bourguignon 1968; Beattie and Middleton 1969). We still understand very little about altered states, and Western prejudice against entering non-normal states has hampered serious research in this area. These heightened states may be induced by inhaling fumes, as in northern Ghana (Field 1969:7), or by a combination of shaking gourds and chewing the possibly psychoactive *ojo* bulbs, as Lugbara diviners do (Middleton 1969:225, 1971:271). Another mechanism is sound: the classic relationship of trancing shamans and percussion is found in the "auditory stimulus" of the Mandari diviner's rattle (Buxton 1973:300), and throughout southern Africa diviners are known by names ending in the common root for drum, *-goma* (Hammond-Tooke 1980:350). For most diviners a variety of factors contribute to their heightened awareness: "At divinations, the physiological stimuli provided by drummings and singing, the use of archaic formulae in questions and responses, together take him out of his everyday self and heighten his intuitive awareness: he is a man with a vocation" (Turner 1972:43). These intensifying activities facilitate communication between worlds by permitting direct participation of suprahuman entities in this world through their possession of the diviner.

Even in such little-understood systems as olfactory sensing, where the diviner remains in a relatively normal state of consciousness, the nature of the divinatory enterprise clearly demonstrates the heightened abilities of the diviner. Especially in southern Africa, diviners commonly "smell out" witches and lost objects (see, for example, Buxton 1973:315).[14] Yaka divination begins with olfactory sensing (see the essay by Devisch above), and the association with dogs has already been noted. Intriguingly, recent research has proven that our olfactory sense is among the earliest developed abilities and that we continue to remember smells long after we have forgotten other sensory memories (Weintraub 1986). Tactile communication also is encountered in several divination systems in which diviner and client hold hands, as among the Lobi (Meyer, above), the Senufo (Glaze 1981:64), and the Bena Lulua, who term it "hand-shaking-muscle-reading" divination (McLean and Solomon 1971:33).

The primary senses utilized in divination are vision and hearing, and their enhancement is manifest throughout the divination process. Divination's liminality demands special visual acuity by the diviner ("the man who sets in motion intensive seeing," as the Mende say [Harris and Sawyerr 1968:n. 9]) in order to receive and interpret the revealed information correctly. The very goal of the divination session is, in fact, to see better, more clearly, and thereby act appropriately because "re-vision" of the problem has revealed the proper solution. Not only is the diviner endowed with special sight, as among the Igbo (Uchendu 1965:81) and as noted by several essays in this volume, but rituals are performed to further enhance the diviner's special vision. Kalabari Ijo (Horton 1964:6), Jukun (Meek 1931:329), and Zulu (Ngubane 1977:86–87) diviners use special medicines to ensure the clarity of their perception.

Often the divination apparatus itself must be treated to ensure that its sight is correct. For the Shona, "new *hakata* [divining bones] are considered completely blind and cannot be expected to see until they have been prepared for contact with the spirit world" (Gelfand 1959:109), a custom found elsewhere in southern Africa (Junod 1927:549; Bucher 1980:116). The broken calabash pieces used in Jukun divination must not come from beer containers or their message will be like "the babbling of a drunken man" (Meek 1931:326).

Two other observations may be briefly made concerning divinatory vision. The transcendence of this extraordinary non-normal sight is reflected in its association with human blindness for the Dinka, whose blind diviners are considered especially effective (Lienhardt 1970:68), and for the Mundang, who compare the blindman's cane to divination because both guide the otherwise sightless (Adler and Zempléni 1972). Despite the obvious importance of sight in divination (and the increased use of written materials, usually in symbolic fashion), we must be cautious of referring too readily to the "reading" of divinatory casts or oracular media. In oral cultures, the diviner does not, cannot "read" but looks and listens, sees and hears. This perspective is perfectly expressed by the Xhosa term for books: "a mirror for speaking" (Lévy-Bruhl 1966:369). Bohannan reports that Tiv diviners cock their heads to listen carefully to their divining chains (1975).

What is seen and heard is then transmitted by the diviner to the congregation in the session's next stage. Whether the message emerges through spirit possession, a numerical configuration, or a pattern of symbolic objects, it is the diviner's role to translate these esoteric codes. The objects in a diviner's basket, the shells on a chain, or marks on a board are polysemic morphemes from whose multireferent contexts the diviner constructs meaningful metaphoric utterances (see figure).[15] The oracular message is usually ambiguous and too full of meaning (Werbner 1973), and Parkin (above) aptly refers to the diviner's "straightening the paths" as he transforms the communication's simultaneity of images into a comprehensible sequence.

Often the speech initially produced, whether through spirit mediumship or mechanical means, is not simply metaphoric or archaic but is intelligible only to the diviner and must be translated. Although the uniqueness of divinatory speech is often observed, seldom have the languages been analyzed. Sometimes glossolalia occurs, or the language of a neighboring people may be heard (see Horton 1969: 29). Elsewhere esoteric speech is employed, as in southern Nigeria, where a dis-

Isoko diviner Eture Egbedi (left) and his assistant casting their pairs of *eva* divining chains for a client (far left) with a stomach ailment, Ole, Bendel state, Nigeria, February 12, 1971. *Photo by Philip M. Peek.*

tinct language accompanied the divining chain system as it was adopted by diverse peoples (Peek 1982).

Whatever the literal nature of the words heard or used in divination, this communication is considered very special and caution is always exercised in seeking and expressing it. As Kirwen (1987:87) was told by a diviner who refused to divine for him, "one does not demonstrate or play at divination. It would offend the ancestral spirits to do so." Bascom notes that Yoruba diviners are not allowed to tell folktales, although some Ifa verses contain folktales (1969:131). Thus it appears that, owing to the "power of words" (Peek 1981), the *babalawo* ("father has secrets" [Bascom 1969:81]), cannot confuse the revealed truth of Ifa with the created truth of folktales.

Just as divination can be said to give sight to the blind, so it gives speech to the dumb. The Lobi (and some Senufo groups) say that the spirits which govern all aspects of life have no tongues and can only communicate through divination (Meyer, above; see also Suthers 1987). In addition to communication, the speech of divination may also function as a dissociative technique, as Lienhardt (1970: 234) and Jackson (1978) suggest.

The ritualization of divination separates it from normal discourse and dispute settlement in order to ensure the necessary shift in cognitive processes. We must now attempt to understand how these alternate ways of knowing and thinking, generated by all this difference making—the symbolism, complex communication, and elaborate ritual—is finally brought together to help the client formulate a specific plan of action. As the manager of this process, the diviner is a translator between worlds as much as between modes of thought. And these communications must be organized as well as translated.

Divination systems create configurations of symbols (verbal or material) whose correct order or pattern must be revealed. As Jules-Rosette describes the process, "The pattern is the diviner's finding, and it is precisely this discovery that characterizes his expertise. He strengthens the discovery by showing the correspondence between an apparently random system and the train of misfortunes that the client reveals" (1978:557). This discovery process is similar to Lévi-Strauss's description of shamanistic curing, with its structuring of a broad range of elements relevant to the afflicted's case:

> First, a structure must be elaborated and continually modified through the interaction of group tradition and individual invention. This structure is a system of oppositions and correlations integrating all the elements of a total situation, in which sorcerer, patient, and audience as well as representations and procedures, all play their parts. (1967:176)

Zuesse (1979:215) discusses the diviner's "profound quest" to discover and articulate these deeper levels of existence. Among the Dogon, the fox "is endlessly going and coming to sketch the living pattern of the world to disclose how men must move to bring that pattern forth" (Pelton 1980:218).[16] Young describes how Amaharic divination reveals "an order imminent in the otherwise random course of everyday events" by means of "the image of a universal grid on which all people and all agencies (including pathogenic threats) can be located in space and time" (1977:192). This echoes the processes of Antemoro and Yaka divination (see the essays by Vérin and Rajaonarimanana and by Devisch above).

The persistent search for meaningful patterns is presented by Jahoda as his "alternative interpretation" for the presence of superstition (1971:120). Despite divination's universality and the great reliance on resultant plans of action, not just revealed patterns, a psychological need to relieve anxiety is sufficient explanation for Jahoda (and many anthropologists). Still, it is correct to say that divination reveals signs when none are forthcoming from other sources. If there is a dream or omen and the general espistemological system readily provides an explanation, divination may not be necessary. But if there are ambiguities with the immediately apparent associations of elements or no pattern vividly emerges, then divination must be resorted to.

Not only does divination reveal the basic patterns underlying human activities; it also reveals individual life patterns and relationships with others. Divination produces a narrative of a client's life and a correct history of the event in question. As Ahern observes, oracular communication is cryptic and metaphoric and thereby apparently very general, but it is in reality specifically relevant to the problem at hand. Therefore, the diviner and/or client must expand the coded message "to be what the god would say if he were conversing freely" (1981:62). The final divinatory narrative contains all the elements, now placed in proper order and in proper correspondence. Even among peoples who believe that life patterns are established prior to birth into this world, it is possible through correct action based on proper information—information available only through divination—to improve one's life.

But it is the final establishment of these patterns which brings us up against the apparent contradiction of divination systems. How can we reconcile divination's "mystical" process with its immensely practical results? Why are palm nuts, for example, cast in Ifa divination to determine which of the already known verses to recite? It is exactly at this point that earlier analyses of divination floundered. We have seen how divination is marked off from other means of decision making by the nature of the diviner (in terms of dress, behavior, cultural attributes), by location, by myriad symbolic elements, and by the occult communication invoked. Nevertheless, in the end we are firmly grounded in this world of practical action. This transition occurs in the crucial dialogue between diviner and client as the revealed information is discussed and debated. The all-important pattern may be brought forth before or through this dialogue, but it is in this dialogue, which previous studies have largely ignored, that the unique synthesis of cognitive modes occurs.

The divination process reviews all known factors as well as bringing forth new knowledge of the client's problem. The characteristic randomization of divination's presentation of these relevant elements neutralizes them so that each can be closely scrutinized, so that the true and the false can be clearly distinguished.[17] The cognitive process engaged in by the divinatory contingent which generates and interprets these patterns is very similar to what Bateson (1974) calls "muddling" and to Lévi-Strauss's familiar description of the *bricoleur's* activities (1966:18) as the diviner reorganizes cultural elements, finding new arrangements of old ideas. The diviner must mediate between traditional ideals and current realities, old and new, private and public, this world and that world. Equally informative is Pelton's discussion (1980) of the "shattering and rebuilding" theme of Yoruba Ifa divination, with its opposition of Ifa and Eshu, order and disorder. The theme is reminiscent of the Ndembu diviner who, in shaking his divining basket, rearranges the commonly known symbols of the social order to provide better insight.

Once this perspective on the thinking set in motion by divination is raised, a variety of ideas seem to jell and, at least from evidence about African peoples, the cognitive process we are attempting to present no longer seems so singular. For example, Fernandez (1980) presents the idea of "edification by puzzlement" to explain the intensity and enjoyment of Fang and Kpelle deliberations over "right" answers to riddles. Jackson (1982:235) suggests that Kuranko divination functions much as narratives do by bringing forward tradition to be tested against real life; thus, from the abstraction of a problem in the artificial chaos of the divination cast (or of the folktale) order and clarity emerge. We also know that more dilemma tales (narratives which present a problem but no resolution except that provided by group discussion) are found in Africa than in any other part of the world (Bascom 1975). Therefore, divinatory dialogues, which some have rightly compared to debates, perhaps fit within a larger African dynamic in which human energies are devoted to resolving rather than to resolution.

The intense interaction of client and diviner is not simply an intellectual enterprise. Jackson (1978) suggests there is a process of transference and countertransference which brings the two together. Among the Pedi a formal sacred communion is established between diviner and client (Sansom 1972:208).[18] Several studies in this volume stress the close association which develops during a divination session. This is certainly true for the Lobi, who call the client and diviner by the same name (Meyer, above). Also, Suthers reports that Djimini Senufo divination is founded on the principle of the "twinning" of the diviner and client because twins "share perfect knowledge of each other" (1987:88).[19]

Such portrayals of the dramatic bonding of diviner and client help us comprehend the psychological rapport in divination, but they seem to make more difficult the problem Devisch has raised about how such effective interaction can develop between clients and diviners of different ethnic groups. Earlier we noted that many people seek diviners to whom they are unknown in order to ensure the honesty of the oracular communication. Horton reasons that Kalabari Ijo accept foreign divinatory techniques because the matters they treat are "bad" and thereby "non-Kalabari" (1964:15). Devisch (1985:75) suggests that a common core cultural tradition and the dramatic synthesizing transaction between diviner and client are strong enough to override superficial differences. But it is exactly because of these differences that divination is so effective. The Ijo seek "foreign" diviners because their problem is "foreign" in that normal knowledge is insufficient and a different way of thinking is demanded.[20]

Obviously it is not enough to study only the products of divination, only the resultant behavior. It is now clear that the key stage of divination is the dialogue generated by the oracular message (as the texts above demonstrate), but the manner in which that stage is reached is still critical. How are these patterns, these new perspectives, brought forward, recognized, accepted, and then integrated? I would argue that all of the drama of divination serves to move the participants out of their normal modes of thinking, shaking them up in order to change their minds because their current understanding of the situation is inadequate.

Here we need to recall the earlier confusion among scholars concerning the apparently contradictory aspects of intuitive and intellectual, inspirational and rational in divination systems. Significantly, these dichotomies mirror characterizations of the brain's hemispherical specialization in which the left hemisphere is associated with analytical, linear thinking and the right hemisphere with synthetical, analogical thinking.[21] I maintain that much as the brain must first discriminate, then integrate and synchronize the left and right hemispheres for proper problem solving, so the diviner must first establish a non-normal mode of cognition, then (with the client) mediate between two ways of thinking. In other words, through a radical shift, in literal and symbolic fashion, of the character and context of problem solving, the divination process is used to introduce a mode of cognition different from the cultural norm, whatever that might be; and then, even more important, the divination session creates a synthesis of the non-normal and normal modes as the plans of action are developed between diviner and client.

Striking testimony that such a cognitive change occurs is provided by Batammaliba diviners, who say that when the divining spirit enters one's body it "shifts one's mind to the side" (see Blier's essay above). Bucher's observation that the "possessed" diviner's brain waves shift to alpha rhythms supports the contention that a physiological change occurs (1980:99–100).[22]

The balancing of the left and right sides of divinatory configurations is significant because it reflects the overall integration of mind and body. Recall that the left hemisphere controls the right side of the body while the right hemisphere controls the left side. The mediation in divination also reflects the synthesis that is now believed to occur between right and left hemispherical functioning; we use both hemispheres with varying intensity all the time, but each contributes a distinctive perspective to our bimodal consciousness.[23] Just as it is critical to keep the right and left sides of the divining chain separate, so as to read the configurations in proper order, the physiological separation of motor, sensory, and hemispherical functions is essential to permit necessary cerebral discrimination. But equally, there is a critical need for integration of these functions for the survival of the organism. Thus both divination and the brain are two-sided systems that function through differentiation and synthesis of both sides, often in fixed oscillation, for truly comprehensive and effective responses.

By introducing this level of analysis, which takes into account the brain's physiological differentiation of hemispheres and the mind's alternation of cognitive functioning, we are able to better understand divination's universality among human cultures. This approach does not deny earlier functionalist explanations of how the products of divination are utilized within various African communities, but it does allow us greater appreciation of the intricacies and subtleties of the cognitive dimension of the divinatory process, no matter which divination form is employed. All types of divination aid decision making by literally re-viewing the problem in light of different knowledge (whatever its source), and then the process integrates this perspective with contemporary reality by means of discussion between diviner and client.

Certainly we must try to understand African systems of knowledge in their own terms and our own analyses should respect those perspectives. But more important than arguing for one analytical approach against another is to acknowledge that divination is a critical component of human cultures everywhere and to ignore this essential way of knowing and problem solving is to diminish our study of human behavior.

Notes

A shorter version of this essay was given at the National Museum of Ethnology, Osaka, Japan, June 13, 1987. My sincere appreciation to Karen McCarthy Brown and Ivan Karp for helpful suggestions on earlier drafts.

1. As Ray comments,

The general reluctance of anthropologists to attempt broad comparative studies of African religions has meant that this task has fallen to theologically and philosophically trained scholars. Understandably, they have neglected the cultural and social context of African religious ideas and behavior. Inevitably such efforts have resulted in both superficial and distorted representations. (1976:12)

2. Others who consult only diviners who are strangers include the Alur (Southall 1970: 119), Hehe (Redmayne 1970:117), Kalanga (Werbner 1973:1424), Kaguru (Beidelman 1986: 144), Lele (Douglas 1963:22–23), Pondo (Wilson 1961: 336), and various Zambian peoples (Crawford 1967:182); see also the essays by Blier, Devisch, and Whyte in this volume.

3. This is the custom among the Lobi, Yaka, Nyole, Giriama, and Swahili (see the essays by Meyer, Devisch, Whyte, and Parkin in this volume), Dagaaba (Kuukure 1985: 106), and Sisala (Mendonsa 1978:23).

4. Rigby maintains that divination is a strong preserver of cultural tradition because it is "effective in adapting that tradition to rapid change in Kaganda society" (1975:130–31); for further comment on divination and innovation see Bauer and Hinnant (1980), Horton (1964:11 n.1), Huber (1965:48), Kuukure 1985:72), and Parkin's essay in this volume.

5. See Wilson (1961:348), Crawford (1967:202–3), Bucher (1980:113), and Dubb (1980: 449).

6. See also Ngubane (1977:57, 142), Lee (1969:123–40). Gelfand (1959:151), Hammond-Tooke (1975:32), Sibisi (1975:50), and the introduction to section II above. Cross-gender dressing also occurs among the Yoruba (Bascom 1969:95 and 1980:9–10).

7. This theme is central to the ancient Greek tradition about the seer Tiresias, who once saw two snakes coupling, killed the female, and instantly was turned into a woman. He lived as such until seven years later, when he again saw two snakes coupling and,

killing the male, was returned to his male form. Later, in response to Hera's contention against Zeus that men enjoyed sex more than women did, Tiresias asserted that women enjoyed sex far more (as he had experienced both aspects). In her anger at being refuted, Hera blinded him, but Zeus granted him the art of soothsaying (Avery 1962:1105; Halliday 1967:72).

8. The Zande rubbing board has female and male halves (Evans-Pritchard 1968: 362), and throughout southern Africa divining objects are equally divided between male and female pieces; see Junod (1927:539, 604), Gelfand (1959:108), and Parrinder (1969:62). So are divining chains in southern Nigeria (Talbot 1926: 188).

9. Hammond-Tooke (1975:30), Lienhardt (1970:151), and Ngubane (1977:86–93) also note the diviner's permanent liminality. Zahan's emphasis on the diviner's "double" is relevant to this status (1979:87–88).

10. In fact, one Isoko diviner and his assistant cast their divining chains simultaneously and "read" each other's cast (Peek 1982).

11. Ground dwellers are oracular agents elsewhere: mice for the Guro (Fischer and Homberger 1986:8), land crabs among the Marghi (Vaughan 1964), Jukun and Chanda (Meek 1931:328–29), and termites among the Azande (Evans-Pritchard 1968:294ff, 352ff).

12. For illustrations of Dogon divinatory grids, see Mair (1973:98–99). Douglas (1979: 132–36), and Griaule and Dieterlen (1986). Pelton (1980:164–223) offers an excellent discussion of this opposition of "random" nature and "orderly" culture between which divination mediates.

13. Ndembu avoid animals which might confuse their divinatory vision, such as tunneling rodents, zebras, and spotted bushbucks (Turner 1975:229, 285), while Fipa diviners eat cockerels' hearts to "wake up" their heads (Willis 1968:146). Initiation of Hamba and Tetela diviners includes eating a dog's heart to enhance their olfactory abilities (de Heusch 1985: 31–32).

14. For other accounts, see Junod (1927:538), White (1948:96), and Hammond-Tooke (1980:350). Vansina mentions the role of smell in Kuba divination in Central Africa (1978: 200). Gell (1977) presents one of the few studies of smell in religious contexts.

15. Turner's description of Ndembu basket divination's symbols extends this idea: "Their semantic structure has 'brittle segmentation.' I mean by this that a divinatory symbol possesses a series of senses, only one of which is relevant at a time, that is, at an inspection of a configuration of symbols" (1975:232).

16. Pelton characterizes the trickster's relationship to divination:

If the trickster in West Africa provides a way of dealing with discontinuity and change so that human movement through time may become not merely repetition, but an enlargement of sacred frontiers, he does so by linking the acts of re-vision and re-membering in divination, in myth, in dance, in sacrifice. As he teaches West Africans, again and again, how to see, he instructs them, over and over how to piece together their experience and to discover in that new whole the same open-ended order that they have always known as the source of transcendent ordinariness. (1980:275)

17. This is not the same as Moore's thesis (1979) about the value of random behavior, which was severely questioned by Vollweiler and Sanchez (1983) and earlier by Park (1967).

18. Sansom describes this ritual:

The client, after sitting in the correct position, must blow into the skin bag that holds the lots. The doctor then cuts two slivers of skin from the bag. The client slowly chews one while the doctor eats the other. This is a communion which relates doctor and client to each other and to the bag of lots. Regular consultation of one diviner repeats this communion, which becomes deeper and more permanent. The client strikes a lasting alliance with a man who can mediate in the business of supernatural causation. (1972:208)

19. The Lele also associate twins and divination (Douglas 1984a).
20. Bourguignon's mapping of sub-Saharan cultures with and without trance or trance possession reflects the diversity of practices among contiguous peoples (1968:355), and Southall (1972) specifically addresses the issue of antithetical symbolic structures of neighboring peoples.
21. In their important review article and subsequent discussion in *Current Anthropology*, Paredes and Hepburn (1976) argue that cognitive differences between cultures may result from different hemispherical orientations. Springer and Deutsch (1981) summarize relevant research. Crick extends this important issue to anthropology:

But language is particularly associated with the left hemisphere of the brain, the right side being associated with pattern recognition and intuition rather than "rationality." While anthropologists have normally spoken of modes of thought varying cross-culturally, it is obvious that there are different modes of processing information, different types of knowledge, and different methods of apperception within each human brain. (1982:301)

22. Although Jaynes's work is problematic owing to his literalness, it should be noted that he argues that divination was invented "to supplement right hemisphere function . . . following the breakdown of the bi-cameral mind" (1976:240).
23. See Dobkin de Rios and Schroeder (1979) and Gardner (1981) for further discussion of the alternations of right and left hemispheres.

References

Abimbola, 'Wande. 1977. *Ifa Divination Poetry*. New York: Nok Publishers.
Adler, A., and A. Zempléni. 1972. *Le bâton de l'aveugle: Divination, maladie et pouvoir chez les Moundang du Tchad*. Paris: Hermann.
Ahern, Emily Martin. 1981. *Chinese Ritual and Politics*. Cambridge: Cambridge University Press.
———. 1982. "Rules in Oracles and Games." *Man* n.s. 17(2):302–12.
Avery, Catherine B. 1962. *The New Century Classical Handbook*. New York: Appleton-Century-Crofts.
Bascom, William R. 1969. *Ifa Divination: Communication between Gods and Men in West Africa*. Bloomington: Indiana University Press.
———. 1975. *African Dilemma Tales*. The Hague: Mouton.
———. 1980. *Sixteen Cowries: Yoruba Divination from Africa to the New World*. Bloomington: Indiana University Press.
Bateson, Gregory. 1974. *Steps to an Ecology of Mind*. New York: Ballantine.
Bauer, Dan F., and John Hinnant. 1980. "Normal and Revolutionary Divination: A Kuhnian Approach to African Traditional Thought." In *Explorations in African Systems of Thought*, ed. Ivan Karp and Charles S. Bird, 213–36. Bloomington: Indiana University Press.

Beattie, John, and John Middleton, eds. 1969. *Spirit Mediumship and Society in Africa*. London: Routledge and Kegan Paul.

Beidelman, Thomas O. 1986. *Moral Imagination in Kaguru Modes of Thought*. Bloomington: Indiana University Press.

Bjerke, Svein. 1981. *Religion and Misfortune: The Bacwezi Complex and the Other Spirit Cults of the Zinza of Northwestern Tanzania*. Oslo: Universitetsforlaget.

Bohannan, Paul. 1975. "Tiv Divination." In *Studies in Social Anthropology*, ed. J. H. M. Beattie and R. G. Lienhardt, 149–66. Oxford: Clarendon Press.

Bourguignon, Erika. 1968. "Divination, transe et possession en Afrique transsaharienne." In *La Divination*, vol. 2, ed. André Caquot and Marcel Leibovici, 331–58. Paris: Presses Universitaires de France.

Bucher, Hubert. 1980. *Spirits and Power: An Analysis of Shona Cosmology*. Cape Town: Oxford University Press.

Buxton, Jean. 1973. *Religion and Healing in Mandari*. Oxford: Clarendon Press.

Cole, Herbert M., and Chike C. Aniakor. 1984. *Igbo Arts: Community and Cosmos*. Los Angeles: Museum of Cultural History, University of California.

Colson, Elizabeth. 1966. "The Alien Diviner and Local Politics among the Tonga of Zambia." In *Political Anthropology*, ed. M. Swartz, V. W. Turner, and A. Tuden, 221–28. Chicago: Aldine Press.

Crawford, J. R. 1967. *Witchcraft and Sorcery in Rhodesia*. London: Oxford University Press.

Crick, Malcolm R. 1982. "The Anthropology of Knowledge." In *Annual Review of Anthropology*, vol. 11, 287–313.

d'Azevedo, Warren L. 1975. "Sources of Gola Artistry." In *The Traditional Artist in African Society*, ed. Warren L. d'Azevedo, 282–340. Bloomington: Indiana University Press.

Devisch, René. 1985. "Perspectives on Divination in Contemporary sub-Saharan Africa." In *Theoretical Explorations in African Religions*, ed. W. van Binsbergen and M. Schoffeleers, 50–83. London: KPI/Routledge and Kegan Paul.

Dobkin de Rios, Marlene, and Robert Schroeder. 1979. "American Occupations, Leisure Time Use and Left Brain/Right Brain Dialectics: Some Explorations." In *Forms of Play of Native North Americans*, ed. Edward Norbeck and Claire R. Farrer, 1–16. St. Paul, Minn.: West.

Douglas, Mary. 1963. "The Lele of Kasai." In *African Worlds*, ed. D. Forde, 1–26. London: Oxford University Press.

———. 1984a. "Animals in Lele Religious Symbolism." *Implicit Meanings: Essays in Anthropology*, 27–46. London: Routledge and Kegan Paul.

———. 1984b. "If the Dogon . . . ." *Implicit Meanings: Essays in Anthropology*, 124–41. London: Routledge and Kegan Paul.

Dubb, Allie A. 1980. "The Impact of the City." In *The Bantu-speaking Peoples of Southern Africa* (1937), ed. W. D. Hammond-Tooke, 441–72. London: Routledge and Kegan Paul.

Erivwo, Sam. 1979. "Epha Divination System among the Urhobo of the Niger Delta." *African Notes* (Ibadan) 8(1):21–25.

Evans-Pritchard, E. E. 1968. *Witchcraft, Oracles, and Magic among the Azande* (1937). Oxford: Clarendon Press.

Fernandez, James W. 1980. "Edification by Puzzlement." In *Explorations in African Systems of Thought*, ed. I. Karp and C. Bird, 44–59. Bloomington: Indiana University Press.

Field, M. J. 1969. "Spirit Possession in Ghana." In *Spirit Mediumship and Society in Africa*, ed. J. Beattie and J. Middleton, 3–13. London: Routledge and Kegan Paul.

Fischer, Eberhard, and Lorenz Homberger. 1986. *Masks in Guro Culture, Ivory Coast*. Zurich: Museum Rietberg and New York: Center for African Art.

Gardner, Howard. 1981. "How the Split Brain Gets a Joke." *Psychology Today* 15:74–78.

Gebauer, Paul. 1964. *Spider Divination in the Cameroons.* Milwaukee, Wis.: Milwaukee Public Museum Publications in Anthropology, no. 10.

Gelfand, Michael. 1959. *Shona Ritual.* Cape Town: Juta.

Gell, Alfred. 1977. "Magic, Perfume, Dream . . ." In *Symbols and Sentiments,* ed. I. M. Lewis, 25–38. London: Academic Press.

Glaze, Anita J. 1981. *Art and Death in a Senufo Village.* Bloomington: Indiana University Press.

Griaule, Marcel, and Germaine Dieterlen. 1986. *The Pale Fox* (1965). Trans. Stephen C. Infantino. Chino Valley, Ariz.: Continuum Foundation.

Hallen, Barry, and J. O. Sodipo. 1986. *Knowledge, Belief and Witchcraft: Analytic Experiments in African Philosophy.* London: Ethnographica.

Halliday, William R. 1967. *Greek Divination: A Study of Its Methods and Principles* (1913). Chicago: Argonaut.

Hammond-Tooke, W. D. 1975. "The Symbolic Structure of Cape Nguni Cosmology." In *Religion and Social Change in Southern Africa,* ed. M. G. Whisson and M. West, 15–33. Cape Town: David Philip.

———. 1980. "Worldview I: A System of Beliefs" and "Worldview II: A System of Action." In *The Bantu-speaking Peoples of Southern Africa* (1937), ed. W. D. Hammond-Tooke, 318–66. London: Routledge and Kegan Paul.

Harris, W. T., and H. Sawyerr. 1968. *The Springs of Mende Belief and Conduct.* Freetown: Sierra Leone University Press.

Hertz, Robert. 1960. "The Pre-eminence of the Right Hand." In *Death and the Right Hand* (1909), trans. R. and C. Needham, 89–160. Aberdeen: Cohen and West.

de Heusch, Luc. 1985. *Sacrifice in Africa.* Trans. L. O'Brien and A. Morton. Bloomington: Indiana University Press.

Horton, Robin. 1964. "Kalabari Diviners and Oracles." *ODU* 1(1):3–16.

———. 1969. "Types of Spirit Possession in Kalabari Religion." In *Spirit Mediumship and Society in Africa,* ed. J. Beattie and J. Middleton, 14–49. London: Routledge and Kegan Paul.

Huber, Hugo. 1965. "A Diviner's Apprenticeship and Work among the Bayaka." *Man* 65(35):46–48.

Jackson, Michael. 1978. "An Approach to Kuranko Divination." *Human Relations* 31(2):117–38.

———. 1982. *Allegories of the Wilderness: Ethics and Ambiguity in Kuranko Narratives.* Bloomington: Indiana University Press.

Jahoda, Gustav. 1971. *The Psychology of Superstition.* New York: Penguin.

Jaynes, Julian. 1976. *The Origin of Consciousness in the Breakdown of the Bicameral Mind.* Boston: Houghton-Mifflin.

Jules-Rosette, Benneta. 1978. "The Veil of Objectivity: Prophecy, Divination, and Social Inquiry." *American Anthropology* 80(3):549–70.

Junod, Henri. 1927. *The Life of a South African Tribe.* Vol. 2: *Mental Life.* 2d. ed. London: Macmillan.

Kirwen, Michael C. 1987. *The Missionary and the Diviner.* Mary Knoll, N.Y.: Orbis Books.

Kuukure, Edward. 1985. *The Destiny of Man: Dagaare Beliefs in Dialogue with Christian Eschatology.* Frankfurt am Main: Peter Lang.

Lee, S. G. 1969. "Spirit Possession among the Zulu." In *Spirit Mediumship and Society in Africa,* ed. J. Beattie and J. Middleton, 128–56. London: Routledge and Kegan Paul.

Lévi-Strauss, Claude. 1966. *The Savage Mind.* Chicago: University of Chicago Press.

———. 1967. *Structural Anthropology.* New York: Doubleday Anchor.

Lévy-Bruhl, Lucien. 1966. *Primitive Mentality* (1923). Boston: Beacon Press.

Lienhardt, Godfrey. 1970. *Divinity and Experience: The Religion of the Dinka.* Oxford: Clarendon Press.

Mack, John. 1981. "Animal Representations in Kuba Art: An Anthropological Interpretation of Sculpture." *Oxford Art Journal* 4(2):50–56.

McLean, David A., and Ted J. Solomon. 1971. "Divination among the Bena Lulua." *Journal of Religion in Africa* 4(1):25–44.

Mair, Lucy. 1973. *Witchcraft*. New York: McGraw-Hill.

Marwick, M. G. 1965. *Sorcery in Its Social Setting: A Study of the Northern Rhodesian Cewa*. Manchester: Manchester University Press.

Mbiti, John. 1970. *African Religions and Philosophy*. New York: Doubleday Anchor.

Meek, C. K. 1931. *A Sudanese Kingdom*. London: Kegan Paul.

Mendonsa, Eugene L. 1976. "Characteristics of Sisala Diviners." In *The Realm of the Extra-Human: Agents and Audiences*, ed. Agehanada Bharati, 179–95. The Hague: Mouton.

———. 1978. "Etiology and Divination among the Sisala of Northern Ghana." *Journal of Religion in Africa* 9(1):33–50.

Middleton, John. 1969. "Spirit Possession among the Lugbara." In *Spirit Mediumship and Society in Africa*, ed. J. Beattie and J. Middleton, 220–31. London: Routledge and Kegan Paul.

———. 1971. "Oracles and Divination among the Lugbara." In *Man in Africa*, ed. Mary Douglas and Phyllis M. Kaberry, 262–78. New York: Doubleday Anchor.

Moore, Omar Khayyam. 1979. "Divination—A New Perspective." In *Reader in Comparative Religion*, 4th ed., ed. William A. Lessa and Evon Z. Vogt, 376–79. New York: Harper and Row.

Morris, Martha B. 1976. "A Rjonga Curing Ritual: A Causal and Motivational Analysis." In *The Realm of the Extra-Human: Ideas and Actions*, ed. Agehanada Bharati, 237–60. The Hague: Mouton.

Needham, Rodney. 1973. "Right and Left in Nyoro Symbolic Classification." In *Right and Left: Essays on Dual Symbolic Classification*, ed. R. Needham, 299–341. Chicago: University of Chicago Press.

Ngubane, Harriet. 1977. *Body and Mind in Zulu Medicine*. London: Academic Press.

Paredes, J. Anthony, and Marcus J. Hepburn. 1976. "The Split Brain and the Culture-and-Cognition Paradox." *Current Anthropology* 17(1):121–27, 17(2):318–26, 17(3):503–11, 17(4):738–42.

Park, George K. 1967. "Divination and Its Social Contexts." In *Magic, Witchcraft and Curing*, ed. J. Middleton, 233–54. Garden City, N.Y.: Natural History Press.

Parrinder, Geoffrey. 1969. *Religion in Africa*. London: Penguin.

Peek, Philip M. 1981. "The Power of Words in African Verbal Arts." *Journal of American Folklore* 94(371):19–43.

———. 1982. "The Divining Chain in Southern Nigeria." In *African Religious Groups and Beliefs*, ed. S. Ottenberg, 187–205. Meerut, India: Folklore Institute.

———. 1985. "Ovia Idah and Eture Egbedi: Traditional Nigerian Artists." *African Arts* 18(2):54–59, 102.

Pelton, Robert D. 1980. *The Trickster in West Africa*. Berkeley: University of California Press.

Ray, Benjamin. 1976. *African Religions: Symbols, Ritual, and Community*. Englewood Cliffs, N.J.: Prentice-Hall.

Redmayne, Alison. 1970. "Chikanga: An African Diviner with an International Reputation." In *Witchcraft: Confessions and Accusations*, ed. M. Douglas, 103–28. London: Tavistock.

Rigby, Peter. 1975. "Prophets, Diviners, and Prophetism: The Recent History of Kiganda Religion." *Journal of Anthropological Research* 31(2):116–48.

Sansom, Basil. 1972. "When Witches Are Not Named." In *The Allocation of Responsibility*, ed. Max Gluckman, 193–226. Manchester: Manchester University Press.

Sibisi, Harriet. 1975. "The Place of Spirit Possession in Zulu Cosmology." In *Religion* and *Social Change in Southern Africa*, ed. M. G. Whisson and M. West, 48–57. Cape Town: David Philip.

Southall, Aidan. 1970. *Alur Society*. Nairobi: Oxford University Press.

———. 1972. "Twinship and Symbolic Structure." In *The Interpretation of Ritual*, ed. J. S. La Fontaine, 73–114. London: Tavistock.

Springer, Sally P., and Georg Deutsch. 1981. *Left Brain, Right Brain*. San Francisco: Freeman.

Sussman, Robert W., and Linda K. Sussman. 1977. "Divination among the Sakalava of Madagascar." In *Extrasensory Ecology: Parapsychology and Anthropology*, ed. Joseph K. Long, 271–91. Metuchen, N.J.: Scarecrow Press.

Suthers, Ellen Moore. 1987. "Perception, Knowledge, and Divination in Djimini Society, Ivory Coast." Ph.D. dissertation, University of Virginia.

Talbot, P. Amaury. 1926. *The Peoples of Southern Nigeria*. Vol. 2. London: Oxford University Press.

Thompson, Robert Farris. 1985. *Flash of the Spirit*. New York: Vintage.

Tucker, Leona S. 1940. "The Divining Basket of the Ovimbundu." *Journal of the Royal Anthropological Institute*, 171–201.

Turner, Victor W. 1967. "Muchona the Hornet, Interpreter of Religion" (1959). In *Forest of Symbols: Aspects of Ndembu Ritual*, 131–50. Ithaca, N.Y.: Cornell University Press.

———. 1972. *The Drums of Affliction*. Oxford: Clarendon Press.

———. 1975. *Revelation and Divination in Ndembu Ritual*. Ithaca, N.Y.: Cornell University Press.

Uchendu, Victor C. 1965. *The Igbo of Southeastern Nigeria*. New York: Holt, Rinehart, and Winston.

Vansina, Jan. 1971. "The Bushong Poison Ordeal." In *Man in Africa*, ed. M. Douglas and P. M. Kaberry, 245–61. New York: Doubleday Anchor.

———. 1978. *The Children of Woot: A History of the Kuba Peoples*. Madison: University of Wisconsin Press.

Vaughan, James H., Jr. 1964. "The Religion and World View of the Marghi." *Ethnology* 3(4):389–97.

Vollweiler, Lothar Georg, and Allison B. Sanchez. 1983. "Divination: 'Adaptive' from Whose Perspective?" *Ethnology* 22(3):193–209.

Weintraub, Pamela. 1986. "Scentimental Journeys." *Omni* 8(7):49–52, 114–16.

Werbner, Richard P. 1973. "The Superabundance of Understanding: Kalanga Rhetoric and Domestic Divination." *American Anthropologist* 75(5):1414–40.

White, C. M. N. 1948. "Witchcraft, Divination, and Magic among the Balovale Tribes." *Africa* 18(2):81–104.

Willis, Roy G. 1968. "Changes in Mystical Concepts and Practices among the Fipa." *Ethnology* 7(2):139–57.

Wilson, Monica. 1961. *Reaction to Conquest: Effects of Contact with Europeans on the Pondo of South Africa*. London: Oxford University Press.

Young, Alan. 1977. "Order, Analogy, and Efficacy in Ethiopian Medical Divination." *Culture, Medicine and Psychiatry* 1(2):183–99.

Zahan, Dominique. 1979. *The Religion, Spirituality, and Thought of Traditional Africa*. Chicago: University of Chicago Press.

Zuesse, Evan M. 1979. *Ritual Cosmos: The Sanctification of Life in African Religions*. Athens: Ohio University Press.

James W. Fernandez

Afterword

Let me ground my observations on this highly interesting collection of essays by reflecting on my own experience of divination in Africa, a series of revelatory if ultimately failed incidents of consultation with Zulu diviners in which the health of my father became central (Fernandez 1967). The women leaders of the Old Men's Cult (Amakahleni, Umulazi District, Durban, Natal), which I was studying, regularly divined the health and life problems of their members and visitors by acting as spirit mediums for the great Zulu dead—Shaka, Dingane, and the other kings—as well as for the male founder of the cult, John Mfene. Thus I had already taken an interest in Zulu divination generally. I had also read Reverend Callaway, and in September 1965 I went out, accompanied by my Zulu colleagues Joseph Manyoni and Harriet Sibisi, to consult a whistling diviner (*inyanga yemilozi*), a diviner by means of familiar spirits, in the Valley of the Thousand Hills.

This woman, decked out in the elaborate robes and headdress of the diviner, did not offer me a satisfactory divination. She did not really, for example, discover the nature of the hidden object which was to be an initial test of her power, a coin hidden under Mrs. Sibisi's right thigh. Also the whistling voices of the spirits, which seemed to be coming from outside the hut rather than from within it, were not, for me at least, convincing. And the diviner did not really succeed in "seeing" my case very clearly, although she rather quickly divined that I was far away and not in satisfactory contact with my family, particularly with my father, who had been in precarious health for more than a year. She recommended that I should endeavor to be in better contact. That seemed to me a useful if rather obvious observation, so we agreed to terminate the seance for the time being and return another day. I never did.

In late November, however, several of the women leaders and diviners of the Old Men's Cult urged me to sacrifice a sheep to the ancestors on behalf of myself and my family and as a gesture of solidarity with the cult. Indeed, the cult members treated me with the greatest hospitality and kindness, and so I made the sacrifice, dedicating the sheep to the dead founder, John Mfene, and bringing my case before him. I retired to an adjacent rondeval and, just before lying down to sleep, drank a potion of herbs, sheep's blood, and gall. I was advised to be attentive to any dreams.

Indeed I dreamed! I dreamed, as I recalled, that I was halfway up a ladder that was leaning against a side wall of the Old Men's Chapel. The wall was almost blindingly white, and in the center was a metallic blue window. As I was trying to adjust my eyes, I suddenly felt a shake on the ladder. I looked up, and there at the top of the ladder was the face and shoulders of my father. He either waved or beckoned to me, calling me up the ladder. That ended the dream.

The next morning I took my place among those consulting the leader of the cult, MaMfene, who was divining in the chapel. I recounted my dream. MaMfene seemed momentarily disconcerted but went ahead and consulted the ancestors. I was rather disappointed to find that the ancestors were said to be showing their acceptance of my place in the cult and indicating that I was to contribute to the repainting of the exterior of the chapel and also to the reglazing of any broken windows. As to my father, I should call him in America.

Well, as I was flying back to America in several weeks' time, I did not make the call. To my sorrow, when I did return I found my father very gravely ill. The family and he had wanted to keep the knowledge from me in the field. A scant two weeks after I returned he died. Shortly after, in a letter thanking my friends at Amakhehleni for their kindnesses, I communicated the facts of my father's death to them. I soon received a letter in return in which among condolences they allowed that the ancestors were well aware of my father's imminent death; in fact, this event had been communicated to me in his farewell gesture at the top of the ladder. But as I was soon returning and nothing could be done anyway, they had not wanted to trouble me with that aspect of my dream.

Though these Zulu diviners had surely divined my worries—worries not really apparent to me, incidentally, in the intense involvement of fieldwork—I recall being highly skeptical of the whole experience throughout. Subsequently I came to credit diviners with much deeper insight into the human condition and my place in it than I had at first allowed. My impatience, anchored in my research agenda and my professional social science position, apparently had to exclude me from the deeper "ways of knowing" that they were offering had I had the time and wisdom to explore them.

While I was, I think, listening carefully to the discourse in other arenas of African religious life (Fernandez 1966), for some reason I conceived of divination as an arena of rather mechanical, probably fraudulent, communication between gods and men and between diviners and clients. I focused on the recommendations contained in the divination and not on the complexities of the communication itself. If only I had had this collection of essays before me at the time!

Given the shortcomings of my fieldwork in this respect, let me orient my afterword to this question: how might my field study of divination have been deepened had I had this collection of essays before me? This question is useful and apt as an afterword, although, of course, it presumes not only this volume as an aid to a former state of mind but twenty subsequent years of anthropological theory and research which also informs this volume. So in part an afterword framed in this way is a commentary on twenty years of anthropology.

The Anthropologist as Diviner

In the first place, I might have been made aware of the degree to which my unexamined positivist attitudes toward divination, my intellectualist impatience with it as an explanatory activity, and my suspicion of its probable fraudulence as an investigative and predictive activity were a function, as Philip Peek notes in his introduction to this volume and Rosalind Shaw so well points out in her essay, of my own "epistemological politics," a politics carrying an "emotionally charged normative weight" which protected from critical scrutiny knowledge of the role of interests and powers in producing Western scientists and African diviners. Jules-Rosette (1978) made a similar point about the "unexamined positivist ideology"—our preferred Western mode of divination—which shields us from the "parti pris" in our work. Jules-Rosette spoke of the "veil of objectivity" maintained by both diviners and ethnographers so as to "guarantee" their method from scrutiny. Similar caution was expressed by Jackson (1978), who added the perspective of anthropologist as client in his pragmatic analysis of Kuranko divination. Jules-Rosette and, at least implicitly, several essays in this volume follow Turner (1975) in showing the similarity between divination and anthropological interpretation.

Had I been privy to these arguments in 1965 I would perhaps have understood that my impatience with my divinations had both an ideological basis and a basis in an implicit dispute over—would it be too much to call it—professional privilege, a sense that both I and the *inyanga yemilozi* were diviners trying by our separate and, hence, competitive methods to make some sense out of the turmoiled, anomalous, ambiguous circumstances and the pain and suffering of human social life. Such an insight in 1965 might have created in me greater collegial interest in the Zulu diviner's "ways of knowing."

The Uses of Typologies

One value of this volume and of knowledge of the diverse types of divination of which it gives evidence is the comparative perspective we obtain. In 1965 I would have benefited in having a comparative perspective on the difference between the whistling diviner of the Valley of the Thousand Hills and the dream diviners at the Old Men's Cult. For while both of these diviners were inspirational and mediumistic, the latter were much more interpretive and the former more ritualistic in procedure. Of course, in respect to my case, the whistling diviner had much less to go on than the dream diviners. The whistling diviner was suddenly confronted with a member of another culture about whom neither she nor her

method could presume very much and who otherwise offered little information
to go on in the framing of questions. The dream diviners had the advantage of
my many months working in their kraal, which gave them much contextual
knowledge of me and my situation. Moreover they were presented with the relatively rich materials of my dream of initiation.

What this volume achieves, then, is a sensitizing of the student to the diverse
forms of divination, the diverse ways that diviners and clients have of coming
to know each other and their situation. In Madagascar Vérin and Rajaonarimanana
show us both astrologically oriented diviners (*mpandro*) and geomantics (*mpisikidy*) relatively tightly bound into a system of divinatory interpretation. Among
the Batammaliba, on the other hand, Blier describes an unusually open interaction
between the consultant, the diviner proper, and the adviser to the client. Both
work together, mutually suggestive, to resolve the problem of the client's health.
Both keep in mind community health as a goal. Callaway, for the Zulu, gives
us the contrast between the relatively mechanical "thumb diviner," the "stick diviner" more open in interpretation, and the inspired spirit mediums who depend
little on mechanical interpretative devices. Almquist gives us insight into the variety of oracles and oracular practices among the Pagibeti. The object of his essay
is to show us the substantial variation within cultures as regards divinatory practices. Among the Lobi, Meyer describes a very rapid question and answer session
between diviner and clients, directed at circumambient spirits, that is unusual
among either the more reflective and interpretive divinations or the more delibera-
tive mechanical, geomantic procedures described.

In general this volume enables us to understand the number of continua along
which systems of divination vary: as, for example, between inspired divination
and learned divination; as between open and closed systems of divination; as
between collaborative and consensual divination (in respect to the relation between
diviner and client) and unilateral and authoritarian procedures. While respecting
this variety as a source of insight, I direct myself here primarily to divination
of the inspired, open, collaborative and consensual kind.

The Logic of Divination as a Logic of World Building

This open and collaborative variety of divinatory practice should make us wary
of being able to identify *a* logic of divination. But since the question of the logic
of divination has been a perennial one, as the introduction and various essays
make clear, we may look back at it again in the light of this collection. In 1965
I certainly took divination to be an illogical procedure for human problem solving,
a position all the more strange since I was studying African religions as imaginative
cosmological constructions both redemptive and therapeutic in effect. But I was
not prepared to understand divination as having the world-building import many
of these chapters so clearly show it to have.

One conclusion we arrive at through our reading here is that the old debate
over Western and primitive logics as it is focused on divination is a comparison

that, at best, is all too likely to embody an "epistemological ideology" and at worst to be plainly invidious. The task is not, as this volume shows, to disqualify divination as lacking in the power of Western logic to identify causes and reflect upon premises but rather to try to see the powers of synthesis in divination, the ways that it enables its clients to see and know a better world in which to live. A number of these essays do enable us to see divination as such a cosmological activity. Indeed it is not too much to argue that systems of divination such as Yoruba Ifa are complex enough in their ontological implications to constitute an academic discipline (see Abimbola 1976).

So various essays here move us satisfyingly beyond "epistemological ideology" and invidious comparisons to a pragmatic understanding of what divination achieves in ministering to affliction and by its powers of synthesis in discovering alternative worlds to the afflicted one. Burton, for example, shows us how Atuot divination provokes a reexamination of world view. That is, it provokes philosophic reflection on social order in its participants and leads them to a deeper understanding of the verities of human social life lived out amid suprahumans. He finds in the "dialectic of divination" between diviner and client, which is to say the dialectic between a "social definition of experience" as provided by the diviner and the individual's sense of suffering but uncertain identity as provided by the client, the basis for philosophic reflection. But, of course, this dialectic works best, as Whyte points out, where the "model of misfortune" is "contextual" or "sociocentric." That is, it works best where the person is defined in terms of relations to external agents rather than in terms of relations to autochthonous selves and autochthonous bodies.

I like to call this process whereby a religious world view is constructed in the process of religious communication "edification by puzzlement." It certainly occurs in divination, which is often characterized by puzzling discourse that gives to it a "cryptic potency," as Shaw calls it.

The "Cryptic Potency" of Divination

If I had only paid closer attention to the "performative utterances" that accompanied my experience with divination, I might have better grasped this "cryptic potency." For, as Shaw goes on to say, it is not the logical truth properties, the intellectual aspects, but the performative powers, the "efficacy" that lies in divination to transform social realities, that is most interesting. This is the fundamental "truth" of divination, a truth more fundamental than any positive truth. This point is made effectively in this collection by a number of writers.

The extensive Nyole divination text recorded by Whyte well demonstrates the abundance of meaning brought forth by the diviner which is then clarified through resistance and response by diviner and client. Parkin, in his essay, also provides us with the actual discourse of the Giriama and Swahili divining sessions. He shows us how the initial ambiguous, muddled, "wilderness" speech of diviners obtains its "cryptic potency" by being subsequently straightened out for purposes of providing counsel to the client upon which he can act. The diviner makes sense out of the afflicted world brought to his attention by rescuing sequence out of the muddle of simultaneity and synchronicity. For, in the end, if the client is to be brought to act, if not efficaciously, at least with some confidence, a sequence of activity must be proposed to him. The "cryptic potency" of the diviner's session, therefore, lies in its production of domesticated sequences of action out of the wild, existential simultaneity of experience. It is this simultaneity that is simulated if not constituted originally in the diviner's initial, muddled, wilderness speech. In a like manner Devisch shows us how the Yaka diviner works from his own production of ambiguous dreamlike images, as cryptic and potent in themselves as my dream upon the ladder, which the diviner then, in the act of interpretation, transposes to the client's problem situation. This transfer leads to the therapeutic restoration of social reciprocity.

Figuring Out the Inchoate Human Condition

Insofar as divination is not strictly bound to mechanical procedures—and many mechanical procedures themselves manipulate multivocal symbolic elements subject to variable interpretation—there is a figurative process going on in divination that is well captured in a number of these essays. This is a process by which the diviner and the client often enough together "figure out" (with figures of speech in mind) a pattern of knowing that will meet the existential anomalies and ambiguities, the aleatory and inchoate qualities, of the social situation that has brought them together. This "figuring out" in my view is largely accomplished in primary process language rich in dreamlike images, metaphors, metonyms, synechdoches, and other figurative devices which are put forth as relevant to the divinatory problem but whose relevance has to be subsequently "figured out" in a more straightforward cognitive fashion.

I recall the way my ladder dream was "figured out" by MaMfene, the Zulu dream diviner. I was told, it will be remembered, to contribute to the chapel building fund and to call home. Had this collection of essays been in my hand at the time I would have paid much closer attention to the initial discussion of the dream diviner of the ladder image, the steel window, the brilliant white chapel walls. I was, as I say, too focused on the practical instructions that were subsequently "figured out" from this initial "play of tropes."

In some respects I could have been informed, to be sure, more than a decade and a half ago. Richard Werbner (1973) alerted us to the figurative, if enigmatic and innuendo laden, richness of Kalanga domestic divination, the "superabundance of understandings" it offered through its language of metaphors about the "common occult." Indeed, as Werbner showed, the divinatory apparatus of the Kalanga, the four two-sided pieces of ivory, could be regarded as a matrix of metaphors, a comprehensive concordance of divination that conditioned the play of verbal art at seances (1419). These ivory metaphors, as cast, offer to the diviner and congregation a "superabundance" of possibilities of interpretation as they reason together about the plausible patterns of meaning before them. This metaphoric matrix enables the diviner to avoid falling into too easy error. It enables him —frees him up—to fit his pattern discovery subtly but suitably into the social and personal intricacies of the case at hand. Werbner's insights were also present in Evans-Pritchard's Azande work, as Werbner made clear.

Several papers in this collection expand on these insights, showing us how divination is, in essence, a "figuring out" of the "figurative," a "play of tropes," really (Fernandez 1986). Jackson (1978), in his discussion of Kuranko divination, also wanted us to understand the playfulness of it, the way it creatively manipulates the client's beliefs for pragmatic purposes, that is, for purposes of social order. In this volume, Parkin gives us a careful, text-anchored account of the "metaphors of change" employed in Giriama and Swahili divination and the way these metaphors are simultaneously manipulated—linked—so as to eventually lead to the instructive and admonitory propositions that can be sequentially applied to resolve troubled behaviors.

Synthesizing Worlds in Which to Live

Reading through this collection and thinking back on my own experience with divination, what I feel it teaches, then, is the "constitutive nature" of the diviner's art. It teaches us the way the diviner offers a more acceptable world for his client to live in, more acceptable than the troubled social world that brought the diviner and the client together in the first place. At the heart of this world creation, this therapeutic cosmogony, is, as many of these essays demonstrate, the play of metaphor. Though the reader may already have divined that I, with my long-term interest in the tropes, would have come to metaphor as the final word in my afterword, I simply reiterate Levin's argument (1977) that the putting forth of a metaphor is always the imaginative assertion of a different possible world than the one in which we literally live. There is surely that imaginative assertiveness in much divination.

In response to and as a full step beyond the outmoded debate about primitive mentality and the logic of primitive man, these papers, as the subtitle of this volume so well captures, seek to approach the various forms of divination not invidiously but openly as different "ways of knowing." As Devisch puts it, in divination the diviner's art suggests a structural causality rather than a linear one. The Yaka oracle is performative, and what that performance creates—"reveals," in Devisch's preferred term—is not adequately to be grasped by conventional categorical thought, so often the touchstone in the debate over primitive mentality and primitive logic. For diviners at their best structure a complex world of knowing whose veracity, as Devisch argues, should be judged in its capacity to restructure and restore a world of social reciprocity.

Our master of ceremonies in this volume, Philip Peek, in his valuable essay helps us to see this structurally creative, "synthesizing" role of divination, the way it first shakes up a society, as the divinatory apparatus is shaken up in the diviner's basket, then recreates and reorders that society. Peek speaks, summarizing some of the material in this collection, of the diviner as translator between modes of thought and as mediator between worlds, for example, between left hemisphere and right hemisphere of the brain, between deep structure and surface structure, between inspiration and wisdom, between the supernatural and the natural.

This argument in favor of the "cryptic synthesizing power" of the diviner is all to the good. But since the editor has given me the last word here, let me suggest simply that the best diviners are ones who are exceptionally well tuned in to the primary processes where so many of our problems lie. They are exceptionally attuned to those primary ways of knowing in which the tropes have their primacy in our understanding. But at the same time diviners must also bring this way of knowing revealingly to bear upon troubled social situations. They must provide, in the usual cases, understandable counsel to their clients. They must, thus, synthesize primary process knowing with secondary process knowing, that knowing where the logics of category, concept formation, and cognition hold sway. They must cognize the world as well as perform and express it.

In short, diviners, in my view, are ones who exceptionally sensitively mediate between these two essential ways of human knowing: primary process and secondary process. I personally would not wish to overemphasize the mysterious elements in the "cryptic potency" of diviners. They simply give more credence to primary process thinking than is normal in our world, where secondary process thinking holds sway for a variety of good and bad reasons. But—to be cryptic myself in conclusion—who is to say that we Westerners have not overdone secondary process thinking in human affairs in a non-normal way, if we are allowed to measure normality from the perspective of anthropological knowledge of the human spectrum. To rephrase Marcel Mauss (1967), are the social reciprocities of the modern world what a sensitive and sensible diviner would have them be? As both my Zulu diviners told me after, to be sure, some very recondite discourse: "Spend some money on your fellowman and don't forget to call home."

References

Abimbola, 'Wande. 1976. *Ifa: An Exposition of Ifa Literary Corpus*. Ibadan: Oxford University Press.

Fernandez, J. W. 1966. "Revitalized Words from 'The Parrot's Egg' and 'The Bull Who Crashes in the Kraal': African Cult Sermons." In *Essays on the Verbal and Visual Arts*, ed. J. Helm, 53–64. Proceedings of the 1966 Meeting of the American Ethnological Society.

———. 1967. "Divinations, Confessons, Testimonies—Confrontations with the Social Superstructure among Durban Africans." Occasional Papers of the Institute for Social Research, University of Natal, Winter-Spring.

————. 1986. *Persuasions and Performances: The Play of Tropes in Culture*. Bloomington: Indiana University Press.

Jackson, Michael. 1978. "An Approach to Kuranko Divination." *Human Relations* 31(2):117–38.

Jules-Rosette, B. 1978. "The Veil of Objectivity: Prophecy, Divination, and Social Inquiry." *American Anthropologist* 80(3):549–70.

Levin, S. 1977. *The Semantics of Metaphor*. Baltimore: Johns Hopkins University Press.

Mauss, M. 1967. *The Gift* (1925). New York: Norton.

Turner, V. 1975. *Revelation and Divination in Ndembu Ritual*. Ithaca, N.Y.: Cornell University Press.

Werbner, R. 1973. "The Superabundance of Understanding: Kalanga Rhetoric and Domestic Divination." *American Anthropologist* 75(5):1414–1440.

Contributors

ALDEN ALMQUIST holds a doctorate in anthropology from Indiana University based on intensive fieldwork among the Pagibeti of Zaire. He is now on the staff of the African section of the Library of Congress.

RUDOLPH BLIER, who completed his Ph.D. in sociology at Northwestern University, is a psychotherapist at Coney Island Hospital, Brooklyn, and Adjunct Assistant Professor of Sociology at Iona College. He conducted fieldwork in Togo and Benin (Dahomey).

JOHN W. BURTON. Associate Professor of Anthropology, Connecticut College, carried out research among the Atuot of southern Sudan. He has published several monographs and numerous articles on the Atuot and other Nilotic peoples.

HENRY CALLAWAY served as the first Anglican bishop of "Kaffraria" and compiled several classic works on the Zulu while engaged in missionary activities in South Africa in the late nineteenth century.

RENÉ DEVISCH is Professor of Anthropology at Catholic University of Louvain. Drawing on his anthropological work in Zaire (1971–74), he has conducted research on family medicine in Belgium and is currently coordinating research among traditional healers and healing churches in Zaire.

JAMES W. FERNANDEZ is Professor of Anthropology at the University of Chicago. His most recent works include *Bwiti* (1982) and *Persuasions and Performances* (1986).

PIET MEYER conducted fieldwork in Burkina Faso and curated and authored the catalog for an exhibition of Lobi art at the Rietberg Museum, Zurich.

DAVID PARKIN has written extensively on East African peoples and is Professor and Chair of Anthropology, School of Oriental and African Studies, University of London. He has recently edited *Semantic Anthropology* (1982) and *The Anthropology of Evil* (1985).

PHILIP M. PEEK, Professor and Chair of Anthropology at Drew University, conducted ethnohistorical research among the Isoko clans of the Niger Delta and has published primarily on African visual and verbal arts.

NARIVELO RAJAONARIMANANA has written several articles on Malagasy and has just completed a doctoral dissertation on Malagasy divination at the Institut National des Langues et Civilisations Orientales, Paris.

ROSALIND SHAW, Assistant Professor of Anthropology at Tufts University, has published several articles on Temne (Sierra Leone) divination and Igbo (Nigeria) religion based on her fieldwork. Her co-edited volume, *Dreaming, Religion and Society in Africa*, is in press.

PIERRE VÉRIN is Professor and Vice President, Institut National des Langues et Civilisations Orientales, Paris. He has published extensively on the culture and history of Madagascar.

SUSAN REYNOLDS WHYTE, author of numerous publications on the Nyole of Uganda and on medicines in developing countries, is Associate Professor at the Institute of Anthropology at the University of Copenhagen.

Index

Abimbola, 'Wande: studies of divination by Africans, 13; Ifa history and divination verses, 38

Agnosticism: anthropologists and study of religion, 7

Ahern, Emily Martin: specificity of oracular communication, 203

Alienists: Batammaliba diviner-consultants, 74, 90

Almquist, Alden: typologies and divination systems, 216

Ancestors: traditional religion of Malagasy, 54–55; *sikidy* system, 65; Batammaliba divination, 77, 79; Apagibeti culture, 102

Androgyny: Nyole diviners, 158; diviners and gender, 196–97

Animals: sacrifice and *sikidy* configurations, 65; Batammaliba diviners, 77; Lobi divination, 94–95; foxes and Dogon divination, 140, 198; imagery and world view, 198, 207n

Anthropology: critics of rationalism, 137; anthropologist as diviner, 215. *See also* Scholarship

Apagibeti: ethnographic background, 101–103

Arabic influence: divinatory practices in Madagascar, 39; Malagasy system of astrology, 56, 65; Temne divination, 145; types of Nyole diviners, 156–57; Nyole divination and Arabic books, 159–60, 161–62, 169; Kenyan "Arab" diviners, 175, 177–79

Ardner, Edwin: simultaneity and sequencing in human cognition, 173

Art: *bricolage* and modern science, 184–85

Astrology: origins of in Madagascar, 55; adaptation of Arabic system to Madagascar, 56, 65; Malagasy calendar, 56–60

Atuot: account of origins of divination, 37–38; role of divination in search for knowledge, 38–39, 41, 44–51

Authority: public and private spheres of divination, 149–50; Nyole divination and power structure, 167–70

Barth, F.: view of innovative individual, 187

Bascom, William R.: American study of divination, 6; Yoruba diviners and folktales, 202

Batammaliba: diviners as alienists and annunciators, 73–90

Beattie, J.M.H.: British study of divination, 9; rituals and philosophy, 45

Bena Lulua: initiation ceremonies, 25

Berthier, Hugues: Malagasy calendars, 60

Birds: Temne divination, 143; vultures' hearts, 198. *See also* Animals

p'Bitek, Akot: African scholarship and Western biases, 14

Blier, Rudolph: divination and social order, 69–70; typologies and divination systems, 216

Blier, Suzanne: locomotion and divinatory processes, 12

Blindness: divinatory vision, 200

Boshier, Adrian K.: initiation of Zulu women diviners, 25

Boxes: image in Temne divination, 149

Brain: left and right sides of divinatory configurations, 205

Bricolage: as described by Lévi-Strauss, 183; divinatory diagnosis and schizophrenia, 184; art and modern science, 184–85

Bucher, Hubert: shifts in diviner's brain waves, 205

Bunyole: sexual politics of divination, 168

Burkina Faso: culture and divination among Lobi, 91–99

Burton, John W.: divination's role in search for knowledge, 38–39, 217

Buxton, J.: possession and divination in Nilotic Sudan, 42–43

Calendars: traditional Malagasy astrology, 56–60

Callaway, Henry: European view of divination, 5; study of Zulu divination, 23–26; initiation of Zulu diviners, 27–33; typologies and divination systems, 216

Children: Batammaliba and learning of consultation process, 74–78

Christianity: divination in Madagascar, 53; Apagibeti and Catholicism, 102; Nyole divination, 159

Clairvoyance: Batammaliba diviners, 76–77; Yaka oracles, 118–19

Clients: autonomy of Nyole, 166–67; Nyole ideology and role of diviner, 170–71; innovative power of relationship with diviner, 187–88; quality of divinatory communication, 195; relationship with diviner, 204, 207n–208n. *See also* Patients

Cognition: simultaneity and sequencing, 173; non-normal modes and African divination systems, 193–200, 202–206

Colby, Benjamin N. and Lore M.: American study of divination, 7

Community: truth and orientation of African systems of divination, 135

Consultation club: Batammaliba divination, 83–85

76120